James Cassese, MSW, C⌐ ⌐
Editor

MW00512470

Gay Men
and Childhood Sexual Trauma:
Integrating the Shattered Self

Gay Men and Childhood Sexual Trauma: Integrating the Shattered Self has been co-published simultaneously as *Journal of Gay & Lesbian Social Services*, Volume 12, Numbers 1/2 2000.

Pre-publication
REVIEWS,
COMMENTARIES,
EVALUATIONS . . .

"**A**N EXCELLENT, THOUGHT-PRO-VOKING COLLECTION OF ES-SAYS. Therapists who work with gay men will be grateful to have such a comprehensive resource for dealing with sexual trauma."

Rik Isensee, LCSW
Author of *Reclaiming Your Life*

More pre-publication
REVIEWS, COMMENTARIES, EVALUATIONS . . .

"**E**YE OPENING AND EX-TREMELY COMPELLING . . . of critical importance to every clinician who treats gay men. The topics discussed are valuable as both course content for training graduate students in the area of treating gay male victims of sexual trauma, and for seasoned professionals for whom there is a dearth of culturally relevant and sophisticated clinical resources addressing this issue."

Michael Shernoff, MSW
private practice, New York City, and faculty, Hunter College Graduate School of Social Work, New York

"**A** COMPELLING AND POW-ERFUL COLLECTION of essays about the effects of childhood sexual trauma on gay men. What Cassese brings together in this collection is unique! Truly a must read for academics and practitioners."

Martha A. Gabriel, PhD
Associate Professor,
New York University,
Shirley M. Ehrenkranz School
of Social Work

Harrington Park Press
An Imprint of The Haworth Press, Inc.

Gay Men and Childhood Sexual Trauma: Integrating the Shattered Self

Gay Men and Childhood Sexual Trauma: Integrating the Shattered Self has been co-published simultaneously as *Journal of Gay & Lesbian Social Services,* Volume 12, Numbers 1/2 2000.

The *Journal of Gay & Lesbian Social Services* Monographic "Separates"

Below is a list of "separates," which in serials librarianship means a special issue simultaneously published as a special journal issue or double-issue *and* as a "separate" hardbound monograph. (This is a format which we also call a "DocuSerial.")

"Separates" are published because specialized libraries or professionals may wish to purchase a specific thematic issue by itself in a format which can be separately cataloged and shelved, as opposed to purchasing the journal on an on-going basis. Faculty members may also more easily consider a "separate" for classroom adoption.

"Separates" are carefully classified separately with the major book jobbers so that the journal tie-in can be noted on new book order slips to avoid duplicate purchasing.

You may wish to visit Haworth's Website at . . .

http://www.HaworthPress.com

. . . to search our online catalog for complete tables of contents of these separates and related publications.

You may also call 1-800-HAWORTH (outside US/Canada: 607-722-5857), or Fax 1-800-895-0582 (outside US/Canada: 607-771-0012), or e-mail at:

getinfo@haworthpressinc.com

Gay Men and Childhood Sexual Trauma: Integrating the Shattered Self, edited by James Cassese, MSW, CSW (Vol. 12, No. 1/2, 2000). *"An excellent, thought-provoking collection of essays. Therapists who work with gay men will be grateful to have such a comprehensive resource for dealing with sexual trauma."* *(Rik Isensee, LCSW, Author of* Reclaiming Your Life*)*

Midlife Lesbian Relationships: Friends, Lovers, Children, and Parents, edited by Marcy R. Adelman, PhD (Vol. 11, No. 2/3, 2000). *"A careful and sensitive look at the various relationships of [lesbians at midlife] inside and outside of the therapy office. A useful addition to a growing body of literature."* *(Ellyn Kaschak, PhD, Professor of Psychology, San José State University, California, and Editor of the feminist quarterly journal* Women & Therapy*)*

Social Services with Transgendered Youth, edited by Gerald P. Mallon, DSW (Vol. 10, No. 3/4, 1999). *"A well-articulated book that provides valuable information about a population that has been virtually ignored. . . ."* *(Carol T. Tully, PhD, Associate Professor, Tulane University, School of Social Work, New Orleans, Louisiana)*

Queer Families, Common Agendas: Gay People, Lesbians, and Family Values, edited by T. Richard Sullivan, PhD (Vol. 10, No. 1, 1999). *Examines the real life experience of those affected by current laws and policies regarding homosexual families.*

Lady Boys, Tom Boys, Rent Boys: Male and Female Homosexualities in Contemporary Thailand, edited by Peter A. Jackson, PhD, and Gerard Sullivan, PhD (Vol. 9, No. 2/3, 1999). *"Brings to life issues and problems of interpreting sexual and gender identities in contemporary Thailand."* *(Nerida M. Cook, PhD, Lecturer in Sociology, Department of Sociology and Social Work, University of Tasmania, Australia)*

Working with Gay Men and Lesbians in Private Psychotherapy Practice, edited by Christopher J. Alexander, PhD (Vol. 8, No. 4, 1998). *"Rich with information that will prove especially invaluable to therapists planning to or recently having begun to work with lesbian and gay clients in private practice."* *(Michael Shernoff, MSW, Private Practice, NYC; Adjunct Faculty, Hunter College Graduate School of Social Work)*

Violence and Social Injustice Against Lesbian, Gay and Bisexual People, edited by Lacey M. Sloan, PhD, and Nora S. Gustavsson, PhD (Vol. 8, No. 3, 1998). *"An important and timely book that exposes the multilevel nature of violence against gay, lesbian, bisexual, and transgender people."* *(Dorothy Van Soest, DSW, Associate Dean, School of Social Work, University of Texas at Austin)*

The HIV-Negative Gay Man: Developing Strategies for Survival and Emotional Well-Being, edited by Steven Ball, MSW, ACSW (Vol. 8, No. 1, 1998). *"Essential reading for anyone working with HIV-negative gay men." (Walt Odets, PhD, Author, In the Shadow of the Epidemic: Being HIV-Negative in the Age of AIDS; Clinical Psychologist, private practice, Berkeley, California)*

School Experiences of Gay and Lesbian Youth: The Invisible Minority, edited by Mary B. Harris, PhD (Vol. 7, No. 4, 1998). *"Our schools are well served when authors such as these have the courage to highlight problems that schools deny and to advocate for students whom schools make invisible." (Gerald Unks, Professor, School of Education, University of North Carolina at Chapel Hill; Editor, The Gay Teen.)* Provides schools with helpful suggestions for becoming places that welcome gay and lesbian students and, therefore, better serve the needs of all students.

Rural Gays and Lesbians: Building on the Strengths of Communities, edited by James Donald Smith, ACSW, LCSW, and Ronald J. Mancoske, BSCW, DSW (Vol. 7, No. 3, 1998). *"This informative and well-written book fills a major gap in the literature and should be widely read." (James Midgley, PhD, Harry and Riva Specht Professor of Public Social Services and Dean, School of Social Welfare, University of California at Berkeley)*

Gay Widowers: Life After the Death of a Partner, edited by Michael Shernoff, MSW, ACSW (Vol. 7, No. 2, 1997). *"This inspiring book is not only for those who have experienced the tragedy of losing a partner–it's for every gay man who loves another." (Michelangelo Signorile, author, Life Outside)*

Gay and Lesbian Professionals in the Closet: Who's In, Who's Out, and Why, edited by Teresa DeCrescenzo, MSW, LCSW (Vol. 6, No. 4, 1997). *"A gripping example of the way the closet cripples us and those we try to serve." (Virginia Uribe, PhD, Founder, Project 10 Outreach to Gay and Lesbian Youth, Los Angeles Unified School District)*

Two Spirit People: American Indian Lesbian Women and Gay Men, edited by Lester B. Brown, PhD (Vol. 6, No. 2, 1997). *"A must read for educators, social workers, and other providers of social and mental health services." (Wynne DuBray, Professor, Division of Social Work, California State University)*

Social Services for Senior Gay Men and Lesbians, edited by Jean K. Quam, PhD, MSW (Vol. 6, No. 1, 1997). *"Provides a valuable overview of social service issues and practice with elder gay men and lesbians." (Outword)*

Men of Color: A Context for Service to Homosexually Active Men, edited by John F. Longres, PhD (Vol. 5, No. 2/3, 1996). *"An excellent book for the 'helping professions.'" (Feminist Bookstore News)*

Health Care for Lesbians and Gay Men: Confronting Homophobia and Heterosexism, edited by K. Jean Peterson, DSW (Vol. 5, No. 1, 1996). *"Essential reading for those concerned with the quality of health care services." (Etcetera)*

Sexual Identity on the Job: Issues and Services, edited by Alan L. Ellis, PhD, and Ellen D. B. Riggle, PhD (Vol. 4, No. 4, 1996). *"Reveals a critical need for additional research to address the many questions left unanswered or answered unsatisfactorily by existing research." (Sex Roles: A Journal of Research) "A key resource for addressing sexual identity concerns and issues in your workplace." (Outlines)*

Human Services for Gay People: Clinical and Community Practice, edited by Michael Shernoff, MSW, ACSW (Vol. 4, No. 2, 1996). *"This very practical book on clinical and community practice issues belongs on the shelf of every social worker, counselor, or therapist working with lesbians and gay men." (Gary A. Lloyd, PhD, ACSW, BCD, Professor and Coordinator, Institute for Research and Training in HIV/AIDS Counseling, School of Social Work, Tulane University)*

Violence in Gay and Lesbian Domestic Partnerships, edited by Claire M. Renzetti, PhD, and Charles Harvey Miley, PhD (Vol. 4, No. 1, 1996). *"A comprehensive guidebook for service providers and community and church leaders." (Small Press Magazine)*

Gays and Lesbians in Asia and the Pacific: Social and Human Services, edited by Gerard Sullivan, PhD, and Laurence Wai-Teng Leong, PhD (Vol. 3, No. 3, 1995). *"Insights in this book can provide an understanding of these cultures and provide an opportunity to better understand your own." (The Lavendar Lamp)*

Lesbians of Color: Social and Human Services, edited by Hilda Hidalgo, PhD, ACSW (Vol. 3, No. 2, 1995). *"An illuminating and helpful guide for readers who wish to increase their understanding of and sensitivity toward lesbians of color and the challenges they face." (Black Caucus of the ALA Newsletter)*

Lesbian Social Services: Research Issues, edited by Carol T. Tully, PhD, MSW (Vol. 3, No. 1, 1995). *"Dr. Tully challenges us to reexamine theoretical conclusions that relate to lesbians. . . A must read." (The Lavendar Lamp)*

HIV Disease: Lesbians, Gays and the Social Services, edited by Gary A. Lloyd, PhD, ACSW, and Mary Ann Kuszelewicz, MSW, ACSW (Vol. 2, No. 3/4, 1995). *"A wonderful guide to working with people with AIDS. A terrific meld of political theory and hands-on advice, it is essential, inspiring reading for anyone fighting the pandemic or assisting those living with it." (Small Press)*

Addiction and Recovery in Gay and Lesbian Persons, edited by Robert J. Kus, PhD, RN (Vol. 2, No. 1, 1995). *"Readers are well-guided through the multifaceted, sometimes confusing, and frequently challenging world of the gay or lesbian drug user." (Drug and Alcohol Review)*

Helping Gay and Lesbian Youth: New Policies, New Programs, New Practice, edited by Teresa DeCrescenzo, MSW, LCSW (Vol. 1, No. 3/4, 1994). *"Insightful and up-to-date, this handbook covers several topics relating to gay and lesbian adolescents . . . It is must reading for social workers, educators, guidance counselors, and policymakers." (Journal of Social Work Education)*

Social Services for Gay and Lesbian Couples, edited by Lawrence A. Kurdek, PhD (Vol. 1, No. 2, 1994). *"Many of the unique issues confronted by gay and lesbian couples are addressed here." (Ambush Magazine)*

Gay Men
and Childhood Sexual Trauma:
Integrating the Shattered Self

James Cassese, MSW, CSW
Editor

Gay Men and Childhood Sexual Trauma: Integrating the Shattered Self has been co-published simultaneously as *Journal of Gay & Lesbian Social Services,* Volume 12, Numbers 1/2 2000.

Harrington Park Press
An Imprint of
The Haworth Press, Inc.
New York • London • Oxford

Published by

Harrington Park Press®, 10 Alice Street, Binghamton, NY 13904-1580

Harrington Park Press® is an imprint of The Haworth Press, Inc., 10 Alice Street, Binghamton, NY 13904-1580 USA.

Gay Men and Childhood Sexual Trauma: Integrating the Shattered Self has been co-published simultaneously as *Journal of Gay & Lesbian Services*™, Volume 12, Numbers 1/2 2000.

Cover design by Jennifer M. Gaska

Library of Congress Cataloging-in-Publication Data

Gay men and childhood sexual trauma : integrating the shattered self / James Cassese, editor.
    p. cm.
    "Has been co-published simultaneously as Journal of gay & lesbian social services, Volume 12, Numbers 1/2 2000."
    Includes bibliographical references and index.
    ISBN 1-56023-137-8 (alk. paper)–ISBN 1-56023-138-6 (alk. paper)
    1. Gay men–United States–Psychology. 2. Gay men–Counseling of–United States. 3. Adult child sexual abuse victims–United States. 4. Male rape victims–United States. 5. Social work with gays–United States. I. Cassese, James. II. Journal of gay & lesbian social services.
HQ76.3.U5 G389 2000
305.38'9664–dc21
                                                               00-063234

Indexing, Abstracting & Website/Internet Coverage

This section provides you with a list of major indexing & abstracting services. That is to say, each service began covering this periodical during the year noted in the right column. Most Websites which are listed below have indicated that they will either post, disseminate, compile, archive, cite or alert their own Website users with research-based content from this work. (This list is as current as the copyright date of this publication.)

Abstracting, Website/Indexing Coverage .... Year When Coverage Began

- *BUBL Information Service, an Internet-based Information Service for the UK higher education community <URL: http://bubl.ac.uk/>* **1995**

- *caredata CD: the social and community care database* **1994**

- *CNPIEC Reference Guide: Chinese National Directory of Foreign Periodicals* **1995**

- *Contemporary Women's Issues* **1998**

- *Criminal Justice Abstracts* **1997**

- *ERIC Clearinghouse on Urban Education (ERIC/CUE)* **1995**

- *Family Studies Database (online and CD/ROM) <www.nisc.com>* **1996**

- *Family Violence & Sexual Assault Bulletin* **1999**

- *FINDEX, free Internet Directory of over 150,000 publications from around the world <www.publist.com>* **1999**

- *Gay & Lesbian Abstracts* **1999**

(continued)

Special Bibliographic Notes related to special journal issues (separates) and indexing/abstracting:

- indexing/abstracting services in this list will also cover material in any "separate" that is co-published simultaneously with Haworth's special thematic journal issue or DocuSerial. Indexing/abstracting usually covers material at the article/chapter level.
- monographic co-editions are intended for either non-subscribers or libraries which intend to purchase a second copy for their circulating collections.
- monographic co-editions are reported to all jobbers/wholesalers/approval plans. The source journal is listed as the "series" to assist the prevention of duplicate purchasing in the same manner utilized for books-in-series.
- to facilitate user/access services all indexing/abstracting services are encouraged to utilize the co-indexing entry note indicated at the bottom of the first page of each article/chapter/contribution.
- this is intended to assist a library user of any reference tool (whether print, electronic, online, or CD-ROM) to locate the monographic version if the library has purchased this version but not a subscription to the source journal.
- individual articles/chapters in any Haworth publication are also available through the Haworth Document Delivery Service (HDDS).

Gay Men and Childhood Sexual Trauma: Integrating the Shattered Self

CONTENTS

ABOUT THE EDITOR

James Cassese, MSW, CSW, is a private practice psychotherapist in New York City specializing in the treatment of adult male survivors of childhood sexual trauma. His experiences as an AIDS activist and psychotherapist working with gay and lesbian clients drew him to explore the connections between childhood sexual trauma and subsequent HIV risk behavior in adulthood. These links formed the focus of his work for nearly a decade in a variety of settings and informed his interest in the Harm Reduction movement, and the work of Brazilian educator Paulo Freire.

In recognition of the significance of this approach and his achievement in this area, Mr. Cassese was named J. William Fulbright Foreign Scholar for Brazil 1998-1999. He offered course work and intensive trainings regarding strengthening HIV prevention efforts by understanding the connections between childhood sexual trauma and HIV risk behavior at the post-graduate level at the University of Sao Paulo. As part of his Fulbright duties, Mr. Cassese gathered information from and developed relationships with Brazilian CBOs/NGOs with whom he continues on-going cultural exchange, participating in conferences and providing site-specific workshops throughout Brazil.

Mr. Cassese is on the faculty at New York University Graduate School of Social Work, and provides workshops and designs curricula on these and related topics throughout the United States.

ABOUT THE CONTRIBUTORS

Dennis Balcom, MSW, LICSW, is a clinical social worker in private practice in Brookline, MA. He is a Board Certified Diplomate in Clinical Social Work, a member of the Academy of Certified Social Workers, a clinical member of the AAMFT, and a member of the EMDRIA. He has taught at local universities, presented at national conferences, and published on topics related to men's issues, shame, couples and family therapy, and EMDR.

Franklin L. Brooks, MSW, LCSW, ACSW, is in private practice in Portland, ME. His clinical practice includes working with individuals, couples and families on a wide range of issues including past sexual abuse, sexual orientation, and transgender issues. He has presented workshops on gender atypical/nontraditional issues as well as sexual minority youth issues at local, regional, and national conferences. He is an adjunct faculty member in the Social Work Department at the University of Southern Maine in Portland. He is Chairperson of the Sexual Minorities Issues Committee of the Maine Chapter, National Association of Social Workers. He is also a member of the Same-Sex Domestic Violence Task Force of the Family Crisis Services in Portland and The National Organization on Male Sexual Victimization.

James Cassese, **MSW, CSW,** is a private practice psychotherapist in New York City specializing in the treatment of adult male survivors of childhood sexual trauma. Dr. Cassese taught at the post-graduate level at the University of Sao Paulo as part of his duties as J. William Fulbright Foreign Scholar for Brazil 1998-1999. Part-time faculty member at New York University Graduate School of Social Work, he also provides workshops and designs curricula on these and related topics throughout the United States and South America.

Neal King, PhD, CA, is a licensed psychologist and Dean and Professor of Psychology at the California Campus of the University of Sarasota in Orange, CA. He is the author of *Speaking Our Truth: Voices of Courage and Healing for Male Survivors of Childhood Sexual Abuse* (HarperPerennial, 1995) and various related articles and chapters. He is active in the American Psychological Association, National Council of Schools and Programs of Professional Psychology, and the National Organization on Male Sexual Victimization, The American Association for Higher Education and The Society for Psychologists in Management. Dr. King has also trained with the American Red Cross as a Disaster Mental Health Technician.

Mike Lew, MEd, is the author of *Victims No Longer: Men Recovering From Incest and Other Sexual Child Abuse* (HarperCollins). As Co-Director of the Next Step Counseling and Training Center, Dr. Lew has worked with thousands of men and women in their healing from the effects of childhood sexual abuse, rape, physical violence, emotional abuse and neglect. He conducts workshops, public lectures and trainings worldwide for survivors and professionals who serve them. Mike Lew is a Charter Life Member of the American Professional Society on the Abuse of Children, and a professional member of the American Counseling Association, Association for Specialists in Group Work, Association for Gay, Lesbian and Bisexual Issues in Counseling, and the New England Society for the Study of Dissociation.

Patrick A. Meyer, LCSW, is a Licensed Clinical Social Worker in private practice in Santa Cruz, CA, and Assistant Professor with the Graduate Program of the College of Social Work at San Jose State University. He teaches Human, Group and Organizational Development at the College and is considered the local expert in clinical work (group and individual) with male survivors of childhood sexual abuse. His practice focuses on work primarily with men, with gay and lesbian individuals and families and with staff development in organizations and businesses working with highly stressed populations. In his free time he is a devoted gardener, uncle and poet.

Ernesto Mujica, PhD, is a clinical psychologist and psychoanalyst in private practice in New York City, working primarily with adults and couples. His main interests include the treatment of dissociation, the integration and working through of the bodily and emotional effects of childhood trauma, and the impact of social forces, language and cultural issues on interpersonal relations and psychotherapy. Dr. Mujica is an Instructor in Clinical Psychology at Columbia Presbyterian Medical Center, Adjunct Assistant Professor at Teachers College, Columbia University, and Supervisor of Psychotherapy and Director of Research at the William Alanson White Institute for Psychoanalysis and Psychotherapy.

Lawrence G. Rosenberg, PhD, received his doctorate in clinical psychology from Yale University. He is an Instructor in Psychology in the Department of Psychiatry at Harvard Medical School and maintains a practice in Cambridge, MA. He co-teaches Psychotherapy with Gay, Lesbian, Bisexual, and Transgendered Clients at The Cambridge Hospital, where he also lectures and supervises in Behavioral Medicine. Dr. Rosenberg has written and presented on gay development, integrative psychotherapy, hypnosis, trauma treatment, and compulsive sexual behavior. He recently co-authored (with Steven Schwartzberg, PhD) "Being Gay and Being Male: Psychotherapy with Gay and Bisexual Men" in Pollack and Levant's *New Psychotherapy for Men.*

Don Wright, MEd, is Founder and Executive Director of the British Columbia Society for Male Survivors of Sexual Abuse (BCSMSSA), headquartered in Vancouver, BC with a branch office in Victoria. Mr. Wright is currently Chair of the Greater Vancouver and Victoria Regional Victim Services Coordinating Committees; and has worked on two committees with the Provincial Ministry of the Attorney General in developing practice standards and an evaluation framework for Specialized Victim Services and Sexual Assault Programs in British Columbia. Dr. Wright conducts training seminars throughout Canada, and has presented at conferences in both Canada and the United States.

Foreword:
The State of the Art:
Working with Gay Male Survivors
of Sexual Trauma

Mike Lew

At the 1993 March on Washington for Gay and Lesbian Rights, activist Urvashi Vaid began a brilliant and rousing address by saying:

> With hearts full of hope and an abiding faith in justice, we have come to Washington to speak to America. We have come to speak the truth of our lives and silence the liars. We have come to challenge the cowardly Congress to end its paralysis on moral leadership. We have come to defend our honor and win our equality. But most of all, we have come to say to America that this day marks the return from exile of the gay and lesbian people.

> We are banished no more. We wander the wilderness of despair no more. We are afraid no more. This day marks the end of the power of fear, which has defined our lives. For on this day, with love in our hearts, we have come to reach out to all America to build a bridge of understanding and progress, a majestic bridge as solid as steel, a bridge to a land where no one suffers prejudice because of their sexual orientation, their race, their gender, their religion, or their human difference . . .

[Haworth co-indexing entry note]: "Foreword: The State of the Art: Working with Gay Male Survivors of Sexual Trauma." Lew, Mike. Co-published simultaneously in *Journal of Gay & Lesbian Social Services* (Harrington Park Press, an imprint of The Haworth Press, Inc.) Vol. 12, No. 1/2, 2000, pp. xxiii-xxxi; and: *Gay Men and Childhood Sexual Trauma: Integrating the Shattered Self* (ed: James Cassese) Harrington Park Press, an imprint of The Haworth Press, Inc., 2000, pp. xvii-xxv. Single or multiple copies of this article are available for a fee from The Haworth Document Delivery Service [1-800-342-9678, 9:00 a.m. - 5:00 p.m. (EST). E-mail address: getinfo@haworthpressinc.com].

xvii

Vaid went on to challenge the Far Right for their profound un-truth–their use of language to distort and mislead. Her insights about anti-gay zealots are equally true of the opposition to the survivor recovery movement: in many instances they are the same people and organizations. Vaid spoke of how they are wrong spiritually, morally and politically.

I would add that they are wrong psychologically. They are wrong because they twist and deny the reality of abuse. They are wrong because they ignore and belittle the needs of children and the severity of their wounds. They are wrong to dismiss all abuse memories as fantasies or lies. And they are wrong when they promulgate pseudoscience as fact, when they attempt to twist the arts of healing into the shameful practices of denial and deceit. They are wrong when they offer glib answers and simple solutions to complex problems. They are wrong when they blame and shame victims while making excuses for those who victimize. And they are shamefully wrong when they equate same-sex child abuse with homosexuality.

Some are merely mistaken. Others have been misled and deluded. Still others intentionally lie and misrepresent in order to further their own political, economic or sexual agendas. And some derive pleasure from inflicting harm. But all of them are wrong. They are wrong because harming a child is evil. Because, as AIDS activists have so clearly pointed out, SILENCE = DEATH. Those who attack survivors and their allies, like those who attack gays and lesbians, distort the true meaning of sexual freedom, family values, religion, science, healing and civil liberties. Whether they call themselves defenders of the sanctity of the family, religious fundamentalists, detectors of false memory, advocates of inter-generational love, or balanced journalists. Whether they name themselves the False Memory Syndrome Foundation, Family Research Council or the North American Man-Boy Love Association, these so-called crusaders only care about power and control.

This volume, written as a clinical text, provides voices of calm and reason to counteract the distortion and fanaticism surrounding discussions of both sexual orientation and sexual child abuse. Much as we might wish it to, our professional work does not occur in clinical isolation. Our clients, as well as their treatment, exist within a social and political environment. If we ignore that reality, we fail to understand an essential aspect of healing.

Gay Men and Childhood Sexual Trauma: Integrating the Shattered

Self explicates many ways that homophobia and heterosexism create a climate that permits, and even encourages, sexual exploitation of boys (gay and straight) and interferes with treatment and recovery. This incorporation of the sociopolitical with the scientific and therapeutic is vital if we are to establish an environment of true healing.

Many gay men in recovery find it useful to explore the parallel between coming out (a necessary early step in the healing of one's sexuality) and disclosure of the abuse (a beginning to the survivor's recovery process). An "out" gay man who is new to working on sexual abuse issues can employ the coming out metaphor to help him understand what may be in store. Similarly, a survivor who has been having difficulty coming to terms with his homosexuality may be able to see how the coming out process mirrors his recovery work.

This is a collection of essays whose time has come. It is time for recognition of the complexity of issues facing gay male survivors of childhood sexual trauma. It is time to understand the interrelationship of the politics of abuse and homophobia. It's time to understand the specific therapeutic needs of gay men in recovery. At the same time, we must recognize commonalities with other groups, forging connections to the larger community of humanity.

We have come a long way from the days when isolation seemed the only available alternative to abuse–or aching loneliness drove many survivors to endure the pain and distress of unhealthy relationships. We've made tremendous progress over the past decades, but we're not yet home free. Many obstacles continue to challenge survivors and their allies.

The backlash against survivors who stand up against abuse continues unabated. Memories are still labeled "false" when they are not precise or continuous.

While there are many dedicated, caring people within the legal system and mass media, there are also unscrupulous individuals, eager to profit from pain. Therapists and counselors working with survivors are still accused of "instilling false memories" in their clients. Therapist-bashing has become a popular sport among some reporters and lawyers. A number of the leading advocates for survivors have been subjected to vicious attacks, lies, character assassination and frivolous, harassing lawsuits. Although they are frustrating, costly and time-consuming, these attacks have not succeeded in their aim of silencing the voices of healing.

There are other problems facing survivors and those who care about them. Some professionals try to co-opt recovery, taking power away from survivors. They seek to establish a rigid professional hierarchy of abuse treatment, complete with licensing examinations, official organizations, approved courses, and other manifestations of self-seeking careerism. Professionals must avoid pathologizing our clients by taking a "healthier than thou" attitude.

Some people attempt to profit from the natural desire for a "quick fix" or "magical solution"–offering simplistic formulas or marketing gimmickry, "one size fits all" techniques. Whether in the form of books, therapeutic techniques, or recovery programs, it is important to be wary of easy answers to complex questions. No one has the knowledge or the right to tell a survivor what he or she must do in order to heal. Recovery consists of a series of courageous, individual acts.

There are those who continue to belittle survivor issues. Even now, women and men (and especially gay men) who were abused as children may encounter ridicule, contempt, dismissal, denial and minimization. While this is less frequent, it should never happen.

There still are attempts to keep survivors separated from their natural allies, producing isolation that would keep them weak. This sabotage takes many forms: criticizing individuals or groups, creating false distinctions, playing on fears and doubts, fomenting racism, sexism, homophobia, heterophobia, ageism and other damaging "isms," encouraging misunderstanding, stereotyping and jealousy, and hindering recovery for all.

There needs to be far greater funding of prevention programs, education of professionals, informing the general public, and treatment of child victims and adult survivors. This is especially true for poor people who require access to resources that are available to wealthier individuals. It is true for racial, ethnic and religious minorities, who have ample reason to be suspicious of agendas imposed by outsiders who don't understand their cultures and values. There must be opportunities for minority communities to educate their own members, creating services consistent with the values of the group.

We need far greater recognition of the difficulties experienced by survivors' spouses, partners and other loved ones so that supportive resources can be developed. We need and deserve more services of all kinds, provided by government, professionals or survivors themselves.

There is ample evidence that male survivors–with significant help from female survivors and other allies–have made important progress over the years. And in many instances it was gay male survivors who took the lead in creating services. Some years ago, at the National Lesbian and Gay Health Conference, Claudia Black, PhD, was asked why there are so many gays and lesbians in recovery programs. Her answer was that oppressed groups have always had to advocate for themselves.

It is unlikely that ten years ago it would have been possible to make films that address male survivor issues (such as the excellent and heart-wrenching "The Boys of St. Vincent"), let alone have them distributed in theaters and video stores. We did not see major sports figures like Canadian star hockey player Sheldon Kennedy and Olympic gold medalist diver Greg Louganis speaking out about having been abused–and being taken seriously–or baseball superstar Mark McGwire donating millions to the fight against child abuse. Books by non-celebrities, like Richard Hoffman's superb memoir, *Half the House*, would not have found a mainstream publisher–nor would a major television network have picked up his story for a prime time program (Dateline NBC).

A decade ago churches, schools and other institutions were not held accountable for abusive actions by their personnel; governments were more likely to cover up sexual child abuse than provide help. We did not have such a great number of books, articles, TV shows, films and plays with survivor themes. There were far fewer resources available for survivors.

We have come a long way, but we have far to go. And we must–and will–get there. The struggles of the gay rights and survivor recovery movements parallel those of other oppressed groups. The understanding gained from their experiences–including psychological insights–informs our work with gay men in recovery from sexual trauma. With this collection, Cassese and his colleagues provide much-needed resources for professionals working in all areas of trauma recovery.

It is rare that I read a psychological text that leaves me wanting more, but *Gay Men and Childhood Sexual Trauma: Integrating the Shattered Self* is one such work. Offering theory based on a solid marriage of research and clinical experience, presenting a range of theoretical orientations, clinical modalities and literary styles, it comes to a surprisingly compatible mixture of the academic and anecdotal.

The tone of this work reflects an essential aspect of the healing arts–one that is, sad to say, too often ignored in the current drive to "manage care" and medicate a patient rather than help a person. Here we find, as a primary focus, the humanity and individuality of gay male survivors in their recovery from the dually devastating effects of sexual child abuse and homophobia.

In his excellent introductory essay, Cassese sets a tone of clear-eyed clinical expertise, fearless self-examination and a shining core of humanity.

Recent years have brought a resurgence of right-wing ideologues who prey on fears and doubts. They offer "reparative therapy" and "ex-homosexual" poster boys who claim to have "cured" their sexuality through prayer, self-denial and (no doubt) significant monetary contributions to the local "ex-gay ministry." What a perversion of language! What a distortion of reality! And what a relief to see erroneous assumptions being challenged by Cassese, and replaced from the outset with clear realities of language. How refreshing to see the phrase "the gay child" used matter-of-factly in a professional text. We can no longer accept as "professionals" those who insist that the validity of one's sexual orientation is a topic open to debate.

It is vital that sexual trauma be presented as the harming of the powerless by the powerful. Cassese, perhaps through his cross-cultural and bilingual experience, understands that the power of language is as great as the power of silence. The telling of truth–reclaiming the language of truth–begins the process of overturning the lies and reclaiming power.

Richard Hoffman, poet, author, survivor (and admitted heterosexual), has taken up the struggle to reclaim language, writing:

> With NAMBLA on the one hand crying out "we're gay too, and persecuted for our sexual preference," and rightist homophobes on the other busily scapegoating gay men for crimes against children, it becomes difficult to get anyone to see that these violations are first of all crimes of abusive power, oppressive, exploitative power, and that they are a human rights issue. Add to that such psychobabble as "the incest family," "the cycle of violence," and statistically inaccurate representations that suggest to the public that those who are violated as children go on to

violate children, and you have a paralyzing confusion about who is responsible and what, if anything, can be done.

In a commentary on WBUR (the Public Radio station at Boston University), Hoffman said:

Most insidious of all is the homophobia that equates those who assault little boys with gay men. In fact, for young boys, there is probably nothing that silences them more effectively than homophobia. By the age of eight, boys are using the term "faggot" as a verbal weapon. How can they tell us then if they are lured and entrapped by a coach, an uncle, a teacher, a neighbor?

In an Op-Ed piece in the *Boston Globe* following the murder of young Jeffrey Curley, Hoffman continues his mission to reclaim truth in language. He wrote:

Let's begin by refusing to use the word "pedophile." The word comes from Greek and means, literally, "one who loves children." What an Orwellian inversion! To use this word to describe those who violate children, and in many instances kill to silence them, is to help the wolf into his sheepskin.

The term pedophile is more than a poor word choice, however; a pseudo-medical term, it asks us to see such evil as arising from disease or illness, evil in its effect, perhaps, but no more intentional than other natural misfortunes like diabetes, say, or muscular dystrophy. This makes the violation of children a part of the natural order and the perpetrator one who cannot help himself.

In place of the term pedophile, then, let me offer an alternative: pedoscele, from Latin "scelus," meaning "evil deed." Try it. Pedoscele: one who does evil to children.

And let's stop calling them "sex offenders," as if their crimes had anything to do with sex. (Perhaps Jeffrey Dahmer was a "food offender.") As the poet Linda McCarriston once pointed out, "Saying 'the man had sex with the child' is like saying, 'The man had dinner with the pork chop.'"

The rape of a child is a violent act of contempt, not an expression of sexuality or affection. Pedosceles want us to believe otherwise. This is why they talk of "love" between men and boys. All too often we fall for it. For example, in a newscast about the man who had devastated the childhoods of several generations in my hometown, including mine, a TV commentator said that the defendant had "admitted that he is overly fond of young boys." (The word "pedophile" is there, in the shadows.) At that pre-trial hearing, one boy said the man had threatened to cut off his genitals if he told. Another boy testified that the man threatened to shoot his little brother. Overly fond indeed.

This collection of essays helps to set the language–and the record–straight.

We have Neal King's fine explication of internal and external conflicts faced by gay male trauma survivors developmentally, his guidance to clinicians, and discussion how culture-based gender expectations play out in gay male relationships.

Lawrence Rosenberg offers a well-researched piece on "phase-oriented psychotherapy" for gay men recovering from trauma. He presents a specific theoretical and clinical perspective on the nature of sexual trauma and how it affects the gay male survivor in his treatment and the therapist participating in that treatment. It provides guidance, comfort and suggestions of specific techniques to therapists who are new to the area of treating sexual abuse recovery and those who favor a more structured approach to the therapeutic process.

Patrick Meyer contributes a guide for potential facilitators of male survivor groups. This essay is an excellent clinical resource that should be required reading for anyone contemplating starting a group. In addition to warning of pitfalls and making suggestions for group guidelines, Meyer makes a powerful case for groups of mixed sexual orientation.

James Cassese's essay on HIV and the cycle of trauma in gay men is an excellent framing of the issues by an experienced and compassionate expert.

Perhaps because my initial graduate work was in cultural anthropology, I'm pleased to see emphasis placed on cultural issues in psychotherapy as in the essay by Mujica and Cassese. The material here is so rich, so important, that I wish there were more. I hope the authors will consider expanding it into a book. For now, I'm glad to have this much. Cassese's courageous use of self in presenting the issues is impressive.

There's lots more that is helpful here. Our attention is drawn to crucial issues of self-care for the professional in the face of vicarious trauma. That is worth at least another whole book, but it is important that it was raised in this context.

For a number of years I've been asking male survivors what they think professionals need to hear. This book offers evidence that at least some professionals are listening. It should help us provide services that our gay male survivor clients truly need. Its time has come.

REFERENCE

Hoffman, R. (1995). *Half the house: A memoir.* New York: Harcourt Brace.

Introduction:
Integrating the Experience
of Childhood Sexual Trauma
in Gay Men

James Cassese

SUMMARY. The field of sexual trauma developed from the sociopolitical movements of the feminist, rape, and child protection movements. As thinking in the field developed, however, it has been difficult to integrate the perspective of the male survivor of sexual trauma into these perspectives. Gay men, in particular, have been notably absent from the literature, except when their abuse history is discussed as an etiology for their sexuality. It is clear that gay men suffer violence and oppression in the form of homophobia–an abuse with a sexual focus. Integrating the experience of gay men who have suffered trauma into perspectives regarding sexual trauma offers a possibility to enhance understanding about, as well as prevention efforts against, the sexual abuse of children. This includes expanding definitions and vocabulary regarding sexual trauma, as well as recognizing the impact on mental health professionals of working with survivors of sexual trauma. *[Article copies available for a fee from The Haworth Document Delivery Service: 1-800-342-9678. E-mail address: <getinfo@haworthpressinc.com> Website: <http://www.HaworthPress.com>]*

KEYWORDS. Dissociation, feminism, gay men, homophobia, oppression, powerlessness, sexual trauma, vicarious traumatization

Developments in clinical understanding regarding sexual trauma since the 1970s have followed the strides of the Feminist Movement.

[Haworth co-indexing entry note]: "Introduction: Integrating the Experience of Childhood Sexual Trauma in Gay Men." Cassese, James. Co-published simultaneously in *Journal of Gay & Lesbian Social Services* (Harrington Park Press, an imprint of The Haworth Press, Inc.) Vol. 12, No. 1/2, 2000, pp. 1-17; and: *Gay Men and Childhood Sexual Trauma: Integrating the Shattered Self* (ed: James Cassese) Harrington Park Press, an imprint of The Haworth Press, Inc., 2000, pp. 1-17. Single or multiple copies of this article are available for a fee from The Haworth Document Delivery Service [1-800-342-9678, 9:00 a.m. - 5:00 p.m. (EST). E-mail address: getinfo@haworthpressinc.com].

1

Without the shift in perspective precipitated by that movement, current conceptualizations of crimes and abuses of violence and power would be impossible. Feminism clarified our understanding of, and the *language* for, the unequal balance of power between the genders, seeking to liberate the oppressed, redefining "rape as a method of political control, enforcing the subordination of women through terror" (Herman, 1992). Early Feminist activism illustrated what Paulo Freire (1970) considered the first stage in humanist/libertarian pedagogy wherein "the oppressed unveil the world of oppression and through praxis commit themselves to its transformation."

In the second stage of Freire's pedagogy, "the reality of oppression has already been transformed, and this pedagogy ceases to belong to the oppressed and becomes a pedagogy of all people in the process of permanent liberation." For a variety of reasons, Feminism alone was not able to move to this next level. While components have indeed been addressed by Feminist and subsequent child protection movements, the reality of oppression has not been fully transformed. Common in liberation movements, there has been a retention of the dynamics essential to oppression (Freire, 1970). Freire (1970) notes that often, "during the initial stage of the struggle, the oppressed instead of striving for liberation, tend themselves to become oppressors or 'sub-oppressors' " (Freire, 1970).

There is a poignant irony in a movement setting into motion philosophical investigation which ultimately evolves to the point that it returns to scrutinize its original postulates. While Feminism was responsible for a revolution in thought, time and subsequent theorizing have allowed for recognition of some of early Feminism's limitations. The oppressive forces within the dominant culture necessitated that the early Feminists argue within the confines of the entrenched gender binary where non-heterosexual sexualities were unrecognized. Consequently, even the "radical" assertions of early Feminism which sought to establish balance and reduce oppression, maintained the dynamics of oppression in the form of an oppressor/oppressed relation based on gender.

It is long past time, however, for the need to question some of the movement's early assumptions such as rape is "nothing more or less than a conscious process of intimidation by which *all* men keep *all* women in a state of fear" (Brownmiller, 1975; Herman, 1992). When *all* men, by virtue of their gender, are seen as universal offenders, no real transformation can occur. The oppressive bonds are instead reconfigured. Identifying the oppressor in categorical terms engenders a risk that offenders of different types may be overlooked. While the oppressed may be recognized, the oppressor defies categorical identification. This is to say that *all* people possess the vulnerability to be oppressed and traumatized. *Gay Men and Childhood Sexual Trauma: Integrating the Shattered Self* seeks to examine the dynamics and aftereffects of the traumatization of gay males, a phenomenon which is allowed for and fueled by the forces of oppression in the form of homophobia.

The unwitting retention of oppressor dynamics is illustrated by the categorization of men as perpetrators by virtue of their gender. Such a categorization fails to consider the experience of the gay male. Although he is categorized as "male," the gay male does not possess the same rights and powers as does the heterosexually-identified male. His will, his choices, and his power are limited: he cannot legally marry; he can rarely be open about himself in the workforce; he can seldom hold a lover's hand in public without the fear of assault. He is vulnerable to discrimination in employment, housing, medical care. He is belittled as "girlish," "less than a man" by a dominant misogynist culture that demands that he behave according to oppressive standards. He is teased and tormented in school and consequently often performs below his potential academically. This often results in his being restricted from further education. He may flee from the torture of school, or be afraid of or unwelcome in extracurricular activities that often help gain scholarships or entrance to prestigious colleges. As a result he is at an educational, and ultimately socioeconomic, disadvantage.

At the same time he is identified by some as an oppressive perpetrator. When he "acts like a man," the gay male is imbued with a false power essential to his gender by a perspective which retains the dominant culture's priority of his maleness over any other characteristic. In this sense, homophobia is a disguised extension of misogyny directed at the gay male.[1]

In this respect, gay men represent one of the last frontiers of victim-blaming. They are alleged to possess power as a result of their gender, and yet excluded and vilified by the very power-identified group to which they are supposed to belong. They are located along a fault-line, a pressure point between two rejecting factions. Located in this chasm, the gay male experience is often undervalued and indeed the sexual trauma suffered on a daily basis seems to simply not exist in the literature. The liberational activism of the early Feminist movement began the process of identifying the gender oppression in the dominant culture which added fuel to the child protection movement. The work of subsequent waves is to *integrate* the various voices of the traumatized and understand their needs. *Gay Men and Childhood Sexual Trauma: Integrating the Shattered Self* represents an effort in that direction by generating discussion and developing a language to clarify the experience of sexually traumatized gay men.

Most of the major literary contributions to the field of sexual trauma (and often those texts taught at the graduate level) exclude the male experience. Many rely on data that suggest, for example, that "males perpetuate incest in far greater numbers than females, most often abusing female children" (Courtois, 1988). Some authors insist "there can be little doubt that the problem of childhood sexual abuse is one that overwhelmingly involves males" (Newton, 1992). Confidence in such statements is made possible by research which fails to accurately capture the experience of males and authors who are willing to accept the resultant data. This validates a tendency to configure perpetration and consequently victimhood, in categorical terms. Messler-Davies and Frawley (1994) make little reference to male survivors except to observe that "a more comprehensive understanding of the male survivor awaits additional empirical and clinical investigation." Matthew Mendel's (1994) *The Male Survivor* is a thorough and informative text which provides a comprehensive discussion of the issues and a thorough review of the literature. However, even those few texts which explore the male experience have little information which applies to the gay male experience.

When homosexuality and sexual trauma are discussed, there is almost always some discussion of a cause-effect relation (Finkelhor, 1984; Mayer, 1983; Newton, 1992; Van Wyk & Geist, 1984). The idea of some causational relation between these phenomena implies an interest in an etiology of homosexuality. This might be appropriate in terms of a clinical exploration a patient's thoughts and fantasies (Lew, 1988). In other words, to the degree the *patient* wonders about a connection, it is worth pursuing as it relates to clinical material. However, in terms of research, the usefulness of exploring a traumatic etiology for homosexuality seems questionable despite its prominence in the literature. This tendency becomes further suspect in the context where the term "homosexual" is used to identify same-sex childhood sexual abuse (Newton, 1992; Raybin, 1969). The use of terms "homosexual incest" or "homosexual pedophilia" (despite the absence of analogous heterosexually identified terms) combined with a willingness to consider a traumatic etiology to adult homosexuality, speaks to the degree to which the homosexuality is subject to scrutiny. Homosexuality is (as is heterosexuality, bisexuality, and asexuality) a distinct mature sexuality which involves adults. Pedophilia is not. The ease with which homosexuality is used as an adjective in this context is misleading. It illustrates the lack of knowledge and understanding available regarding both homosexuality *and* the effect of trauma on adult sexuality.

Gay men are not entirely absent from the literature, however. Mike Lew (1988) devotes an entire chapter in *Victims No Longer* to issues specific to gay men. A subtle, but extremely powerful, contribution was made by Mic Hunter's (1990a) inclusion of the ridicule of "the child's sexual development, preference or organs" as a sexual trauma. Herman (1992) mentions a gay man in the widely read *Trauma and Recovery* in the context of the need for a safe environment in which the survivor may heal. Stephen Parker (1990) discusses the group experience in treating the gay male survivor (Hunter, 1990c). However, to a great extent, the language with which to comprehend, process and understand the sexual victimization of gay children has not yet been coined.

The entrenchment of oppressive dynamics not only influences research, but limits the ways in which the traumatization of men is discussed. These dynamics distort the male child's perception of the childhood sexual events. Fromuth and Burkhart (1987) found that 20%-24% of undergraduate males reported childhood sexual activity with adults. However, only 4% identified these events as abuse. "Men are more apt to label a childhood sexual experience with an adult as neutral or positive rather than abuse, especially in the case of a female perpetrator" (Mendel, 1994). This renders it difficult to obtain accurate prevalence data, as it is tricky to establish a comprehensive definition of abuse that is universally recognizable. This is further complicated in that some theorists might accept, for example, the 4% figure from the Fromuth and Burkhart (1987) study as correct and perpetuate in *theory* largely inaccurate and faulty information. This would then impact subsequent research hypotheses, the construction and phrasing of research tools and measures, and the funding available to study this problem.

As was the case in the early days of Feminism, where the redefinition of terms such as rape were vital to the movement, much needs to be done to expand our understanding of terms such as consent, power and coercion. We cannot accept the accuracy of research regarding male sexual victimization. While more recent studies have focused on "nondirect abuse" (which includes showing pornography to the child or exhibitionism), most studies have focused on what has been termed "direct abuse" (where physical touch was involved) (Mendel, 1995). These categories fail to capture the unique experience of the gay child for a variety of reasons.

Freire (1970) posits that "any situation in which 'A' objectively exploits 'B' or hinders his or her pursuit of self-affirmation as a responsible person" is oppression, an act of violence. Gay men suffer this violence from all directions and many levels. "Psychological trauma is an affliction of the powerless. Traumatic events overwhelm the ordinary systems of care that give people a sense of control, connection and meaning" (Herman, 1992). Powerlessness, a risk factor for psychological trauma (Herman, 1992), is "the expectancy or belief that an individual cannot determine the occurrence of outcomes" (Seeman, 1959; Wallerstein, 1992), and is a common experience for gay men. The sense of powerlessness fostered by a culture and legal system that does not validate homosexuality is often internalized into self-blame (Wallerstein, 1992), absolving the forces of discrimination and oppression.

Trauma shatters beliefs of trust, safety, reliability, physical integrity and, in many cases, conceptions of the future. A sexual trauma separates the victim's physical being from his psyche. It becomes the survivor's legacy to integrate the shards of his shattered self into a cohesive whole. The sexual trauma "movement" provided an opportunity for this integration to be supported by social recognition for the issues. To the degree that the experience of gay men is overlooked, the safety of that context does not exist.

Psychological trauma is a relentless, chronic reality in the life of the gay child. The prevalence as well as the variety of these assaults and acts of violence against gay children are horrifying. Ironically, this universality of experience further obscures the visibility and comprehension of these events. Discounting the intensity of the experience is fostered by a dominant culture which stigmatizes male vulnerability and recognition of victimization. In this respect the culture itself takes the role of the perpetrator silencing the victim.

> In order to escape accountability for his crimes, the perpetrator does everything in his power to promote forgetting . . . Secrecy and silence are the perpetrator's first line of defense. If secrecy fails, the perpetrator attacks the credibility of his victim. If he cannot silence (the victim) absolutely, he makes sure that no one listens.

Further perpetuating this silence, men are socialized to consider vulnerability as existentially shameful and wrong. In the case of an abuse, in particular sexual abuse, the stigma attached to victimization in males is enhanced. "A male victim may assume that he is 'less of a man' due to his inability to protect himself . . . (he) may equate being abused with being weak, homosexual, or female" (Mendel, 1994). Nasjleti (1980) observes that in the mind of the male survivor, "victimization = passivity/helplessness = homosexuality" (Mendel, 1994). It is common for a survivor to be confused about his adult sexuality. When the victim is indeed homosexual, the association between his trauma and his sexual orientation become fused in silence.

Further, as Mendel (1994) points out, men are socialized to expect that they "should be eternally sexually willing and eager." This social mandate sends the message to the male child or adolescent that he should enjoy any sexual contact, and if he does not, that there is something wrong with him. Feelings of self-doubt or judgment in this situation would be particularly sharp when the perpetrator is female. Indeed, in various media, the sexually active male child who engages in sexual contact with an older female is seen as precocious, rather than victimized. The gay child may hesitate to identify this as abuse for fear of being exposed as homosexual or for fear of retribution.

Additionally, "if sexual arousal occurs or pleasure is obtained then the victim assumes that he must have actually wanted the sexual interaction" (Mendel, 1994). For gay men, there is greater occasion to attribute their physical sexual trauma to their own homosexuality fueled by cultural mythology and the bias of the literature outlined above. A gay man may interpret his sexuality as inviting or seducing the perpetrator. The survivor may believe that he was targeted because of his sexuality (Dimmock, 1988; Lew, 1990). This is engendered and fostered by, for example, the analogous misperception that gay children are teased in childhood because they are different (rather than assigning responsibility to the victimizing behavior of the perpetrator). Neal King discusses in Article 2, that an Imprinted Arousal Pattern (IAP) may result from a traumatic sexual encounter and be identified in adulthood as the authentic sexuality. Some gay men may therefore remember and locate their sexual involvement with an adult in the context of a rite of passage (especially when the adult is male).

The gay child who is verbally assaulted by name-calling has his sense of difference simultaneously identified, rejected and ridiculed. A piece of him is broken off from the whole and magnified. This will be echoed in the resultant psychological symptomatology where fragments of the shattered psyche are dissociated from and split off into the unconscious. It is in this respect that the gay child's identity is *forged* in a traumatic context.

Additionally, he needs to split off authentic feelings related to this trauma. To acknowledge the pain of being humiliated and rejected from peer membership may be seen as weak or girlish. This creates a spiral of shame, attached to the victimization as well as to the validity of the feelings engendered by these events. In the misogynist binary which divides the suitability of behaviors by gender, the gay/lesbian child is caught in a perpetual limbo state of being in-between and therefore an easy target (Cassese, 1993). To the extent that the child believes he is a "sissy" then he will at least accept (if not assume) responsibility and blame. He accepts belonging to a category of people who are in the minority, have less power and are treated as deviant.

Even some well-meaning clinicians "do not realize that they are serving only to dehumanize" (Freire, 1970) and formalize the relegation of the gay child from the binary socially assigned to the genders with terms like "gender-atypical behavior."[2] Allegedly used to empathically locate the gay child's difference, these perspectives do little to address the dehumanization inherent in terms such as typical/atypical, or normal/abnormal. Consequently, those children who are perceived as "gender typical" and, by implication, "heterosexual" *have more power.* It is the minority that is kept powerless.

While the experience is, if not traumatic, at least psychologically shocking for the child who suffers racial/ethnic/religious discrimination, there are a number of differences for the sexual minority. The minority race/ethnicity/religion child often has a family that mirrors his minority characteristics and to which he may return. There are laws specifically protecting these minorities against bias and discrimination which can encourage the frightened child. His family may be less likely to verbalize assaults against their own race/ethnicity/religion. However, within an ostensibly heterosexual family, ridiculing homosexuality would not appear blatantly self-contradictory. This potential source of family reassurance is not implicit for the gay child whose parents apparently differ in their sexuality.

There is a further singularity when the attack targets a child's perceived sexuality. The assaults against the gay child are *sexual* in nature; they are directed against intimate sexual self-expression. These childhood traumas occur before the individual has had a chance to experience intimate sexual contact in maturity. He has not yet had the opportunity to establish for himself his relation to and understanding of his sexual tastes on his own terms, within his own boundaries. Don Wright, in this collection, explores the boundary damage further in terms of the adult gay male survivor's resultant difficulties distinguishing between sex and intimacy. During the course of his childhood and adolescent development, his sexuality and the assaults against it become traumatically fused. In adulthood, intimate sexual contact must accommodate the abuse and damage that the gay male's sexual sense of self has endured.

In keeping with this perspective, the term sexual trauma is applied throughout this text to events perpetrated by a more powerful agent involving a less powerful victim's sexual boundaries, sexuality, sense of sexual orientation, identity or sexual integrity. The term "sexual trauma" as used here includes incest, extra-familial contact with an older or more powerful other, verbal assaults on the child's sexual orientation or viability as well as witnessing any of these actions perpetrated against another victim with whom the child has a bond. The range of behaviors that constitute trauma here are not delineated in terms of "direct" or "nondirect" contact. These actions produce aftereffects that may not be observable until adulthood. These aftereffects put the survivor at risk for further victimization or harm; correspond with an impaired and highly reactive self-esteem; and often have a sexual or erotic theme. Absent from this definition is the criterion of an age differential, replaced by a *power* differential, which more accurately speaks to the experience of powerlessness of the sexual minority.

In gay men, recognition of sexual trauma is elusive for a number of reasons. The symptoms often present in extremes as a result of the fragmentation that occurs during the natural dissociative response to, and psychological splitting resulting from, a traumatic event. Certain nuances of perception are lost such as subtlety and ambiguity as though the viewpoint shifted from 3-dimensionality to 2-dimensionality. Thoughts and feelings are experienced as monochromatic, all-or-none and often the symptomatology is similarly polarized. The person may, for example, be highly active sexually or, conversely, sexually anorexic. He may trust no one, or indiscriminately trust everyone. These complex and seemingly contradictory symptoms make accurate recognition and assessment difficult.

Further, traumas that occur to the gay child are often peculiar to circumstance and temperament of perpetrator and victim. For the reasons outlined above, the child's coping is often forged in isolation and the resultant symptomatology is often similarly unique. Indeed, for some survivors, the aftereffects will reflect their resilient talents and skills. Some survivors may be particularly intellectually gifted (or so split off from their feelings that as a result their intellect becomes hyper-developed), and in an environment where their intellect provided rewards or respite from the abuse. This set of circumstances, along with the aftereffect of perfectionism, could combine to produce a highly successful, dynamic adult. Unfortunately, however, that person might also be unable to appreciate or take true joy in their achievements as perfectionism is a constant infinite process and overreliance on intellect sacrifices the expression of deep emotion.

The idiosyncratic nature of the resultant aftereffects, including the seemingly "positive" presentations, further contribute to the difficulty in identifying trauma in gay men. As Herman (1992) points out, the central dialectic in psychological trauma is the wish to deny and the wish to disclose the events. In gay men this is exacerbated by a history of having to hide oneself, especially anything that marks him as different (and therefore a vulnerable target). At the same time, he often wishes to have his difference, that which makes him special, be seen and noticed. Because the natural wish to be noticed places the gay child at risk for victimization (Cassese, 1993), it is often inhibited by defense mechanisms or experienced as shameful. This defensive maneuvering may color the gay man's memories of the event (when accessible) as fond or sexually arousing.

Memories are often obscured in particular by dissociation. Through the mechanisms of this sophisticated psychological defense strategy, "more information is available than accessible to consciousness" (Erdelyi, 1994). Dissociation is the means by which the survivor preserves his sanity by psychically withdrawing from the traumatic situation. As the possibility for trauma exists in various locations within the gay child's environment, he may be chronically terrified that he will be teased, tormented or abused. He may intuitively sense which hallway contains the greatest risk for humiliating attack. He may be in a perpetual state of preoccupied arousal as a result of being sexually overstimulated. Each of these circumstances can activate a dissociative response, consequently configuring a spiral of dissociative triggers.

The gay male survivor eventually learns to routinely function within a dissociated state. Combined with the mandate of secrecy about his sexual orientation, the survivor constructs an elaborate facade to avoid detection, with dissociation proving a strong ally. However, as dissociation functions at the mind-body junction, the survivor's thoughts/feelings and physical states may as a consequence not operate in harmony. His body may present, for example, sexual arousal when he is frightened, or he may be sexually impotent when he feels emotionally intimate. Drugs or alcohol may be used (or overused) to blur the discrepancy between his feelings and behavior, or to bolster the amnestic or derealizing properties of dissociation.

Substance overuse as an aid to, or substitute for, dissociation is a common aftereffect of sexual trauma that is not unique to gay men. Despite unique *constellations* of symptoms, many of the individual aftereffects related to sexual trauma are consistent and thematic. Whether it is blind trust or total paranoia, for example, the issue is one of trust. What is different for gay men is the context in, and frequency with which traumatic events occur and the dominant culture's willingness to overlook or indeed minimize the power of these events. Standard aftereffects are translated through the gay male existential and cultural experience. For example, issues regarding sexual behavior often present in the sexual trauma survivor as compulsive in nature. These issues are often seen in relation to other behavior management disorders such as eating disorders or substance overuse. Substance use and sexual behavior are highly responsive to peer influence (Bandura, 1994). For gay male survivors, the available sexual as well as drug using partners have also often been traumatically sexualized.[3] The gay male survivor, following intense self-scrutiny in the face of social criticism (*"How can they tell I'm different?" "What is it they see?"*), becomes hypervigilant to social cues. This produces an intense awareness of the social cues fueled by the wish to belong to the dominant group.

When the factors of a group of potential survivors, observing each other for cues as to how to fit in, and the peer influence of sex and drug use converge, the facade of a cohesive culture may result. In other words, the authentic desires of an entire community of people may be assumed to be represented by recognizable stereotypic behaviors. As a result, it is difficult to identify what is genuine desire and what has been induced. This is represented on a "micro-" level by the aftereffects induced by trauma that may seem authentic/organic to the individual.

It is painful to identify that we might seek validation through sexual contact or that we are petrified of sexual contact. It is torturous to recognize that some of us drink or drug to forget the pain of childhood traumas. It is psychologically shocking to realize that the intimacy issues that we have believed to be our individual struggles may not be essential to our nature but the legacy of childhood sexual trauma. The process of identifying these elements of our personality and of integrating the fragments is extremely painful. It is a similar pain, an overwhelming stunned shock that often is provoked when an adult survivor understands the effect that his sexual trauma has had on his life. The mind of the survivor will seek to avoid these realizations until it is ready.

This project speaks to the hope that the field of sexual trauma is ready to acknowledge and try to understand the experience of the gay male. The papers in this collection represent various perspectives and observations of the phenomena of sexual trauma in gay men. As this is the first such project, to my knowledge, and we are breaking new ground, the papers were written to provoke thought and to invite problem-solving. Although in some papers direct treatment approaches are offered, these articles are exploratory and discursive in content. Comprehensive and detailed research on the topic of gay men and childhood sexual trauma is long overdue. Lawrence Rosenberg's paper "Phase Oriented Psychotherapy" presents a sound integrative model for the treatment of adult survivors of sexual trauma. It is particularly exciting to have a sound approach developed with gay men in mind that can be extrapolated onto the majority population, instead of the usual translating developments from the majority to be used for the minority.

To that end, *Gay Men and Childhood Sexual Trauma: Integrating the Shattered Self* includes Dennis Balcom's informative article applying the techniques of Eye Movement Desensitization and Reprocessing (EMDR) to the needs of gay men. EMDR is an innovative rapid change brief treatment approach which also relies on the more recognized cognitive, behavioral, and psychodynamic models. A variety of psychodynamic and psychoanalytic models, such as Self Psychology and the Interpersonal School, are represented in this collection as well. It is beyond the scope of this paper to offer a thorough explanation of the similarities and contrasts of each of the models. Those discussed in *Gay Men and Childhood Sexual Trauma: Integrating the Shattered Self*, however, share an interest in understanding how the client's issues dynamically exist within the treatment room. They may differ in conceptions, for example, about the origins of symptomatology.

In Self Psychology for instance, the self is understood to be an amalgam of three spheres of need, and individual personalities and motivations reflect how adequately those needs have been met. Emphasis is placed on self-cohesion, and symptomatology is understood to reflect the self's best efforts to ward off fragmentation. From the perspective of the Interpersonal School, however, personality is "the relatively enduring pattern of recurrent interpersonal situations which characterize a human life" (Sullivan, 1940). From this perspective psychopathology is understood to arise from anxiety which "operates as a disintegrating tendency" that had been set in motion through early childhood experiences with a caregiver (Mitchell & Black, 1995). Both perspectives, however, share an understanding of the self that differs from the classical Freudian view of humankind being essentially animals "pursuing simple pleasures with ruthless abandon" (Mitchell & Black, 1995). The psychodynamic approaches included in this text reflect progressions in thought and view the human as more suited to its world and existing within a more humane or humanistic context than the "traditional" Freudian perspective.

A similar revolution in thought, such as was provoked by the Feminist movement, needs to occur with regard to the minority sexualities. *Gay Men and Childhood Sexual Trauma: Integrating the Shattered Self* represents a step in that direction in terms of gay men.

As with any information regarding sexual trauma, however, the reader is at risk. By taking in this information, trauma is witnessed and vicariously experienced. With that in mind, the papers and information presented in *Gay Men and Childhood Sexual Trauma: Integrating the Shattered Self* maintain a focus on presenting the information with minimal provocative case material. The impact of vicarious traumatization will be, of course, especially true for the clinician working with sexual trauma patients. We hear horror stories, and we recognize cycles of re-traumatizing aftereffects. More so than most, we witness the scope of the damage with only the therapeutic distance and our internal resources to comfort us. At times we note the traumatic roots of a symptom before the patient sees it. However, to facilitate the healing and empowerment process we quietly observe as the patient finds a way to a connection. When a connection is made, we then hear the story of the trauma, often in vivid detail. We are given the privilege of being with the client experiencing the full range of emotions associated with the trauma.

With this privilege comes dangers and burdens. This is one of the risks of the work. Not only are we present for our patients, but we must also be constantly vigilant for the effect that the material has on us. We may be vicariously traumatized, we may absorb anger, terror, or anxiety. Our behavior may unconsciously mimic that of our patients. We may find ourselves overusing substances or feeling depressed. Our sexuality may be influenced: We may avoid sexual contact or conversely become vicariously traumatically sexualized. Bearing witness may fill us with anger and rage which we may direct at ourselves. While as clinicians we have a categorical responsibility to behave ethically, we also need compassion for our mistakes and errors. How is it possible that we can listen without bias to our patients and yet hold ourselves to impossible standards, judging ourselves when we fall short?

Colleague and friend Martha Gabriel has reminded me that there are no "bad guys." This is a difficult concept for clinicians working in the field of sexual trauma. I learned, however, that when we vilify, when we make someone the bad guy, we undoubtedly overlook significant information, fail to appreciate nuance and subtle dynamics. This is a mistake of Feminism from which we can learn. This does not identify 1970s Feminism as a "bad guy"–it made enormous strides in a profoundly restricting environment. However, in identifying what the oppressor "always" looks like, it could not do justice to the enormous cunning, shape-shifting dynamics of the oppression that fuels sexual trauma. If we continue to identify the oppressor in relation to the oppressed, we continue the dehumanizing of oppression. We cannot dehumanize the Other–even when the Other appears monstrous–in order to appreciate the pain of the victim. If we do, oppression is not transformed; rather, roles are simply exchanged.

Instead, the next step in liberationalist humanism begins in recognizing the damage done to the oppressed in an attempt to heal and grow.

> Liberation is . . . a childbirth, and a painful one. The man or woman who emerges is a new person, viable only as the oppressor-oppressed contradiction is superceded by the humanization of all people. Or to put it another way, the solution of this contradiction is born in the labor which brings into the world this new being: no longer oppressor, no longer oppressed, but human in the process of achieving freedom.
>
> –Freire (1970)

Gay Men and Childhood Sexual Trauma: Integrating the Shattered Self represents a collective move toward developing a comprehensive understanding of sexual trauma. That understanding can only be whole when a full appreciation of victimhood and survivorship in all its forms is established.

NOTES

1. While this and other papers within this text discuss issues in terms of gay men specifically, some of this information will have obvious applications to the minority sexualities such as lesbians, transsexuals, and bisexuals.

2. Franklin Brooks' sensitive and compassionate paper discussing what he terms non-traditional/gender atypical boys offers a context within which to understand the plight of boys who are different. We both struggled with the terminology, and ultimately accepted that "gender atypical" functions as a descriptive term. We also both were uncomfortable with the language and invite our readers and colleagues to help coin new terminology that is freer from oppressive implications.

3. See Don Wright's paper for a further exploration of this issue.

REFERENCES

Bandura, A. (1991). Self-efficacy mechanism in physiological activation and health promoting behavior. In J. Madden (Ed.), *Neurobiology of learning, emotion and affect.* New York: Raven.

Bandura, A. (1994). Social cognitive theory and exercise of control over HIV infection. In R. DiClemente & J. Peterson (Eds.), *Preventing AIDS theories and methods of behavioral interventions*. New York: Plenum.

Briere, J., Evans, D., Runtz, M., & Wall, M. (1988). Symptomatology in men who were molested as children: A comparison study. *American Journal of Orthopsychiatry, 58,* 457-461.

Brownmiller, S. (1975). *Against our will: Men, women and rape.* New York: Simon & Schuster.

Cassese, J. (1993). The invisible bridge: Childhood sexual abuse and the risk of HIV infection in adulthood. *Journal of Sex Information and Education Council of the US, 21,* 4 Apr/May, 1-7.

Courtois, C. (1988). *Healing the incest wound: Adult survivors in therapy.* New York: W.W. Norton.

Dimmock, P. T. (1988). Adult males sexually abused as children. *Journal of Interpersonal Violence, 3,* 203-221.

Erdelyi, M. (1994). Dissociation, defense and the unconscious. In D. Spiegel (Ed.), *Dissociation: Culture, mind and body.* Washington, DC: APA Press.

Finkelhor, D. (1981). The sexual abuse of boys. *Victimology: An International Journal, 6,* 76-84.

Finkelhor, D. (1984). *Child sexual abuse.* New York: The Free Press.

Finkelhor, D., & Browne, A. (1985). The traumatic impact of child sexual abuse: A conceptualization. *American Journal of Orthopsychiatry, 55,* 530-541.

Freire, P. (1970). *Pedagogy of the oppressed.* New York: Continuum.

Fromuth, M. E., & Burkhart, B. R. (1987). Childhood sexual victimization among college men: Definition & methodological issues. *Violence & Victims, 2,* 241-253.

Gaventa, J. (1980). *Power and powerlessness.* Illinois: U. Illinois Press.

Gerber, P. N. (1990). Victims becoming offenders: A study of ambiguities. In M. Hunter (Ed.), *The sexually abused male: Vol 1. Prevalence, impact and treatment* (pp. 153-176). New York: Lexington Books.

Herman, J. L. (1992). *Trauma and recovery.* New York: Basic Books.

Hunter, M. (1990a). *Abused boys: The neglected victims of sexual abuse.* New York: Fawcett.

Hunter, M. (1990b). *The sexually abused male: Vol. 1.* New York: Lexington Books.

Hunter, M. (1990c). *The sexually abused male: Vol. 2.* New York: Lexington Books.

Lew, M. (1990). *Victims no longer: Men recovering from incest and other sexual child abuse.* New York: Harper Collins/Perennial.

Mayer, A. (1983). *Sexual abuse: Causes, consequences and treatment of incestuous and pedophilic acts.* Holmes Beach, FL: Learning Publications.

Mendel, M. (1994). *The male survivor: The impact of sexual abuse.* California: Sage Publications.

Messler-Davies, J., & Frawley, G. (1994). *Treating the adult survivor of childhood sexual abuse: A psychoanalytic perspective.* New York: Basic Books.

Mitchell, S. A., & Black, M. (1995). *Freud and beyond.* New York: HarperCollins.

Nasjjleti, M. (1980). Suffering in silence: The male incest victim. *Child Welfare, 59,* 269-275.

Newton, D. (1992). Homosexuality and child sexual abuse. In W. O'Donohue & J. Geer (Eds.), *The sexual abuse of children: Theory and research* (pp. 329-358). New Jersey: Lawrence Erlbaum Associates.

O'Donohue, W., & Geer, J. (Eds.). (1992). *The sexual abuse of children: Theory and research.* New Jersey: Lawrence Erlbaum Associates.

Parker, S. (1990). Healing abuse in gay men: The group component. In M. Hunter (Ed.), *The sexually abused male: Vol. 2.* (pp. 177-198). New York: Lexington Books.

Raybin, J. (1969). Homosexual incest. *The Journal of Nervous & Mental Disorders, 48,* 2.

Seeman, M. (1959). On the meaning of alienation. *American Sociological Review, 24,* 783-791.

Spiegel, D. (Ed). (1994). *Dissociation: Culture, mind and body.* Washington, DC: APA Press.

Sullivan, H. S. (1940). *Conceptions of modern psychiatry.* New York: Norton.

Van Wyk, P. H., & Geist, C. S. (1984). Psychological development of heterosexual, bisexual and homosexual behavior. *Archives of Sexual Behavior, 13,* 505-544.

Wallerstein, N. (1992). Powerlessness, empowerment, and health: Implications for health promotion programs. *American Journal of Health Promotion, 6* (3), 197-205.

Childhood Sexual Trauma in Gay Men: Social Context and the Imprinted Arousal Pattern

Neal King

SUMMARY. Social context is a crucial lens through which to see and understand the experience of gay men who have been sexually abused as children. Clinicians who recognize the complex interplay of forces within this context will be better able to serve their gay male sexual abuse survivor clients. Given the trauma inherent in a cultural context which stigmatizes, devalues, pathologizes and punishes homosexuality, the added trauma of childhood sexual abuse in effect exponentially intensifies the trauma and the task of healing. It is particularly important that clinicians assist clients to separate sexual abuse and its effects from sexual orientation. Ideally, the former comes to be seen as imposed from without due to another's pathology, and the latter as an intrinsically good and positive part of self that exists entirely apart from the former. The phenomenon of an "Imprinted Arousal Pattern" (IAP), common among sexual abuse survivors, induces the individual to continue to be eroticized by stimulation and circumstances that overtly or covertly resemble the abuse circumstances. Case illustrations are provided to aid the reader in understanding and assisting others to work through this dynamic. *[Article copies available for a fee from The Haworth Document Delivery Service: 1-800-342-9678. E-mail address: <getinfo@haworthpressinc.com> Website: <http://www.HaworthPress.com>]*

KEYWORDS. Childhood sexual abuse, homophobia, homosexuality, imprinted arousal pattern, sexual trauma, social context

---

[Haworth co-indexing entry note]: "Childhood Sexual Trauma in Gay Men: Social Context and the Imprinted Arousal Pattern." King, Neal. Co-published simultaneously in *Journal of Gay & Lesbian Social Services* (Harrington Park Press, an imprint of The Haworth Press, Inc.) Vol. 12, No. 1/2, 2000, pp. 19-35; and: *Gay Men and Childhood Sexual Trauma: Integrating the Shattered Self* (ed: James Cassese) Harrington Park Press, an imprint of The Haworth Press, Inc., 2000, pp. 19-35. Single or multiple copies of this article are available for a fee from The Haworth Document Delivery Service [1-800-342-9678, 9:00 a.m. - 5:00 p.m. (EST). E-mail address: getinfo@haworthpressinc.com].

19

THE SOCIAL CONTEXT

Little has been written about the clinical issues of gay men who have been sexually traumatized. On one level, while this is emblematic of neglect, it also contributes to the lack of a comprehensive understanding of the gay male experience. Clinical understanding of this population and its clinical presentation begins with a sociocultural context/perspective.

Gay men and lesbians in the USA are *de facto* traumatized by a devaluing and stigmatizing culture whose primary institutions (from religious to legal to mental health) have traditionally defined them as sinners, criminal and sick. Statistics and case examples of young lesbians and gay men attempting or completing suicide are powerful testimony to the force and reality of these traumatic institutional rejections (Martin, 1982; Schneider, Farberow, & Kruks, 1989; Aarons 1996). Further, the dominant culture is overwhelmingly rigid in its pervasive equation of heterosexuality with normalcy in all avenues of media, ritual, law, custom and other forms of social embrace. The consequences of this prevailing heterosexism and its accompanying social stigma are reflected in many ways, including anti-gay violence and the uses made of homosexuality by the religious right for fundraising and other political purposes (Herek, 1996). There remains a lack of knowledge about homosexuality in the culture at large, with a consequent distortion, misunderstanding, and accompanying dependence on mythology to comprehend the phenomenon of homosexuality. This is reflected in cultural attitudes, for example, regarding HIV, its origins and "risk populations," gay parenting and child custody, same-sex marriage, and gays in the military. These factors alone can result in a loss of social affiliation or belongingness, and marginalization in social identity, where gay men and lesbians feel outside the sanctioned legal, ecclesiastical and psychological parameters of social normalcy.

Further, there have historically been few visible positive role models within the larger social context for gay men or lesbians. This has begun to change with the present generation of openly gay professionals, politicians, athletes and entertainers. However, many, if not most, gay men and lesbians are left with a solitary internal dissonance between who and what they feel themselves to be and what is approved or sanctioned by the larger culture. For lesbians and gay men of color, little is known about the intersections of their experience as sexual and ethnic/cultural minorities (Greene, 1997); even less is known about the psychological experience of gay men from within these groups who have been sexually abused. This writer assumes that at a minimum they, like their Euro-descendant counterparts, are vulnerable to attacks on their identity ranging from narcissistic injury to physical assault.

While the case examples in this chapter focus on the realities of Euro-descendent gay men who have been sexually traumatized, there may be generalizable concepts that extend beyond cultural parameters. However, it is the hope of this author that needed additional research will emerge regarding non-Euro-descendent gay male survivors.

Gender Socialization as Context

Gender socialization within the cultural parameters discussed above provides a context within which the differential experience of gay men may be conceptualized. This is offered in contrast to, for example, lesbian women, who are sexually abused. The dominant culture is invested in a misogynist and patriarchal bias valuing men over women. For a man (or male child) the message is learned early in life: to be identified as homosexual is to lose gender status. Gay men are devalued by being associated as being not "real men" but rather "like women" (the implication being that this is less than being a man). In this way the cultural forces of homophobia are linked with those of sexism (Herek, 1986).

The vulnerabilities created by social forces can become actualized or more profoundly internalized by sexual trauma. A male's core gender identity is threatened when a male perpetrator sexually abuses him. Jordan et al. (1991) observe that "boys . . . [are] socialized to be good soldiers or effective competitors in a largely alienated work world . . . are encouraged to pursue individual 'mastery' of tasks and to contain affect, particularly if it suggests to them need of another, fear, or inability to act on one's own." They describe boys' gender socialization as including active encouragement to " . . . suppress certain relational sensitivities" (e.g., feeling pain or crying when saddened or hurt by another or when seeing someone else in pain) and as "taught to accept peer standards of 'toughness' and invulnerability." As a result, the male child will often "tough it out" when abused rather than admit his hurt, fear, confusion and need. His sense of masculinity may have already been injured by the abuse; he will often be reluctant to deepen the insult further by admitting to his reactions (Hunter, 1990; King, 1995; Lew, 1990).

Cultural mythology also serves to encourage the boy to associate his abuse with homosexuality. This is often a painful and confusing relation, which may appear to him to be grounded in reality in the case where the boy is homosexual. Even for the heterosexual male who is molested by a male perpetrator, this is no easy association to resolve (King, 1995). For the boy who attempts to integrate early childhood sexual abuse into later psychosexual identity formation, regardless of eventual adult sexual orientation, the task of disentangling these apparent links is very complex.

The pairing by the dominant culture of sexual trauma with sexual orientation ("molestation causes homosexuality; pedophilia is a manifestation of homosexual pathology; gays can't procreate, so they molest to perpetuate themselves") (Newton, 1992) complicates the gay male sexual abuse survivor's process of healthy identity formation. The victim is at risk to attribute the abuse to the orientation as a causal factor, or vice versa ("I was abused because I'm gay"; "I'm gay because I was abused.") (Anderson, 1982). As context for treatment, this phenomenon directs the clinician's attention to valuable information regarding the client's internal experience. The internal experience of the abuse and the sexual orientation can become intertwined in the individual psyche, often with little or no differentiation between the two.

Gay men who are sexually traumatized, as children and/or as adults, are in effect subjected to trauma squared. The trauma of the molest/incest/rape experience is often incorporated into the internal understanding of one's sexual identity, with developmental implications in the areas of will, responsibility and blame. One's homosexual identity, as a result, can develop in *relation* to the traumatic events rather than as a separate phenomenon. This manifests as an exponential intensification and complication of the emotional and psychological developmental tasks involved in acquiring a healthy adult psychosexual identity. Within this context both gender and sexual orientation identities may not be viewed as prized and positive aspects of self, but rather as dystonic aspects of self. Profound identity confusion and self-blame are classic consequences of these combined traumas. A core sense of self wrapped in shame, and the self-destructive ideation and behaviors that can result, are common outcomes. Some of the manifestations of these internal states, as seen in clinical contexts, will be discussed below.

APPROACHING THE PROBLEM CLINICALLY: PROVIDING APPROPRIATE CARE

Understanding the expression of a client's sexuality can provide both challenge and direction to the treating clinician. The challenge includes the extent of the clinician's knowledge base about, and willingness to investigate, personal bias regarding homosexuality. The prevailing heterosexism of the dominant culture makes it very difficult for even the healthiest among us, regardless of sexuality, not to have internalized homophobic cultural values. The clinician's ability to discern clinical meaning, without bias, in the sexual/relational/interpersonal behavior(s) of the client is essential for the appropriate treatment of gay male sexual abuse survivors. The direction taken by the clinician and provided to the client rests in the meaning discerned from and assigned to the clinical material presented (e.g., hyper or hypo sexuality; intimacy complications or avoidance; sexual objectification of self and/or others; the absence or presence of "re-victimizing" scenarios in the client's life).

WHAT THE CLINICIAN SEES

News media focused in 1997-1998 on a landmark sexual harassment case before the US Supreme Court, where the complainant and the accused were both male (*New York Times*, 1997). Commentators seemed puzzled and unsure how to discuss the apparent contradiction in the fact that both parties were "married" and "heterosexual." While the behaviors seemed "homosexual," at the same time (in the words of one broadcaster) "there is no homosexuality present." At least two elements of cultural ignorance and misunderstanding present themselves here: one, the perception that human sexuality is fixed, an "either/or" (homosexual or heterosexual) phenomenon, and two, the fact that homosexual activity often manifests in the lives of people who are heterosexual by social identity. (Prison, military and "celibate" religious environments are obvious scenarios, although many men practice bisexuality or have had same-sex experience(s) while identifying publicly as heterosexual.)

A person who is homosexual or bisexual (in terms of predominant sexual fantasy and attraction) may choose not to identify as such. He may instead enjoy a heterosexual marriage and all attendant social status, and either act or not on his homosexual desires. Conversely, an individual may actually be heterosexual in orientation, but engage in same-sex behavior that is directed by an Imprinted Arousal Pattern (IAP). The phenomenon of an IAP, common among sexual abuse survivors, induces the individual to continue to be eroticized by stimulation and circumstances that overtly or covertly resemble the abuse circumstances. This is a type of learned behavior that is imprinted as a traumatic effect of the abuse. It is repeated in an often excruciatingly dystonic cycle which is ultimately in the service of the person attempting to recover from the trauma.

Van der Kolk (1987) discusses the probable biological base of "hyperarousal following trauma" as a conditioned response to the traumatic circumstances themselves. He posits that several aspects of the trauma victim's adult experience can be explained by this phenomenon, including poor modulation of affect and " . . . physiological hyperactivity, subjective loss of control, chronic passivity alternating with uncontrolled violence, and nightmares." While the complex range of neuro-physiological responses to trauma are beyond the scope of this article, useful understandings of otherwise puzzling behaviors of the victim of sexual trauma can be found in these ideas. Carnes (1997) in his discussion of "trauma bonds" and "cross-addictions" draws our attention to similar concepts. Herman (1992) does as well when she observes that:

> Abused children generally discover at some point in their development that they can produce major, though temporary, alterations in their affective state by voluntarily inducing autonomic crises or extreme autonomic arousal. Purging and vomiting, compulsive sexual behavior, compulsive risk taking or exposure to danger, and the use of psychoactive drugs become the vehicles by which abused children attempt to regulate their internal emotional states. (p. 109)

As seen in the case examples provided below, compulsive behaviors in their many forms (patterns of sexual activity and relationship, addictive "cruising" for sex, use of various substances, risk taking, gambling) are frequently found in combination in gay male trauma survivors. These behaviors, predictable and classic aftereffects of trauma, can be understood in terms of the IAP. From this perspective, the survivor is unconsciously trapped in a traumagenic heightened state of arousal. He experiences little control and is constantly poised to act, often in a repetitive fashion. He wants, on the one hand, to control his affect and not continue as victim to the trauma. On the other hand, he repeats or surrenders to the intensity of the affect introduced by the trauma, which he recognizes as oddly familiar and comfortable. He will frequently appear to defend against intimacy and its attendant vulnerability, as his lack of ability to protect himself against the unwanted intrusions of the powerful Others have taught him that he cannot afford for others to have power over him. This often manifests as a classic split between encounters or relationships including sexual behaviors, and relationships where true attachment/intimacy exists. It is important for the clinician to understand that the deeper meaning and function of the client's behaviors are most frequently outside conscious awareness.

The gay male survivor of childhood (and/or adult) sexual abuse struggling to psychologically master and integrate the trauma attendant to both his sexual orientation and his sexual trauma, may present a range of symptoms and behavioral manifestations consistent with the context discussed above. Effective intervention will result from careful attention paid to the matrix created by the sources of trauma: their intersections and manifestations, as well as their differentiation, in the life of the particular individual.

Where another boy or man has molested a boy or a man, one might anticipate volatile reactions including anti-gay violence from the victim. This would be particularly true when the victim is not gay, or is strongly conflicted about his sexuality. This dynamic illustrates Jung's concept of "infection of the psyche," where the (often toxic) psychic material belongs to another party, and is not native to the infected party. The survivor strikes out at what he sees as an externalized representation of an unwanted part of himself (which has been imprinted by the IAP), attempting (through intimate contact) to purge himself of this residue (Herek, 1990). Any survivor of sexual trauma can be left with an IAP.

Despite the confusion that an IAP may produce in creating a pattern of sexual behavior that suggests an identity, the clinician must seek to understand the survivor's authentic sexual identity. For example, with a heterosexual survivor, the therapeutic task would not be to assist him in accepting and valuing his bi- or homosexuality. Rather, the task would be to assist the client in resolving his repetition compulsion(s), making conscious the origins of the IAP, and regaining his unfragmented identity as a heterosexual man.

For gay male survivors who evidence repetition compulsions in their sexual behaviors and suffer IAPs, however, there is a different avenue to healing. For gay survivors, the "positive pole" of heterosexual identity (with its accompanying affirming sanctions) is not an option. Instead, the gay male survivor must sort all this out within the context and confines of a homosexual (and, as discussed above, negatively sanctioned) reality. When the abuse-orientation connection is experienced internally as a negative association ("The abuse caused me to be gay"; "I hate my homosexuality"; "I deserved to be abused because I'm gay"), distinguishing between what belongs to the abuse and what belongs to the orientation is extremely complex, and requires great clinical skill (Parker, 1990).

Some case illustrations follow shortly, but first some cautionary/contextual comments about attaching meaning to sexual activity in the gay male community. The community can at times be very confusing for an abuse survivor. Given the historical repression and persecution of homosexuality, there has been a prevailing and ferociously guarded norm of "anything goes" where all should be free to express themselves sexually as they please, certainly when consenting adults are involved. Many feel strongly that it is anathema simply to copy heterosexual models and norms of sexual expression and relationship. Creativity, freedom of expression and innovation in these realms are seen as positive, desirable and even indigenous to the territory of gay sexuality. Fantasy roles and identities (cowboys and leather men; drag queens and bodybuilders) all coexist in the gay male sexual universe. Casual, anonymous sex and committed relationships between two men are both normal ways of relating in the gay community, often in the same context. One gay man in a serious, loving and committed relationship might carouse in a sex club and then return home to his partner with no contradiction; another may never have sex outside the relationship.

In the context of a cultural socialization of men as aggressors, in control, and deriving meaning from sexual conquest, the sexual culture can appear to be a jungle of permissions, excesses, few boundaries, little prohibition and no direction except perhaps "play safe and have a good time." To complicate matters further, there can be the reality of rape or other forms of sexual abuse within a gay context, where the survivor is left to distinguish what is normal gay sexual activity and what is not. Finding one's unique and appropriate personal psychosexual identity in this community, even without a sexual abuse history to deal with, can be a daunting undertaking.

For the abuse survivor (and the clinician assisting him) this is a particularly challenging task. For example, a gay male client may present as having or having had multiple sexual partners, often in anonymous circumstances. This might be a matter of individual choice, where the man prefers to live his sexuality in a manner that, while non-traditional, is not trauma-based. Conversely, this behavior might be reflective of a sexual abuse survivor who has learned through his early abuse that sex and affection do not coexist, perhaps that sex is most familiar in a context where one or both parties are objectified. He may be acting out his own IAP. He may feel greater safety in keeping the experience of affection and vulnerability separate from his sexual experience. Within the unconscious cycle of his private IAP he may remain confused about whether the traumatic circumstances were perpetrated upon him or whether he was himself somehow agent or willing participant in the abuse.

The identification of this confusion is a key component to successful clinical intervention. The client may, consciously or unconsciously, believe that he can never again afford to feel as vulnerable as he did when he was the victim of his sexual trauma. He is then, paradoxically, protecting himself against what has already happened (Miller, 1997) not realizing, so long as he remains in the grip of the early trauma, the greater depth and range of resources available to him now as an adult. The clinical task here is to revisit the intact wound from the initial trauma. This occurs in the context of the safety and trust established in the therapeutic relationship, where the client is once again risking experiencing vulnerability . . . this time with the therapist, and with positive and healing results. The clinician may then introduce the client to the adult resources, internal and external, he has at his disposal to protect himself against further trauma. Trauma victims often remain frozen in their reactions to the trauma and unaware of personal resources they have to protect themselves from revictimization until the complex dynamics of the trauma residue, including the IAP, are made conscious (Herman, 1992). The clinician should never assume which meaning lies behind the client's behavior, but should rather discover in careful exploration with the client what particular meaning(s) are being expressed in the presenting behaviors.

Some case examples are provided to assist in illustrating the points made so far:

> Bryan was referred by the university counseling center during his tenure as a graduate student. Comfortable in his gay identity, he was nonetheless concerned about a pattern that had emerged in his intimate relationships. He seemed always to form relationships with men significantly older than himself. More than the age difference, however, what concerned Bryan were the roles that he saw himself consistently playing, again and again, in his relationships. While he felt "special" being with these men, he felt diminished, disempowered, infantalized, used, and objectified by his partners. He did not feel either seen or known by the men with whom he had partnered. He felt that all the power and control in the relationship rested in the other person. He presented as confused, helpless, frustrated and mildly depressed at this stubborn pattern.

> Bryan's sexual history revealed an ongoing incestuous relationship with his father, a military officer, from the time he was 5 or 6 until he was 15. Bryan's mother worked nights; when he and his father heard the garage door open in the morning, Bryan would leave his parent's bed and return to his own. Conspiracy and secrecy bound Bryan and his father for a prolonged and very significant period of Bryan's childhood.

Bryan was caught as an adult in a "repetition compulsion" based upon an IAP, which resulted from the incestuous relationship with his father. His IAP compelled him to be invariably drawn to much older men as partners, despite clear emotional incompatibilities. This prompted a repetition compulsion in which he was essentially repeating his relationship with his father in his adult life. Resilient, psychologically minded, and remarkably intact despite the trauma which had marked such a long period of his childhood, Bryan was able to engage the therapeutic process in the service of resolving his "stuck places." He eventually began to date younger men, with whom he formed relationships of greater parity and satisfaction. When he stopped therapy, somewhat abruptly, he had been in a relationship with an age peer and fellow graduate student for about a year. Testifying to the depth and stubbornness of the trauma residue, however, were the facts that Bryan clearly held the emotional and psychological power in this relationship, and had, on more than one occasion, suggested casual three-way sexual encounters involving himself, his partner, and an older man.

> Curtis referred two consecutive boyfriends to therapy before appearing himself, each of whom reported a strong sense that Curtis had a sexual "secret life" and was both angrily in denial about this part of himself, and not fully available to his partner for relationship. They would describe scraps of paper with men's phone numbers which Curtis would deny knowing anything about when confronted, or phone calls for Curtis from men he would deny knowing when the boyfriend would take the call. The first boyfriend left Curtis; the second, a serious alcoholic who would intermittently stop drinking, was eventually left by Curtis. Curtis was in treatment for most of his 20s, nearly ten years, with varying consistency. The advent of Curtis's thirtieth birthday, more than any other factor, turned out to be powerful motivation to change long ingrained patterns.
>
> Curtis was the classic "invisible child" in his family of origin. He was only acquainted with his biological father, his mother was depressed and preoccupied with herself and his stepfather, and his younger sister required his attention as protector and nurturer. Curtis's stepfather was harsh and critical, never affectionate or supportive of Curtis or his sister. Curtis was a champion athlete during his school years, accomplishing this feat on his own, with little support from his family.
>
> Around the time that Curtis became pubescent, the father and older brother of a neighborhood chum molested him. Sworn to secrecy, Curtis was at once confused by this activity, but even more strongly intoxicated by the attention and "affection" he

received from this adult and much older boy. There were several instances of this scenario repeating itself with the same perpetrators, which then became an aspect of Curtis's blueprint for adult functioning.

In therapy, Curtis presented himself as frustrated at the patterns of his relationships. Like Bryan, he was quite comfortable in his identity as a gay man. What kept occurring, however, was that Curtis (a very bright, attractive and engaging young man) was repeatedly approached in social settings by somewhat older men with money and some social station. At one point, he suggested that being simply an "ornament" in the accomplished lives of these men was sufficient for his satisfaction. Each relationship ended after the intensity of the initial courtship phase, with Curtis simultaneously finding fault with his partner and beginning to enter into serious flirtation with another man who fit his pattern, each time convinced that this was "the one" who was "different from the rest."

Curtis was more than two years into treatment before he confessed his sexual "secret life." He was deeply ashamed of this part of himself, as his identity was very closely associated with both a highly romanticized (and somewhat caricatured) notion of monogamous relationship and being seen as "good." At first, he admitted that he became highly aroused simply reading the "sex ads" in the local gay papers. He then admitted that he on occasion had called the numbers in the ads. Most difficult to own was the fact that he would sometimes visit a downtown sex club not far from his place of work. He would engage in public, anonymous sex, more excited that others were watching than by the act itself. He would be consumed by guilt and shame when he returned to his office, and often would fall into a deep depression for days afterwards. When the experience would repeat, Curtis would describe feeling powerless over the urge to seek out the attention.

The advent of Curtis's 30th birthday was the "break" needed for him to plummet to his "bottom." Curtis was able to realize that attention was his drug (and the core of his IAP); shame and self-punishment were the shadow side of the same dynamic. He was addicted to both sides of his IAP, and willing to sacrifice and pay almost anything for the attention which perpetuated his cycle (he was always deeply in debt to his wardrobe and travel to attend all the "right" parties). Attention was becoming less and less available to Curtis as he aged. His relational patterns repeated more quickly; he saw what was coming before it happened and he stopped the cycle. Curtis saw himself replaced by a younger generation of "boys," and became severely depressed. He had no idea who or how to be if not the center of attention.

Curtis manifests many of the classic symptoms of a gay man caught in the unresolved residue of childhood sexual abuse. He epitomizes the vulnerability to sexual victimization of a child who is hungry for adult attention, receiving far too little in his home life. Perhaps most striking in Curtis's adult life are the split between the romanticized and the shadow aspects of his sexuality, both extreme, neither fully workable for him, and the compulsive nature of each aspect.

The patterns of Curtis's IAP (both the relational and the anonymously sexual) and their repetition give greatest direction to the clinician. His IAP shows him as locked simultaneously in seeking attention from the older accomplished male, and his exhibitionism, wherein he repeats having learned that he can obtain attention on demand as a sexual object. The clinician's task is to find out what put the patterns in place, what defensive purposes they serve, what unmet needs they point to, and what sorts of corrective intervention are needed to allow them to stop. For Curtis, learning the safety to experience attention, affection, sexual love and respect and appreciation for his true self in the same context/relationship, was key. Once this safety had been established in the clinical relationship, further exploration was possible, including: the etiology of his addiction; the underlying unmet needs; the distorting influence of the molestation; and healthy alternatives to getting his legitimate needs met. Curtis missed the intensity of his life in the limelight, but began to organize an identity around the possibility of being a man with intrinsic value of his own, and to claim the right to structure a life of substance for himself. Poignant beginnings of this new identity included taking a studio apartment of his own and spending painful evenings alone face to face with his bewildered isolation, without turning to the behaviors which had previously insulated him from this pain. At treatment's end, Curtis was increasingly able to tolerate his own and boyfriends' imperfections and had begun to investigate various graduate professional programs.

Compassion for self, and beginning to heal the split by bringing all parts of self into one accepting environment, are essential beginnings of mastery over the IAP and the first stages of adult functioning as a healed and whole sexual being. The therapeutic relationship serves as laboratory for the initial experience of a caring relationship; this can then be carried as a reference point out into the world and expanded to include all the facets mentioned above.

Adam was determined to save a rapidly disintegrating relationship, and reluctantly agreed to his partner's insistence that he seek therapy as a condition for "keeping the door open." He initially saw his acquiescence in this demand as a manipulation of his partner, assuming that his perceived "control" over their life together was strengthened by this move. The relationship ultimately ended, acrimoniously. Adam was surprised. He remained, however, in therapy, where he discovered a few more surprises.

At age 12 or 13, Adam "confessed" his sexual feelings for males to his parish priest. The priest was not condemnatory; instead he warned Adam that these feelings would result in a complicated life that many would not accept. He told Adam about a public restroom in an isolated spot near their town, where people like Adam met for sex. Adam visited the restroom, encountered men who wanted to have sex with him, and frequented the spot for some years during his childhood and adolescence.

Adam was very religious and much of his identity came from his active relationship with his church. Adam's partner at the time he entered therapy was a minister. Church activity had been a key part of their bond. Both were open about their sexuality in their church activities.

Adam recounted, in therapy, memories of nightmares and nocturnal terrors that he would relate to his mother, who dismissed them. He remembered being left for hours in the family car outside a local tavern with his siblings while his parents drank inside. A very creative and intuitive man, Adam painted and wrote stories as a part of his therapy. A memory emerged of a drunken father coming into his bed when he was a young boy and a mother unable or unwilling to protect him.

One aspect of Adam's experience is the susceptibility to re-victimization on the part of the young victim. He has already learned by his experience that someone who has power can take what he wants from him and there is no one to protect him or prevent this from happening. This, therefore, can come to seem normal and even acceptable as attention to a child who receives little other attention. The fact that a trusted adult in a position of moral authority, the local priest, directed Adam as a boy to sexual activity with adult males, further reinforces the apparent normalcy of this activity. It is difficult to know what the priest intended. Perhaps he was naïve, perhaps well-intended, perhaps a pedophile himself. His directive to Adam as a boy seems at best inappropriate, if not in itself abusive. It is also difficult to know who the men were who Adam interacted with at the public restroom. Did they identify as gay men and see activity with a boy as normal and acceptable? Were they abuse survivors themselves who were acting from their own IAPs? Were they pedophiles? Were they heterosexually married men who, like Curtis in the previous example, had a secret "shadow" aspect to their sexual lives?

Adam's experience illustrates another complicating variable in the recovery experience of the gay man who has been sexually victimized. The initial victimization, or some aspect of re-victimization, can occur or appear to occur within the gay community and the context of somehow "sanctioned" or "normal" gay sexuality. Certainly Adam, at the time unconscious of the early abuse by his father, must have thought his experience at the public restroom so, as his parish priest directed him to it! Adam's IAP involved sexual activity with older men who held all the power; even his uncritical susceptibility to the parish priest's directive is an example of this. His distorted perception of his own power in his adult relationships bordered on the delusional, even as he attempted to live them out according to the same template of power and control which formed the base of his IAP.

As discussed above, the gay community, with its sexual permissions and variations, can be very confusing for the victim of sexual victimization. Already, a child victim has learned to distrust his own experience and perceptions. When he encounters a sort of experience which feels familiar to the initial circumstances of his abuse, he can become reinforced in his lack of confidence in his own judgment and even more susceptible to further victimization than before. In this way, the victim's IAP can be triggered or reenacted within an apparently appropriate gay context. Sorting out what, from a client's sexual history, represents injurious or otherwise undesirable activity can represent a profound challenge in discernment and treatment strategy for clinicians assisting gay male victims of sexual victimization. The goal of treatment is always the client's trauma recovery and finding a way to live in the present in an integrated and conscious state of maximum emotional and psychological health.

SUCCESSFUL TREATMENT

Successful treatment of the gay male sexual abuse survivor necessitates the careful separation of the client's abuse experience from his sexual orientation. The survivor must be able to deeply prize the latter as a positive aspect of self while appropriately externalizing blame for the former as resulting from the pathology of another. Identifying and making conscious the client's IAP as a primary focus for clinical intervention with this population can facilitate this process.

REFERENCES

Aarons, L. (1996). *Prayers for Bobby: A mother's coming to terms with the suicide of her gay son.* San Francisco: HarperCollins.

Anderson, C. L. (1982). Males as sexual assault victims: Multiple levels of trauma. *Journal of Homosexuality, 7,* 145-162.

Carnes, P. (1997). *The betrayal bond: Breaking free of exploitative relationships.* Deerfield Beach, FL: Health Communications, Inc.

Greene, B. (1997). *Ethnic and cultural diversity among lesbians and gay men.* Washington, DC: American Psychological Association.

Herek, G. M. (1996). Heterosexism and homophobia. In R.P. Cabaj & T. S. Stein (Eds.), *Textbook of homosexuality and mental health* (pp. 101-113). Washington, DC: American Psychiatric Press.

Herek, G. M. (1990). The context of anti-gay violence: Notes on culture and psychological heterosexism. *Journal of Interpersonal Violence, 5* (3), 316-333.

Herek, G. M. (1986). On heterosexual masculinity: Some psychical consequences of the social construction of gender and sexuality. *American Behavioral Scientist, 29* (5), 563-577.

Herman, J. L. (1992). *Trauma and recovery.* New York: Basic Books.

Hunter, M. (1990). *Abused boys: The neglected victims of sexual abuse.* New York: Fawcett Columbine.

King, N. (1995). *Speaking our truth: Voices of courage and healing for male survivors of childhood sexual abuse.* New York: Harper Perrenial.

Lew, M. (1990). *Victims no longer: Men recovering from incest and other sexual child abuse.* New York: Nevraumont.

Martin, A. D. (1982). Learning to hide: The socialization of the gay adolescent. In S. C. Feinstein, J. G. Looney, A. Z. Schwartzberg, & A. D. Sorosky (Eds.), *Adolescent psychiatry: Developmental and clinical studies.* Vol. 10 (pp. 52-65). Chicago: University of Chicago Press.

Miller, A. (1997). *The drama of the gifted child: The search for the true self.* New York: Basic Books.

Newton, D. (1992). Homosexuality and child sexual abuse. In O'Donohue, W. & J. Geer, *The sexual abuse of children: Theory and research.* Volume 1. New Jersey: Lawrence Erlbaum.

New York Times. 4 December 97 "Supreme Court Weighs Same Sex Harassment" 28 UMI journal code NYT, UMI Article no. NYT-26622-119.

Parker, S. (1990). Healing abuse in gay men: The group component. In M. Hunter (Ed.) *The sexually abused male, Volume 2: Application of treatment strategies.* Lexington, MA: Lexington Books.

Schneider, S. G., Farberow, N. L. & Kruks, G. N. (1989). Suicidal behavior in adolescent and young adult gay men. *Suicide and Life-Threatening Behavior, 19* (4), 381-394.

Van der Kolk, B. (Ed.). (1987). *Psychological trauma.* Washington, DC: American Psychological Association.

Phase Oriented Psychotherapy for Gay Men Recovering from Trauma

Lawrence G. Rosenberg

SUMMARY. Gay men live in a culture of trauma in the United States. Phase Oriented Psychotherapy offers an integrative treatment model for helping gay men overcome the helplessness and disconnections that result from trauma. Successful recovery in this model yields a basic cognitive shift from indiscriminately attributing traumatic significance to present events to accurately differentiating discomfort from danger and responding to situations with aware choice. The model is a synthesis of the phase-oriented model of recovery with the principles of gay-affirmative psychotherapy. Recovery occurs over stages: (a) Stabilization of symptoms and the development of coping skills; followed by (b) Integration of dissociated or fragmented aspects of experience (including affects, sensations, beliefs, memories, identity); leading to (c) New Self and Relational development. This type of work will present distinct challenges to both therapist and client. Specific techniques are offered to aid the therapist both to assist the client and protect him/herself. *[Article copies available for a fee from The Haworth Document Delivery Service: 1-800-342-9678. E-mail address: <getinfo@haworthpressinc.com> Website: <http://www.HaworthPress.com>]*

KEYWORDS. Dissociation, gay, helplessness, Post Traumatic Stress Disorder, sexual trauma, vicarious traumatization

---

The author would like to acknowledge the wisdom and caring of his colleagues at The Center for Integrative Psychotherapy/Daniel Brown, PhD, & Associates, Cambridge, MA over many years of thinking together about the challenges and richness of trauma treatment, and to appreciate the unwavering encouragement of James Cassese.

[Haworth co-indexing entry note]: "Phase Oriented Psychotherapy for Gay Men Recovering from Trauma." Rosenberg, Lawrence, G. Co-published simultaneously in *Journal of Gay & Lesbian Social Services* (Harrington Park Press, an imprint of The Haworth Press, Inc.) Vol. 12, No. 1/2, 2000, pp. 37-73; and: *Gay Men and Childhood Sexual Trauma: Integrating the Shattered Self* (ed: James Cassese) Harrington Park Press, an imprint of The Haworth Press, Inc., 2000, pp. 37-73. Single or multiple copies of this article are available for a fee from The Haworth Document Delivery Service [1-800-342-9678, 9:00 a.m. - 5:00 p.m. (EST). E-mail address: getinfo@haworthpressinc.com].

INTRODUCTION

Gay men live in a culture of trauma in the United States. From childhood abuses to hate crimes to subtle homophobic jokes aimed at shaming and silencing, gay men are routinely vulnerable to abuse and its traumatic effects (e.g., De Cecco, 1985; Herek, 1996; Herek & Berrill, 1991; Neisen, 1993). This paper presents an integrative treatment model for helping gay men overcome the helplessness and disconnections that result. Successful recovery in this model yields a basic cognitive shift from indiscriminately attributing traumatic significance to present events to accurately differentiating discomfort from danger and responding to situations with aware choice. The individual aims to be in "the driver's seat" rather than continuing to be the helpless passenger in the careening post-traumatic stress disordered (PTSD) vehicle. He learns to control the cognitive-affective-somatic aftereffects of trauma, utilizing different strategies of thinking and behavior (or consciously continuing with old survival patterns). He sheds his self-image as a victim by forging a fresher identity founded on self-acceptance. This transformation brings a stronger sense of self-image and purpose, greater tolerance of emotions, and capacity to develop and sustain satisfying personal relationships. Sometimes the survivor experiences a deepening of spiritual or moral beliefs as well.

The model described here is a synthesis of the phase-oriented model of recovery with the principles of gay-affirmative psychotherapy. The standard of care that has evolved in the field of PTSD assumes that recovery occurs over stages, which are broadly conceptualized as: (a) Stabilization of symptoms and the development of coping skills; followed by (b) Integration of dissociated or fragmented aspects of experience (including affects, sensations, beliefs, memories, identity); leading to (c) New Self and Relational development (e.g., Brown & Fromm, 1986; Brown, Scheflin, & Hammond, 1998; Courtois, 1988; Crowder, 1995; Davies & Frawley, 1994; Herman, 1992; Kluft, 1996; McCann & Pearlman, 1990; Meichenbaum, 1994; Phillips & Frederick, 1995; Putnam, 1989; Ross, 1989). The individual must first experience safety in the therapy relationship and develop skills to achieve the first phase: stabilization of symptoms. It is only after this safety is established that he can embark on making sense of earlier traumatic events and can integrate split-off emotions, sensations, images, actions, and relationships. The tasks of the three phases of trauma treatment may overlap, as an actual therapy will contain unique elements and not unfold as smoothly as the ideal model. However, the sequential trajectory always emphasizes symptom stabilization first (as opposed to, for example, emotional catharsis or beginning with memories of past trauma) followed by integrative tasks, all carefully paced to the readiness and capacities of the client.

The road to recovery can be rocky, sometimes sorely testing the relationship between therapist and client. With each phase of treatment, the therapist is called upon to be flexible in style, conceptualization and feeling. This paper outlines the consequences of traumatization, guidelines for conducting trauma treatment, and the tasks and challenges specific to each phase of treatment. For the trauma therapist who is unfamiliar with conducting a gay-affirmative psychotherapy, some of the principles of this stance will be reviewed before turning to the phase-oriented model.

GAY AFFIRMATIVE PSYCHOTHERAPY

A therapist working with a client from any subcultural minority group of the dominant culture should at least be sensitive to, if not competent with, the values, social-familial organization and networks, and experiences of oppression, stigmatization, and difference associated with that subcultural group. Without an understanding of the normative attitudes and developmental life experiences of the subcultural group, the therapist is at risk for biases and egregious assumptions about the client, which could impair communication, shame or anger the client, lead the client to drop out of treatment, or even re-traumatize the client. Almost a century of psychotherapy with gay clients has been filled with the prejudices that heterosexuality is the only expression of normality and health–that homosexuality is pathological, sinful, and threatening to masculinity and male power (e.g., Herek, 1986; Hocquenghem, 1972/1978; Morin & Garfinkle, 1978; Rich, 1983). While there are many cases of homosexually-oriented persons who were severely harmed by this outlook, the conversion therapy movement perpetuates this damage today (Haldeman, 1994; Nicolosi, 1991; Stein, 1996).

With therapists' growing appreciation of minority experience, the rise of the gay liberation movement, and the eventual and hotly contested removal of homosexuality from the American Psychiatric Association's diagnostic manual in 1973, a new therapeutic perspective gradually evolved which emphasized an affirmative stance toward gay people (Bayer, 1981; Davison, 1976; Silverstein, 1991; Ross, 1988; Stein & Cohen, 1986). The tenets of this perspective are that (a) homosexuality is a normal expression of human sexuality and (b) as part of normal development, non-heterosexually-oriented and non-gender-conforming persons must face, internalize, and work through the homophobia, sexism, and heterosexism of the dominant heterosexual culture as part of the "coming out" process in forming a positive gay and gender identity (Beemyn & Eliason, 1996; Cabaj & Stein, 1996; D'Augelli & Patterson, 1995; Garnets & Kimmel, 1993; Gonsiorek, 1985; Isay, 1989). In contrast to persons of other minority groups, whose skin color, speech, name, traditions, or other external features distinguish them from the dominant group, many gay men are different based on an internal characteristic. This hidden yet powerful difference leaves many gay men feeling invisible–their desire concealed. They bear the burden of developing strategies to cope with being different from their families and the broader society (de Monteflores, 1986). These challenges mean that the timing and the form of developmental milestones (i.e., childhood play behavior, adolescent dating and relationships, identity consolidation, sexual experimentation and attitudes, adult partnering) for gay/lesbian/bisexual/transgender (GLBT)-developing persons often differ from their heterosexually-developing peers (Beemyn & Eliason, 1996; Cabaj & Stein, 1996; D'Augelli & Patterson, 1995; Garnets & Kimmel, 1993; Isay, 1989; Schwartzberg & Rosenberg, 1998).

The gay-affirmative clinician is also knowledgeable about the considerable individual differences (Bell & Weinberg, 1978) and ethnic and cultural diversity among gay men (Greene, 1997), variations in sexual practices and motivations, safe sex and health risks, places for social and sexual contact, and aspects of the local gay communities, politics, humor, and resources. When evaluating a presenting problem, the therapist should not "presume the relevance of the client's sexual orientation to the problem" (Committee on Lesbian and Gay Concerns, 1991). Treatment goals include "assisting a client with the development of a positive lesbian [or gay] identity when the issue of identity is relevant to the therapy," and "actively confronting and countering misinformation or bias about lesbians and gay men with colleagues, students, and clients." Listening for and gradually identifying themes of internalized homophobia to the client and differentiating this problem from other causes of shame and guilt, such as abuse, is essential. Finally, both gay and non-gay therapists do well to seek supervision, workshops, and self-education.

This knowledge and outlook is especially important when assessing the impact of childhood or adolescent abuse on the development of a GLBT person. The victim's age and his stage in the coming out process influence the effect of traumatization. Boys who appear to be different stand out as targets for scapegoating and abuse (Grubman-Black, 1990; Hunter, 1990; Lew, 1988). When sexual abuse has occurred, a boy must cope with the double shaming effects of a personal violation and a sexual orientation branded as unacceptable. The normative developmental process of learning about and accepting one's sexual identity is sidetracked when the boy must first survive the effects of bodily and spiritual abuse (see Introduction to this volume). Not only will he likely suffer traumatic symptoms, but he may also vacillate in his attraction and repulsion to men (or women), experience fear and inhibitions in sexual intimacy, and/or develop a pattern of acting out sexually as an attempt to master unresolved helplessness, anger, and humiliation associated with the abuse.

CONSEQUENCES OF TRAUMATIZATION

The phase-oriented model aims to help clients understand and work through the effects of traumatization. This paradigm identifies helplessness, distortions in awareness and dissociation, breakdown of existential meaning, and repetition compulsion as essential consequences of trauma.

Helplessness

Whether the trauma is acute or chronic, occurs as an accident, natural disaster, war combat, rape, childhood physical or sexual abuse, hate crimes, or political torture, a fundamental consequence of traumatization is helplessness. During a traumatic event an individual has no control over what is happening and is subjected to the force of the event. He can neither fight nor flee. Terror compounds this experience when the victim realizes that he cannot get away, stop the abuse, or get help (e.g., Garnets, Herek, & Levy, 1993). The duration and intensity of the state of helplessness vary widely depending on: (a) the severity (i.e., life-threatening), quick vs. gradual onset, longevity, repetitiveness, and degree of sadism of the trauma; (b) the victim's biopsychological temperament and resilience, mental health and personality style, anticipation of the trauma, participation in vs. witnessing the trauma, and previous traumatic history; and (c) the interpersonal context, i.e., others' awareness of and willingness to talk about the trauma vs. others' overt or covert involvement in and denial of the trauma (e.g., Herman, 1992; Horowitz, 1986; Van der Kolk, McFarlane, & Weisaeth, 1996). The loss of subjective control can affect behavior (e.g., compulsions and inhibitions), emotion (e.g., dysregulated flooding or numbing), sensation (e.g., startle reaction), and knowledge (e.g., memory flashbacks) (Braun, 1988). Helplessness is often experienced as chronic hyperarousal of the autonomic nervous system, which has lost its capacity to "turn off" following the cessation of a stressful event. This physiological dysregulation contributes to hypervigilance, muscular tension, disrupted sleep, depression, suicidality, sexual dysfunction, substance abuse, and physical illness (Van der Kolk, McFarlane, & Weisaeth, 1996).

Awareness and Dissociation

Due to the particular effects of traumatization on perception, cognition, and memory, the individual's awareness of the external event and/or his internal phenomenological experience is altered (Brown, Scheflin, & Hammond, 1998; Van der Kolk, McFarlane, & Weisaeth, 1996). Relative to ordinary processing of information, the traumatized individual typically struggles with an imbalance of awareness, alternating between intrusive reexperiencing and a numbing of responsiveness (Horowitz, 1986). A person may be unable to remember events that had occurred in a specific context or when he was in a particular state of mind until that context or state of mind is re-invoked. The individual may lose perspective on whether a current situation is in fact dangerous and responds as though he is in a traumatic situation. Overwhelming aspects of the trauma can be dissociated or split off from awareness, creating discontinuities, fragmentations, and amnestic barriers in the experience of the self and relations with others, with different states of consciousness representing beliefs and affects associated with particular aspects of the abusive relationship (Kluft & Fine, 1993; Putnam, 1989). The person may feel that the world is unreal (derealization) or he goes through life like a robot, observing himself from the outside (depersonalization). The relationship between helplessness and awareness is illustrated in Figure 1.

The alternation between intrusion and dissociation is matched by a dialectic between the survivor's urge to reveal and make known what happened versus his urge to deny and keep the reality secret (Herman, 1992). There are parallels to the gay man's decisions to come out or hide his gay identity. Both the trauma survivor and the closeted homosexually- or bisexually-oriented man struggle with living in a place of shame. A man who does not acknowledge and accept his sexual attraction to men will likely suffer intrusive thoughts and feelings (in the form of unbidden fantasies, guilt, anxiety, and possibly somatic symptoms) and dissociative problems (such as compartmentalizing parts of his life; seeking sexual gratification with men in a clandestine manner, possibly with limited awareness and responsibility; and lying about his personal activities).

FIGURE 1. The Relationship Between Self-Control (Helplessness) and Awareness

Self-Control

High

(Voluntary, Mastery)

Normal Attention – Balanced Internal and External Awareness
e.g., Problem-solving or coping skills
Performance (athletics, dance)
Mindful of self in relation to the world

Heightened Internal Awareness
e.g., Hypnosis, Meditation, Mental Imagery
or
Heightened External Awareness
e.g., Concentrating on a movie, pinball game

Awareness   High   Low

Startle
Hypervigilance
Intrusive Re-experiencing

Dissociation
Fragmentation
Dissociative Identity Disorder

Low
(Involuntary, Helpless)

Shattered Meanings and Cognitive Distortions

The ordinary assumptions that buttress our everyday existence–that people are trustworthy, benevolent, and predictable and that the self is worthy–are shattered when trauma strikes (Janoff-Bulman, 1992). The traumatized individual is thrown into an existential crisis, facing potentially massive disillusionment regarding significant people in his world and himself. He may have difficulties finding meaning and safety in life and others may be seen as unreliable and potential perpetrators. He may view himself as "bad" and "deserving punishment," and, in extreme cases, lacking a core self. Basic values and spirituality involving good and evil and the role of God are thrown into question.

Many gay, bisexual, and transgendered men do not grow up with the ordinary benign assumptions. Instead, they face the traumatic effects of the United States mainstream culture, which treats people whose behavior, appearance, or desires do not conform to conventional gender and/or sexual orientation standards with prejudice, disgust, and hostility. That GLBT people are violently assaulted and that these attacks are sometimes condoned by the broader community (Comstock, 1991; Herek & Berrill, 1991) serve as a dangerous backdrop to GLBT development. One way to conceptualize internalized homophobia is as a shattering of the beliefs that the world is safe and that one is a good person. The resulting experience of fear and shame becomes normative in the early development of almost all GLBT persons (Malyon, 1982; Shidlo, 1994). Furthermore, the ongoing trauma of the AIDS epidemic challenges basic assumptions about longevity of life and safety (Cadwell, Burnham, & Forstein, 1995). The fatal danger involved in the sexual transmission of the AIDS virus has brought new meaning to the concept of sexual victimization (see "HIV and the Cycle of Trauma in Gay Men" in this collection). Gay and bisexual men must create meaning of their own HIV status, whether positive or negative (Schwartzberg, 1996), and face the sicknesses and deaths of loved ones, mentors, and large portions of the gay community (Shilts, 1987).

Relationship Disturbances and Repetition Compulsion

The unresolved effects of traumatization continue to replay in later relationships and behaviors. When trauma occurs at formative developmental periods, there is a disruption in attachment bonds. A boy may suffer the loss of a positive attachment and identification with his father, especially when the father's expectations for a "real boy" are not met by a son who may be sensitive, arty, with "feminine" interests (Green, 1987; Isay, 1989; Isensee, 1991). The nature of the abuse experience, i.e., the sadistic or unpredictable features, influences the qualities of the adult's relationships, fantasies, and preferred forms of sexual expression, such as power dominance-submission role-playing, as well as problematic erotic obsessions and compulsive sexual behaviors. It is important to understand how the "who" or "what" that a person finds erotically arousing relates to the quality of the person's attachments (e.g., monogamous bonding, multiple partnering, anonymous sex, compulsive sex, fetishes), the emotions involved in the attachments (e.g., love, anger, sadness, shame, anxiety), and personality style. In general, childhood abuse influences one's later object relations whereas sexual orientation per se probably follows an independent line of development, which may have biological determinants (e.g., Bailey & Pillard, 1991; Burr, 1996; De Cecco & Parker, 1995; Pillard, 1996).

It is not unusual for a trauma survivor to select a partner whose personality or behavior contains elements of his earlier traumatic association with an abusive and/or non-protective person. This selection often occurs outside of the survivor's awareness. Even when he recognizes a repetitive pattern of entering into hurtful relationships, he may feel unable to extricate himself. Part of the pull of this repetition is the individual's attempt to achieve psychological mastery over the original trauma by trying to recreate its elements and bring about a different outcome. An intense "trauma bond" might glue two survivors in a relationship, in which each projects fantasies on to the other, stimulating an intense attraction and the illusion that they have finally found their longed-for match (e.g., Schwartz, 1992). A potent combination of love and hurt reinforces the yearning that the partner will fulfill the role of a truly nurturing parental figure. As the authentic qualities, needs, and fears of each partner come forth, the fantasy explodes with the reality of the disappointment, leaving the trauma survivor with the sense of frustration and failure of being in a dissatisfying and potentially abusive relationship.

BASIC GUIDELINES AND TECHNICAL CONSIDERATIONS IN TRAUMA TREATMENT

Determination of Client's Present Safety and Readiness for Treatment

Prior to formally starting phase-oriented treatment, the client's current life should be safe and relatively free from ongoing chaos. If the client is presently in an abusive environment, such as a participant in domestic violence or a witness to violence, systemic and perhaps legal interventions must be taken to ensure that he does not remain exposed to danger. Or, if the client is engaging in behaviors that put him or another at risk for serious harm, including suicidal action, compulsive unsafe sex, and substance misuse, the therapist and the client need to establish a treatment framework which spells out what conditions of safe and responsible conduct must exist if the therapy can proceed. These hazardous circumstances, such as attachment to abusive relationships or self-defeating patterns of behavior, create a complicated beginning to therapy. It is difficult for a person to truly stabilize when his everyday life is destabilizing. Whether the therapist insists on a contract of behavior, aims to foster the therapeutic alliance, begins to teach ego-strengthening, self-monitoring, and assertiveness skills while the client struggles to detach from a dangerous situation, or refers the client elsewhere, will depend on the individual client and on the needs, style, and resources of the therapist. Kluft (1993) and Linehan (1993) offer very useful guidelines for making these difficult decisions.

Trauma and the Therapy Relationship–Projections, Self-Disclosure, the Erotic, and Empathy

Given the breakdown of attachment that results from traumatization, the formation of a safe and trusting therapy relationship can be a challenge for the trauma survivor–and his therapist. As a client vacillates between the need to know and reveal and the need to deny and keep hidden, he may fear that his therapist is either overly cautious and afraid of hearing his traumatic story or is too intrusive, "poking" him on the outside or inside to force him to feel, think, and remember. He may project onto his therapist strong wishes and fears ranging from seeing his therapist as an all-benevolent, loving parent (which could set the stage for initial idealization and later disappointment and anger) to experiencing his therapist as an abusive perpetrator who is hurting him (which could be manifested as mistrust and paranoia, rage, repetitive stuckness in the therapy, flight from treatment, or filing a complaint against the therapist). It can be quite provocative to be on the receiving end of these projections, which may produce powerful feelings for some therapists. This may indeed be the client's conscious or unconscious intention. The therapist tries to understand the client's motivations for the particular transference and determine whether and how to tolerate the projections. Often the aggressiveness, even sadism, of the accusation is the client's long-developed protective strategy to ward off anticipated hurt, suggesting that he is not yet ready to face greater emotional vulnerability.

These tough moments also encourage the therapist to examine his or her own motivations. To the degree that the client's perceptions are accurate (i.e., the therapist is being defensive, aggressive, or controlling), the therapist should understand the sources and meanings of these reactions in himself or herself, and perhaps acknowledge aloud when appropriate that the client is correct. Such an admission has powerful healing potential for a trauma survivor, who may be confused about trusting his own perceptions, due to others' dismissal of the client's experience in the past (e.g., the child who receives the message, "That's not what happened. Don't tell anyone. You're stupid. You got it wrong."). The therapist communicates that having and revealing negative feelings or impulses need not ruin a relationship. Indeed, such disclosures can foster trust and a new model for the client to learn how to handle his inner experience. This stance of voicing reality and identifying "what is" contrasts with the more traditional position of letting the client sit with the anxiety of uncertainty. This latter strategy may be more useful during the later phase of treatment when the client has the ego capacities to successfully appraise reality on his own.

Erotic transference and countertransference, which should be attended to in any therapy, may intensify when the treatment is addressing dynamics of sexual power and victimization related to abuse. The therapist (male or female; gay, bisexual, or heterosexual) tries to understand the meanings behind a client's sexual attraction to him or her as well as be aware of his or her own attractions to the client. Despite ethical and legal guidelines that prohibit sexual activity with a client, some therapists sexually exploit and abuse their clients; especially vulnerable are clients who are trauma survivors. The therapist's willingness to examine his or her sexual feelings for a client is an important step toward preventing therapist mistreatment and clarifying the client's possible seductive and sexualized wishes (Pope, Sonne, & Holroyd, 1993).

Trauma can infiltrate the treatment relationship in unexpected ways, requiring modification of the usual therapeutic stance. One example comes from Salter (1995), who has identified that whether or not the perpetrator had taken a sadistic stance toward his or her victim is a crucial influence on the kind of traumatic aftereffects that the person will experience, including those experienced in the therapy relationship. Through her intensive interviews with incarcerated sex offenders, Salter observed that sadistic perpetrators are carefully attuned to their victims, watching their facial and bodily reactions, in order to cruelly increase the suffering of the victim at just the right level. In non-sadistic abuse, the perpetrator tends to be less concentrated on the victim and more focused on fulfilling his or her own desires. Salter found that when sadistically-abused survivors are closely empathized with, they may experience danger, dissociation, or confusion and they usually do not know why. It appears that the fine attunement, which therapists naturally employ as the sine qua non of psychotherapy, triggers the feeling of being scrutinized from the earlier sadistically traumatic relationship. If the therapist perceives anxiety/fear while paying close attention to the client, this could be a transferential clue suggesting that the client had been abused in a sadistic manner.

Flexibility in Conceptualizing and Behaving During Each Phase of Treatment

With the shifts in transference and tasks of treatment, the therapist is summoned, at various points, to be kind, tough, and stable, to set limits, instruct, monitor, contain and express strong feeling, bear witness to suffering and tragedy, receive divergent projections, tolerate ambiguity, balance his or her own needs with those of the client, keep private experience to himself or herself, and disclose personal experience and be genuine. During the stabilization phase, the work may be conceptualized from an Ego-Psychological perspective with the therapist playing an active and educative role in teaching coping skills for the client to gain mastery over symptoms. The therapist's directive stance recedes during some of the integrative work where suggestion is minimized to permit the client to freely recall and create meaning about the past in his own way. Throughout the treatment, object relational, self-psychological, systemic, cognitive-behavioral, social learning, and existential perspectives co-mingle in an integrative manner to guide the evolving relationship and recovery process.

Pacing, Feedback, Assessing Readiness to Move Forward

Clients in trauma treatment vary tremendously in how quickly they want to proceed depending on where they are on the denial-revelation continuum and their personality style. Some move very slowly requiring everything to be just right before they feel safe to go forward a tiny step. Others take a kind of kamikaze approach, eager to uncover past traumas and be finished quickly. They risk re-traumatization by being confronted with overwhelming content and feelings before they have the tools to manage and process these. This might result in a precipitous decompensation, unplanned hospitalization, or swift and premature departure from treatment. The therapist must pace the treatment carefully, regularly eliciting the client's feedback regarding his capacity to handle material and readiness to go forward. This permissive approach encourages the client to be an active participant to develop control in the treatment and ultimately in himself. The client should have an armament of stabilization skills at his disposal and demonstrate improvement in symptoms before proceeding to remembering and integrating past events. If hypnosis or guided visualization is used, then the client may be taught to use finger signaling to communicate nonverbally about his readiness to proceed (i.e., the therapist suggests that the fingers will be able to communicate from the unconscious mind. Together, the therapist and client agree upon the client's raising a specific finger to indicate "yes," another finger to say "no," a third finger to signal "stop.").

Sensory Modalities and Language

The therapist is regularly helping the client to pay attention to and gain voluntary control over his cognitive, emotional, and bodily experience. Early in the treatment, the therapist listens for which sensory modalities are salient for the client in understanding where the trauma infiltrated and where change can occur. The therapist might say, for example, "Notice any feelings, images, thoughts, or sensations that you're experiencing and perhaps you could describe these aloud." One client might have harsh visual images of an attacker that intrude into his consciousness, another may feel the traumatic effects as pain and tightness in his body, still another may hear a voice yelling in his head that he is bad and deserves to die. Many survivors have encoded the traumatic experience on multiple sensory levels, some of which are obvious at the outset and others emerge later in treatment. The therapist attempts to use language that best matches the client's reported modalities as well as gradually directing the client's attention to other modalities.

Memory and Legal Considerations–Informed Consent and Assessment

Trauma treatment provokes an epistemological dilemma for both the therapist and the client when the client is seeking to remember past abusive experiences and/or has any plan to pursue legal action. We can never be certain that our knowledge about the past is truly accurate without external corroborating evidence (Brown, Scheflin, & Hammond, 1998; Scheflin & Shapiro, 1989). The therapeutic goal is to help the client to create a narrative of his experience that brings meaning to his life and permits him to move forward as opposed to uncovering the historical "Truth." This dilemma may become problematic if the client intends to use what he learns in therapy to press charges against an alleged perpetrator or take other confrontational steps that might lead him, and possibly the therapist, to be involved in a legal complaint or a suit.

Contemporary trauma therapists practice in a highly charged climate concerning true and false memories of traumatic events and accusations of abuse (e.g., Brown, Scheflin, & Hammond, 1998; Lindsay & Read, 1994; Loftus, 1993; Yapko, 1994). At the heart of the controversy is the serious concern that therapists can influence their clients about what they recall about past events and their confidence in and beliefs about these memories. It is essential that the therapist inform his or her client about what to expect in the psychotherapy, the bounds of confidentiality, the limits on the accuracy of material about the past that emerges through treatment, and the current forensic and scientific debates over memory and trauma (Brown, Scheflin, & Hammond, 1998; Pope & Brown, 1996). When hypnosis is being considered as part of the treatment, the client must understand that hypnotically-refreshed information may not be admissible as testimony in court (Brown, Scheflin, & Hammond, 1998; Scheflin & Shapiro, 1989). If legal action is anticipated, the client and the therapist need to assess the pros and cons of including hypnosis, eye movement desensitization and reprocessing (EMDR), or another modality which might be viewed by a court as a source of influence on the client's memory and beliefs. Careful documentation is crucial and a legal consultation could be valuable. Formal assessment of the client's dissociation (Dissociative Experience Scale, Bernstein & Putnam, 1986; Structured Clinical Interview for Diagnosis-Dissociation, Steinberg, 1993; Dissociative Disorders Interview Schedule, Ross, 1989), suggestibility (Gudjonsson, 1984) and hypnotizability (Spiegel & Spiegel, 1978; Weitzenhoffer & Hilgard, 1962) should be undertaken. The challenge for the therapist is to incorporate these professional guidelines in a clinically sensitive manner so they do not impede the client's opportunity to examine any aspect of his life in the privacy of the office.

Integrative Approach to Treatment

The integration of psychodynamic, cognitive-behavioral, and psychopharmacological modes of intervention permits the therapist to tailor the treatment to the client's individual capacities and needs (Beutler & Clarkin, 1990). Existentialism is frequently the overarching philosophy in working with trauma survivors (Frankl, 1946/1985): how to make sense of the horrors that humans can perpetrate on one another and still lead a life of dignity, freedom, and responsibility. An initial formulation, which identifies areas of conflict, defense, strengths, secondary gain, narcissistic vulnerabilities, and likely transferential themes, helps guide the therapist in the timing of his or her interventions. At key choice-points during a therapy session, the therapist decides whether to use a psychodynamic intervention (e.g., offering an interpretation or elaborating unconscious fantasies and having the patient sit with the anxiety) or a cognitive-behavioral intervention (e.g., guiding the patient to actively apply skills to reduce the anxiety) (Messer, 1986). These two general approaches are not mutually exclusive and they usually reinforce one another (Beutler & Clarkin, 1990; Wachtel, 1977). A frequent example is teaching coping skills to help a characterologically disturbed trauma survivor stabilize and tolerate relational interventions. A variety of modalities may be incorporated into the treatment, including medication, hypnosis, EMDR, dialectical behavior therapy (DBT), or adjunctive group therapy. Medication may be essential for many syndromes associated with PTSD, especially chronic hyperarousal and startle response (Van der Kolk, McFarlane, & Weisaeth, 1996).

Vicarious Traumatization and Therapist Self-Care

Depending on personal history, personality, and current stressors, some clinicians may be vulnerable to secondary traumatization. The term "burnout" summarizes a variety of symptoms including fatigue, depression, boredom, agitation, and loss of compassion (McCann & Pearlman, 1990). Bearing witness to survivors' accounts of trauma can produce traumatic sequelae in the therapist, such as intrusive images, anxiety, and dissociation.

Trauma therapists can reduce the impact of vicarious traumatization by being attentive to the risks involved in their work. Maintaining a balanced caseload, not only consisting of trauma survivors, is important. The therapist should understand his or her limits regarding what constitutes unacceptable behavior in therapy, and communicate these limits to the client (e.g., some therapists find that they cannot work effectively with a client who yells at them). When a therapist puts forth his or her needs in a manner that is also respectful of the client's needs, he or she is modeling the capacity to take care of oneself to the client. Other valuable strategies include talking with colleagues for support to break through the isolating potential of trauma material, obtaining good supervision, using self-soothing, confidence reinforcing and self-hypnotic techniques, exercising, writing, creating art, taking vacations, and leading a balanced life. For some therapists, social activism can help transform the horror and pain of what they have heard from their clients into broader benefits for the community at large.

PHASE-ORIENTED TREATMENT OF TRAUMA (STABILIZATION, INTEGRATION, SELF-DEVELOPMENT)

The Stabilization Phase

Stabilization is the foundation of treatment for a person recovering from trauma. This phase of therapy consists of having the client learn a set of tools to gain control over the helplessness, intrusions, and other debilitating effects of traumatization. During the initial sessions, the therapist begins by educating the client about patterns underlying seemingly unrelated symptoms and some of the adaptive and problematic functions that these symptoms are serving. A description of how trauma and abuse infiltrate outlooks and relationships is very helpful for the client to develop a new framework for understanding his experience. Relationship building goes hand-in-hand with stabilization as the therapist relies on transference and counter-transference information to guide which stabilization methods are put forth. Stabilization work occurs throughout the therapy. The skills learned during this phase are essential to the subsequent work of integration. When stressful material threatens to destabilize the client, it is crucial to review the stabilization techniques before proceeding.

When symptoms appear to be defensive and obstacles to growth, it is often useful to reframe the symptoms as serving practical and protective functions. The suffering client comes to appreciate the insight that he is already trying to help himself, albeit awkwardly–that, at some level, he knows what to do to help himself. The treatment involves bringing these hidden assets to the surface and teaching new strategies as substitutes for the old patterns to provide protection or relief without the symptomatic pain. For example, many abuse survivors have sleep disturbances and want to be able to sleep restfully without interruption. The sleep disorder should be assessed for possible organic, substance use, and other psychological causes and maintenance factors. If there is evidence that the sleep problem might be linked to past childhood abuse, the insomnia may be interpreted as a form of hypervigilance, which the client learned at a younger age in order to maintain his guard against a perpetrator coming into his bedroom at night. By placing the problem in an interpersonal and historical context, the client develops a new perspective for how he wants to work with the hypervigilance in his current life at emotional, intellectual, and behavioral levels.

Are there times when he can give his mind permission to quiet and not be watchful or ruminating on potential catastrophic concerns? Would he want to relegate a portion of his mind to watch and maintain safety while the rest of the mind sleeps? Might he use relaxation methods or a self-guiding audiotape for soothing? Is he willing to incorporate sleep hygiene techniques into his behavior? Clients have a much easier time managing a symptom when they see its adaptive purpose and see that the therapist is not trying to just get rid of it.

The essence of stabilization is for the client to develop safety and mastery by establishing voluntary control over PTSD symptoms. The client is taught a repertoire of cognitive-behavioral skills to promote self-regulation of mental and physiological processes. Many clients begin with learning self-soothing skills and developing mental representations of safety. The power of the mind is used to alleviate symptoms and modify neuromuscular and cardiovascular functioning. Others may start with self-monitoring–keeping a written log or journal to identify either internal cues, such as specific thoughts or feelings, or external cues, such as a particular setting or charged interaction with another, in order to see a pattern and learn to intervene. There is a general emphasis on helping the client to recognize distorted beliefs about reality, often influenced by past abuse, introduce more accurate appraisals, and rehearse adaptive cognitive and behavioral strategies. Finally, a client's successes are reinforced throughout the stabilization work to foster ego-strength and self-efficacy. For example, a client who has achieved some skill decreasing bodily tension would be asked to notice his ability to relax his muscles. With practice, he will be able to utilize this capacity when he chooses.

Methods for Stabilization

Breathing and relaxation techniques, as well as medication, can be used to help regulate the hyperarousal of the autonomic nervous system. Some people readily respond and benefit from these techniques. Others experience paradoxical reactions, for example, find they become more tense when guided to relax. This reaction might suggest trauma intrusions in some form–the individual fears letting his guard down and loosening a well-honed hypervigilance or loosening the muscular armoring that shields him from distressing feelings. It is possible to modify standard relaxation protocols to accommodate the individual's need to be alert while beginning to learn to relax (e.g., "It is fine that, in some way, you would like to observe how this process of relaxation is going. That part of you that would like to relax will find a way to do so. That side of you that wants to watch and be alert can do so."). Relaxation techniques include diaphragmatic breathing; body-action techniques, such as progressive muscle relaxation or experiencing body tightness flowing into one's fist and then flinging the tension into the air; or body-visualization techniques, such as imagining a wave of relaxation spreading through the body moving the client into a deeper and peaceful place, picturing walking through a rainbow and feeling more deeply relaxed with each color, and hypnotic methods.

In *Safe Place Imagery*, the client develops an internal representational world that contradicts the shattered world that resulted from traumatization. Individual clients vary in their capacity to create a safe space in their mind; some easily gravitate to a soothing nature scene or cuddling under a comforter whereas others do not find anything to be safe. Indeed, for some survivors, the use of the word "safe" may be anxiety-inducing because a perpetrator might have used the word during the abuse (e.g., "We're safe now, no one can find us here."). In this case, the therapist and the client need to select another term, such as a "special" or "beautiful" place. Once one or more safe places have been identified and the client has rehearsed "traveling" to them in his mind, it is beneficial to incorporate these scenes into the ongoing treatment. Later during the integrative phase, when the client may be in the process of recalling past traumatic events, he can alternate between the safe and traumatic scenes, to maintain a psychological distance from the trauma and not get "locked" into it. He will also have had practice by that point in manipulating images in his mind and will be better prepared to alter and re-work traumatic scenes to reduce their impact.

It is possible that a client will identify as safe a place that the therapist would not consider safe. For example, while I was guiding a client in a relaxing scene, he announced that he imagined himself being blown to bits. This image didn't sound particularly safe to me! I suggested (probably to relieve my own anxiety) that he would find a way to come together whole. Later, the client reported that this instruction made his experience worse. I came to realize that being fragmented was more syntonic for him than being integrated at that point in the treatment. I needed to tolerate my anxiety, proceed at a slower pace, and believe that my client instinctively knew where to turn. His next safe scene was being buried in a casket under ground. Again, while not a place that I would have chosen, I appreciated that the degree of sadistic intrusions that this man had endured meant that he could feel safe only if he were certain that he was in a place where no one could find him. From the start of treatment, a client directly or indirectly invites the therapist to enter his world, to be his ally in facing trauma. The therapist must be able to experience his or her own internal stability in order to safely make this journey with his or her client.

Containment Imagery

Trauma survivors commonly suffer from intrusions, existing at every sensory level. The metaphor of containment is used to develop control over the internal disruptions. The client is guided in imagining a sturdy container, such as a strong chest of drawers or a vault, into which he deposits the intrusive material. As he stores away each anxious-making chunk, he is asked to notice any feeling of relief or lightness or freedom. Once he has ascertained that he has put all of the current fearful images and thoughts into the container, then he locks it "vacuum sealed–notice that nothing can get out." Sometimes a client might leave the container with the therapist. The therapist and the client might agree that the client won't unlock the container until a future therapy session, with the understanding that the intrusive material will need to be looked at and worked through at a time when the client has better tools to tolerate it. This containment imagery can easily be modified to handle somatic or auditory intrusions.

A variety of imagery and behavioral methods are available for the client to learn self-regulation over non-volitional cognitive, emotional, and bodily activity. The aim is to gain control by learning to increase or decrease the intensity of a particular experience. One concrete tool is the Feelings Dial, whereby the client and the therapist identify, quantify, and discuss various emotional or body states. The client is asked to imagine a dial with the numbers ranging from one through ten, where "one" represents the slightest awareness of a feeling and "ten" corresponds to an extreme intensity of the feeling. Usually the client begins with a neutral or pleasant feeling in order to practice with the dial and pay attention to the subtle and dramatic changes that occur when the feeling is turned up or down. Then, the client focuses on a more troubling feeling, typically associated with a difficult situation or state that has been discussed in therapy. For example, while thinking about a fight that a client had with his boyfriend, he feels anger, pictures the feelings dial, and rates the anger initially at a "seven." He is guided in noticing what this level of anger feels like in his body, breathing, and what thoughts correspond to it. He is then asked to try to turn down the anger a notch, for example, to "six" and notice any emotional, physical, or cognitive changes that follow and then to turn it up to "eight," and similarly notice his experience. Linking the somatic, cognitive, and emotional levels illustrates early integrative work that begins during the stabilization phase. Clients who repeatedly use these kinds of self-regulation techniques often report that feeling states, which had been amorphous and confusing, become clearer; and that they are less likely to be ruled by internal emotional storms and distressing sensations. This technique may be used at home and work to regulate emotional and behavioral reactions in stressful situations.

Hypnosis is a powerful modality to facilitate relaxation, produce symptom amelioration, discover and rehearse coping strategies, re-work traumatic effects, and explore psychodynamic conflicts. While a discussion of hypnosis and hypnotherapy is beyond the scope of this chapter, one of the benefits of hypnosis for trauma survivors is in managing dissociation. Because there are similarities between a disso-ciated state and a trance state, the client can gain control over involun-tary dissociation by learning to lighten and deepen his level of trance. This process heightens a client's perception of inner experience in a paced manner so that he becomes aware of cues that trigger dissoci-ation and he can decide whether or not he wants to dissociate based on his appraisal of the current situation.

Exposure to Anxious, Intrusive Images

The methods just described emphasize gaining control over the symptoms by creating a distance from or turning down the internal experience. Another valuable approach, following a behavioral model for treating phobias, involves the client's gradually learning to tolerate the source of the fear through systematic exposure to the fearful stimu-li, first in imagination and then in actuality. The client is guided to bring to mind the emotionally-charged images and sensations in doses, think about them, perhaps examine associations and meanings, put them away, and then bring them back again, repeating the process of tolerating and meaning making (Horowitz, 1986). It appears necessary that the client maintains a balance of attention between the present moment (i.e., the office surroundings, the current relationship with the therapist) and the past (trauma material) in order to reduce or extin-guish the intense hold of the past trauma. Eye movement desensitiza-tion and reprocessing (EMDR) (Shapiro, 1995), in which the client's attention shifts between imagining a past traumatic experience and attending to an external perceptual task (watching the back-and-forth movement of the therapist's fingers or feeling alternating taps on the knees), is an illustration of this balance of attention. Many people realize substantial improvement in a small number of sessions with this straightforward exposure and processing approach.

Self-Monitoring

Developing an awareness of patterns which link situations to thoughts, feelings, and actions and modifying these patterns are necessary skills to achieve stabilization. Self-monitoring homework is an excellent method for self-observation of everyday baseline experience. The very act of writing words on the page to document reactions to triggering events and to identify alternative responses hastens the process of mastery over dissociated thoughts and behaviors and depersonalization. It is best to use a structured form (Figure 2) at the outset; later the client can record this information in a looser format in a journal. With the therapist, the client identifies a sequence of feelings, thoughts, and behaviors that have resulted in distress or negative consequences. He is asked to target a particular behavior, thought, emotional state, situation, or some combination thereof which he is aware of occurring early in the sequence.

For example, a client engages in compulsive sexual behavior, which appears related to the unresolved effects of abuse. He might go through the following sequence of events (not all of which he can articulate in the beginning): he feels lonely or bored or stressed, dislikes this mood, thinks he would feel better if he met a guy for sex, starts to fantasize about sex or being with an erotic body, begins to get sexually aroused, figures out how to hook up with a trick, goes on line or to a bar or cruising spot or sex club, drinks alcohol or uses drugs on the way, scans the environment for a guy whom he finds attractive, makes contact through the eyes and body language–few words are exchanged (when on "automatic pilot," words interrupt the fantasy arousal); in a short while or after lengthy persistence, he connects with a guy who shows mutual interest, they determine a location for sex, he feels a rush of mounting anticipatory excitement, the sex itself might or might not be fulfilling (and might or might not be safe), and afterwards, he might feel relieved of pressure yet guilty, depressed, self-chastising, or still lonely. He recognizes that he is unable to control his need for sex as an addictive "fix."

At the start of self-monitoring, he does not realize that distressing emotions trigger his compulsive pattern or that the alcohol or drugs reinforce his dissociative, single-focus mental state. He may be aware of being in compulsive mode only after sex when he is bemoaning "not again" and feeling depressed. Thus, the event that he targets for

FIGURE 2. Daily Self-Monitoring Form

Target Symptom or Experience _____

Time	Situation	Thoughts/Feelings	External Stress (1-10)	Internal Distress (1-10)	Reactions/Coping
5:00					
6:00					
7:00					
8:00					
9:00					
10:00					
11:00					
12:00					
1:00					
2:00					
3:00					
4:00					
5:00					
6:00					
7:00					
8:00					
9:00					
10:00					
11:00					
12:00					
1:00					
2:00					
3:00					
4:00					

the first self-monitoring homework is the act of just having had casual sex. Every time he has sex with another guy he needs to fill out a line on the form (which he may find terribly annoying). He brings the completed forms to the next session and reviews what he has documented with his therapist, with whom he clarifies emotion-thought-behavior-situation patterns. The therapist then congratulates the client on his monitoring efforts.

This discussion could be the springboard for cognitive interventions regarding the client's beliefs about his need to have sex and what he imagines would happen if he were to postpone acting on the compulsion. If the client perseveres with the self-monitoring, he will eventually target an earlier moment in the sequence, such as feeling lonely. He is taught to experience the target event as a cue to implement a coping strategy (e.g., relaxation, rational self-talk, or contacting a friend to counteract the isolation). He might find that pausing to write down his experience in the moment is sufficient as a "wake-up call" to decide whether to proceed with the old behavior or choose an alternative response. His drinking or drugging could also be monitored as a second addictive problem. (In an attempt to foster self-control and separate compulsive sex from substance use, the client might be encouraged to schedule sex at specific times in a planned manner and not have sex at other times. Some men are surprised to discover that they enjoy sex much more–and are safer–when they intentionally choose it rather than seeking sex when compelled to quench urgent needs.) The pattern becomes easier to alter when it is identified at an early point than when it is well underway. The self-monitoring is followed and discussed over many sessions, using instances of poor compliance with the homework as suggestive of the powerful wish to maintain denial of a familiar yet harmful pattern. The goal is not necessarily to eliminate the maladaptive sequence but to develop the freedom to choose or not choose it as one of several options.

Indications that Stabilization Has Been Achieved

Successful stabilization brings the client to living with significant symptom improvement. Depending on the severity of the trauma and the client's personality, this phase may last from a few weeks to many months or even years. From a managed care perspective, stabilization is often the only component of trauma treatment that occurs. While the tasks of stabilization carry on throughout the entire therapy, there are certain signposts that indicate that it is possible to move the focus to the integrative phase (Brown, Scheflin, & Hammond, 1998). The client will have demonstrated significant mastery over his symptoms and achieved substantive relief, with a decrease in affective numbing, depression, and anxiety and greater control over intrusions and hyper-arousal. Serious behavioral problems, such as suicidal action and dissociative "acting out," should be under control. Both the therapist and the client should believe that stabilization tools are effectively in place before proceeding to deeper memory work.

The Integration Phase

Integration is the process of bringing together in a manageable form elements of a person that have been disconnected or dissociated as a result of traumatization. The fragmented components include bodily sensations, emotions, beliefs, knowledge, memory representations about past and recent experience, and behaviors. There are individual differences in how people handle these splits, ranging from conscious awareness of distinct elements of the self to virtually no awareness of discrete "parts," which seem to take on a life of their own beyond the person's volition, as in a severe dissociative identity disorder. The traumatized person has created and maintained these internal divisions for powerful reasons. They often represent his best attempt to survive a horrific situation and continue to cope, sometimes effectively and sometimes marginally.

The goals of the integrative phase are to: (1) understand and respect the reasons why fragmentation exists; (2) discover routes to gradually foster connections among the divisions without threatening the dissociative defenses too quickly; and (3) eventually achieve consolidation among the divisions to form a unified self (e.g., Brown & Fromm, 1986; Brown, Scheflin, & Hammond, 1998; Davies & Frawley, 1994; Herman, 1992; Kluft, 1996; Phillips & Frederick, 1995; McCann & Pearlman, 1990).

Fragmentation and Memory

A thoughtful formulation, drawing on psychodynamic, behavioral, physiological, and systemic perspectives, offers hypotheses for understanding the roots of a trauma survivor's need to exist within a context of fragmentation. Often the client's current functioning and relationships, including with the therapist, reflect the adaptive and defensive functions of the fragmentation. Any intrusive material that had already emerged during the stabilization phase and how the client attempted to handle the intrusions were early hints about the severity and the form of his internal splits. As discussed earlier, the kinds of protective and aggressive projections and beliefs that the client brings to the transference elucidate the specific conflicts, impulses, and fears that he may have tried to keep out of awareness.

The client's descriptions of his history point to the possible fragmenting strategies that he developed to cope with the trauma. Some of the factors to understand the form of the fragmentation include: how he interprets what he remembers, how much he desires to believe or not believe what he recalls, whether he tends to block or intensify his emotions and body sensations associated with the events, whether he experiences the memories in one sensory dimension or on multiple sensory levels, whether he connects past incidents with one another or views them as discrete and unrelated events, whether a part of him tries to censor the material as though he had been warned never to speak this aloud, and whether he describes the events as though they had happened to, and/or are remembered by, someone else and not him.

There is considerable variability among clients in the completeness, clarity, accuracy of, and their interest in their memories of past abuse. Some never forgot what happened, some partially recall the past events, and some are amnestic for past trauma (Brown, Scheflin, & Hammond, 1998). Some trauma survivors enter therapy with complete or mostly complete memories of past abuse whereas others do not. Some appear to have constructed a story of sexual abuse as a dramatic metaphor for intense narcissistic injuries and anger resulting from emotional abuse and neglect during the early years, even when there is no clear evidence for sexual abuse. Some seek therapy explicitly to recover memories and others are extremely reticent to discover almost anything about their past. The questions for the therapist and the client to answer together are: is it beneficial for the client to try to remember more about his past and when and how are the best ways to proceed in this process? To the degree that the client has been successful in gaining control over symptoms and has been functioning well in his contemporary life, it may not be necessary or even helpful to embark on recovering memories. If, however, after substantial efforts, the client appears unable to modify a repetitive pattern that is causing impaired functioning and distress and has reached a plateau in the treatment, then memory work could offer insight and a new perspective for understanding the fragmentation in order to shift this rigid position.

If memory retrieval is undertaken, the goal is to permit the client to remember as much as possible while limiting his chances for becoming overwhelmed by the emerging material and minimizing the potential for memory inaccuracies (Brown, Scheflin, & Hammond, 1998). As fragments of memories begin to surface, the client may temporarily become frightened and less functional. This is the time to reinstate stabilization skills and possibly slow down the memory work until the client can safely move forward. The best strategy for beginning memory work is free narrative recall, in which the client is instructed to say whatever associations come to mind, combined with the therapist's neutral repeated inquiry ("And then" or "notice what happened next"). This approach is the least likely to yield memory errors. Memories sometimes spontaneously surface during treatment as a result of transference interpretations or when the therapist suggests that the client think back to a particular significant time in his life. A method that further increases the chances of bringing forth both memories and inaccuracies involves suggesting that the client can use his present cognitive-emotional state to return to an earlier time when he was in a similar mental state.

While deeper memory uncovering, such as hypnotic age regression, can help some clients remember previously forgotten events, this approach might also produce more erroneous information because the vividness and affective charge of the imagery of such a method interferes with the client's capacity to evaluate the accuracy of the imagery. Finally, any statement, in which the therapist directly suggests that a particular event must have happened, significantly diminishes the likelihood that the client's memories will be accurate (Brown, Scheflin, & Hammond, 1998). The primary objective is for the client to gradually organize memory elements to form a more complete and meaningful narrative of his past experience in order to understand and reduce the influence of the past on his current functioning.

Fostering Internal Connections: Working with Ego-States

The disruption of self-image, beliefs, and relationships that results from abuse may be represented as specific split-off parts or ego-states of the survivor's self. There is debate within the field regarding whether it is clinically useful and accurate to identify and "talk to" discrete parts existing within a dissociative person's whole being. A concern is that using the language of parts or states may reify the parts and release the client from taking responsibility for his behavior: he can blame "that part," over which he seemed to have no control or awareness, for a harmful or antisocial action (Halleck, 1990). Whether one speaks of parts or of unconscious conflicts and drives, the general message, starting in stabilization, is that the client can develop awareness and choice even when these choices are very difficult to make. Within this guideline, the construct of parts or ego-states is helpful for fostering this awareness, highlighting the unconscious motivations, and communicating that the therapist understands that a client genuinely does experience some of his behavior and outlooks as coming from forces outside of, or separate from, himself.

An ego-state is a metaphoric shorthand for describing a concrete set of affects, impulses, memories, and/or sensations that is derived from particular conflictual themes of the abuse and its interpersonal context (e.g., the aggressive violence, the attachment to the perpetrator, the self-blame, the sexual arousal, the secrecy). Each ego-state is dissociated from the rest of the individual because what it represents is too intolerable or undesirable for him to integrate or face at a fully aware level. When a conflict, image, thought, or feeling in the survivor's current interactions, comes close to what he experienced during the earlier abusive relationships, one or more of the ego-states may be "activated," influencing the survivor's perceptions, motivations, and behavior in the current situation. On the surface, these states typically embody resistance to change, to relinquishing a maladaptive symptom. From an object relations perspective, these internal representations embody qualities of the relationships with persons involved in the abuse that the victim has internalized ("introjected").

Identifying the specific ego-states and the functions that each serves is an important step toward mending the dissociative splits and fostering integration. For example, a "perpetrator" or "killer" ego-state, derived from the victim's identification with the abuser's aggression and sadism, operates as an internal cognitive schema for the client's out-of-control aggressive impulses, directed against himself, as in self-injurious or suicidal actions, or against others, such as in domestic violence. A "bad" or "defective" ego-state embodies the intense shame and guilt of having been abused. This is often associated with the negative messages and taunts thrown at the victim and is at the core of the bleak depressions and self-negation that some survivors suffer through. A "failed protector" part represents the relationship with an adult who failed to protect the victim from the abuse and serves as the model for the client's helplessness, denial, and his inability to care for himself and stay safe. Some survivors may have a "child" part that underlies their motivation to perceive the world from a child's perspective, sometimes using the logic and the vocabulary of a child. A "censor" ego-state is the internalization of the command to keep silent, not disclose the abuse, and perhaps remain loyal and attached to the perpetrator. A "watcher" part represents the client's ability to have psychologically removed himself from the abuse and to segregate experiencing from observing ("I was floating on the ceiling when that body got raped at night.").

One method for working with these divisions is ego-state therapy (Phillips & Frederick, 1995; Watkins & Watkins, 1991). This author's variation on the method aims to invite the client's unbidden, socially unacceptable, "bad" part of himself into the office and have a voice, based on the traditional analytic principle of a talking cure: get the person to speak the conflict rather than enact it. The "speaking" is not just talking about the conflict, it's letting the different sides of the conflict speak for themselves, with their full energy, so that the process occurs at somatic and emotional levels as well as at an intellectual level. This may be seen as a direct encouragement of the transference but in the context that the therapist and the patient see what's happening–the client is both participating and observing. This balance of attention appears to be a necessary component for healing changes to occur. Forming a therapeutic alliance with the "bad" ego-state becomes a turning point in the treatment as this part of the client begins to trust another person. This marks a shift from a split-off or disavowed status to greater connection.

This energetic approach can have a gestalt and family therapy quality in that different parts of the client are brought into the room, encouraged to discover safe routes to communicate with one another, and work together as a system to resolve problems. For example, one client, Mike, who was in treatment for abusing others and for depression, was asked to speak from his "abuser" side. With intensity, the "abuser" described how powerful he felt when he got others to do his bidding and how much he despised Mike's usual weak and wimpy behavior. When the "abuser" and Mike began speaking to each other, it became clear that the "abuser" wished that Mike could be tougher in a healthy way and that he was taking out his anger on the world for having been mistreated by his parents and told that he was a sissy. We eventually negotiated a trade in which the "abuser" agreed to stop hurting others and give some of "his" power to Mike in exchange for Mike's assertively standing up for himself with his professional colleagues. Ego-state therapy offers a framework for identifying the sources of power and fear within the internal system and redistributing the power for the client to be able to choose a constructive course of action.

Challenges Encountered During the Integration Phase

As the client begins to integrate previously disconnected elements of past trauma, he and his therapist might face several difficulties, some of which are reflected in dramatic shifts in the client's functioning and the transference. While maintenance of the client's improved functioning continues to be an important focus, erosions do occur. When the client appears to get stuck in the past traumatic material and repeats it without resolution, he might be at risk for reenacting self-destructive and suicidal behaviors. In thinking about significant caring people from his formative years as having been abusive and/or nonprotective, the client may come to view his therapist as abusive. What had been a strong positive alliance seems to derail as fear and rage alter the client's perceptions. This is a stressful period during which the therapist may feel devalued, attacked, and confused, perhaps angry at the client's apparent betrayal of the relationship and harboring fantasies that the client will disappear. The therapist's tasks are to recognize that this phase of the transference process involves the client's asserting himself, albeit awkwardly, in ways that were never safe to do during the original abuse and to tolerate some of the client's anger without personally believing that he or she is a bad therapist. Talking together about what is happening gives the client a framework to navigate. Guided imagery, in which the client might picture going back as an adult and fighting back the perpetrator, can be a powerful healing tool. This intense work may stimulate an abreactive reaction or a release of suppressed emotions which, if handled carefully, can facilitate cognitive insight and re-framing about the trauma. Once some of the transference has been addressed, the treatment would profit from returning to earlier stabilization methods to calm the client and help him see that the therapist is still an ally and not a foe, and that the new knowledge about past relationships can be handled. Supervision or consultation is very beneficial to retain a clear-headed view during this relational tumult.

The complex relationships with meaningful people from the traumatic era may produce additional dilemmas during this phase. Long-standing and sometimes unconscious loyalties to past abusive people might prevent the client from imagining or speaking aloud what had happened during the abuse, as though there was a conspiracy to silence. If a perpetrator was also a nurturing figure in the client's life, then he might struggle with surrendering a harsh black-or-white image of the perpetrator in order to construct a new mental schema that synthesizes both contradictory qualities of the perpetrator and the client's diverse feelings about his relationship with the perpetrator. The client may also want to confront the perpetrator and/or his family. This decision to act on this wish is complicated, requiring considerable discussion about the risks, such as disbelief and excommunication by family members, hoped for results, and timing. In general, if such a confrontation does occur, it is best left toward the end of treatment when the client has completed much of the integrative work and is in a strong and stable frame of mind.

Consolidation

The integrative phase of treatment comes to a close when the client has made meaning of his trauma so that it no longer is the lens through which he experiences the world. Although he will likely never forget the abuse that he suffered, he moves beyond victim status and has developed consolidated strengths to address ordinary problems of living. His dissociative defenses recede and he is able to function well while being aware of different sides of himself. The degree of complete integration varies among people. More severely fragmented and dissociated clients may benefit from guided imagery aimed at fusion and integration. One approach is imagining different parts of the self as patches of snow and ice atop a mountain, gradually melting into individual streams traveling down the mountainside, and eventually forming a whole unified pool of water below. Also, any remaining hyperarousal of the autonomic nervous system would be addressed at this time, using biofeedback, EMDR, self-hypnosis, or meditation. This deeply conditioned physiological reaction is often the last vestige of PTSD and may be modifiable only after the individual can believe that the world is now safe enough for him to learn to relax his body.

THE SELF AND RELATIONAL DEVELOPMENT PHASE

The final phase of treatment builds on the client's integrated aware-ness and skills to achieve a life for himself that had been beyond his capacity while still living under the legacy of trauma. The client brings a fresh and wise perspective to his personal, occupational, relation-ship, and spiritual goals and believes in his future. He may have a sophisticated appreciation of the complexity of human morality and a new or different God-concept. With the lifting of depression and mas-tery over other symptoms, he would experience increased self-esteem. Blame would be reconfigured in this phase, reassigning responsibility to those who perpetrated the abuse. This is especially healing for a gay man whose sexuality had been implicated in his abuse. Permitting himself to be curious and receptive, the client experiments with new interests and talents and forming relationships that are not based on traumatic forces.

One reward during this phase is that the client learns to play. When trauma hits during childhood, ordinary play, through which children rehearse such basic developmental skills as self-soothing, mastery via make-believe creativity, and sharing and negotiation with others, is often interrupted or stopped. Having worked through the effects of trauma, the client can start embarking on adult play with others and by himself. Mental imagery focusing on visions for the future can facili-tate the exploration of new avenues for growth.

With a more realistic and self-loving attitude toward himself, the client is in a powerful position to forge relationships founded on trust and intimacy rather than on insecurity and repetition. Having come through the charged transferences together during the integrative phase, the client and his therapist now typically have a strong alliance. The client figures out which past relationships with a partner, family members, or friends he wants to retain and what forms they will take. He has the ego-strengths to take risks with meaningful people, including direct discussions about the abuse. This includes his choosing to forgive and reconcile with a perpetrator or to completely terminate a relationship with a significant person and mourn this loss with all its associated dreams (e.g., to have had a truly loving and understanding parent). The client may benefit from learning dating and assertiveness skills, from his therapist or in adjunctive group therapy, in order to communicate "Yes, let's get closer" and "No, I do not want that" with a potential partner. For some gay men, who have found the ambiguities of developing an emotional/romantic attachment to be more anxiety-inducing than the relatively clear-cut rules of anonymous or casual sex ("we don't need to talk; I know what to do to please him"), this is a time for the client to practice tolerating uncertainty and to understand and verbalize his desires and limits. With increased self-acceptance, the client has an easier time accepting the real qualities of another and is less trapped by impossibly high expectations and infuriating disappointments. He can determine whether he wants a love relationship and how he would like to create this with another man.

The work of helping survivors recover from abuse is arduous, exciting, exhausting, fulfilling, and transforming of both the client and the therapist. To truly remedy the problem of abuse, changes must continue on a societal level. The research of Herek (1996) makes clear that persons will hold more positive attitudes toward gay men and lesbians when they are exposed to accurate information about homosexuality, learn that someone they know personally is bisexual, lesbian, or gay, or hear that a famous person has come out. These public awarenesses are necessary if men are going to be released from the straight jacketing definitions of manliness, which serve to buttress the fear and rationalize the abuse. This is one step toward men becoming comfortable with all men, regardless of their differences.

REFERENCES

Bailey, J. M., & Pillard, R. (1991). A genetic study of male sexual orientation. *Archives of General Psychiatry, 48*, 1089-96.

Bayer, R. (1981). *Homosexuality and American psychiatry.* New York: Basic Books.

Beemyn, B., & Eliason, M. (Eds.) (1996). *Queer studies: A lesbian, gay, bisexual, and transgender anthology.* New York: New York University Press.

Bell, A. P., & Weinberg, M. S. (1978). *Homosexualities: A study of diversity among men and women.* New York: Simon & Schuster.

Bernstein, E. M., & Putnam, F. W. (1986). Development, reliability and validity of a dissociation scale. *Journal of Nervous and Mental Disease, 174,* 727-735.

Beutler, L. E., & Clarkin, J. F. (1990). *Systematic treatment selection: Toward targeted therapeutic interventions.* New York: Brunner/Mazel.

Brown, D. P., & Fromm, E. (1986). *Hypnotherapy and hypnoanalysis.* Hillsdale, NJ: Lawrence Erlbaum.

Brown, D., Scheflin, A. W., & Hammond, D. C. (1998). *Memory, trauma treatment, and the law.* New York: Norton.

Burr, C. (1996). *A separate creation: The search for the biological origins of sexual orientation.* New York: Hyperion.

Cabaj, R. P., & Stein, T. S. (Eds.). (1996). *The textbook of homosexuality and mental health.* Washington, DC: American Psychiatric Press.

Cadwell, S. A., Burnham, R. A., & Forsten, M. (Eds.). (1994). *Therapists on the frontline: Psychotherapy with gay men in the age of AIDS.* Washington, DC: APA.

Committee on Lesbian and Gay Concerns. (1991). *Bias in psychotherapy with lesbians and gay men.* Washington, DC: American Psychological Association.

Comstock, D. (1991). *Violence against gay men and lesbians.* New York: Columbia University Press.

Courtois, C. (1988). *Healing the incest wound: Adult survivors in therapy.* New York: Norton.

Crowder, A. (1995). *Opening the door: A treatment model for therapy with male survivors of sexual abuse.* New York: Brunner/Mazel.

D'Augelli, A. R., & Patterson, C. J. (Eds.) (1995). *Lesbian, gay, and bisexual identities over the lifespan.* New York: Oxford University Press.

Davies, J. M., & Frawley, M. G. (1994). *Treating the adult survivor of childhood sexual abuse: A psychoanalytic perspective.* New York: Basic.

Davison, G. C. (1976). Homosexuality: The ethical challenge. *Journal of Consulting and Clinical Psychology, 44,* 157-162.

De Cecco, J. P. (1985). *Bashers, baiters, and bigots: Homophobia in American society.* New York: Harrington Park Press.

De Cecco, J. P., & Parker, D. A. (1995). *Sex, cells, and same-sex desire: The biology of sexual preference.* Binghamton, New York: Harrington Park Press.

De Monteflores, C. (1986). Notes on the management of difference. In T. S. Stein & C. J. Cohen (Eds.), *Contemporary perspectives on psychotherapy with lesbians and gay men.* pp. 73-101 New York: Plenum Press.

Frankl, V. E. (1946/1985). *Man's search for meaning.* New York: Washington Square Press.

Garnets, L., Herek, G. M., & Levy, B. (1993). Violence and victimization of lesbians and gay men: Mental health consequences. In L. D. Garnets & D. C. Kimmel (Eds.), *Psychological perspectives on lesbian and gay male experiences.* New York: Columbia University Press.

Garnets, L. D., & Kimmel, D. C. (Eds.) (1993). *Psychological perspectives on lesbian and gay male experiences.* New York: Columbia University Press.

Gonsiorek, J. C. (Ed.) (1985). *A guide to psychotherapy with gay and lesbian clients.* New York: Harrington Park Press.

Green, R. (1987). *The "Sissy boy syndrome" and the development of homosexuality.* New Haven: Yale University.

Greene, B. (Ed.) (1997). *Ethnic and cultural diversity among lesbians and gay men.* Thousand Oaks, CA: Sage.

Grubman-Black, S. D. (1990). *Broken boys/mending men.* New York: Ivy/Ballantine.

Gudjonsson, G. H. (1984). A new scale of interrogative suggestibility. *Personality and Individual Differences, 5,* 303-314.

Haldeman, D. (1994). The practice and ethics of sexual orientation conversion therapy. *Journal of Consulting and Clinical Psychology, 62,* 221-227.

Halleck, S. (1990). Responsibility and the phenomenon of dissociation. *International Journal of Clinical & Experimental Hypnosis, 38,* 298-314.

Herek, G. M. (1986). On heterosexual masculinity: Some psychical consequences of the social construction of gender and sexuality. *American Behavioral Scientist, 29,* 563-577.

Herek, G. M. (1996). Heterosexism and homophobia. In R. P. Cabaj & T. S. Stein (Eds.), *Textbook of homosexuality and mental health.* Washington, DC: American Psychiatric Press.

Herek, G. M., & Berrill, K. T. (Eds.) (1991). *Hate crimes: Confronting violence against lesbians and gay men.* Thousand Oaks: Sage.

Herman, J. L. (1992). *Trauma and recovery.* New York: Basic Books.

Hocquenghem, G. (1972/1978). *Homosexual desire.* London: Allison & Busby.

Horowitz, M. J. (1986). *Stress response syndromes* (2nd ed). New York: Aronson.

Hunter, M. (1990). *Abused boys: The neglected victims of sexual abuse.* New York: Fawcett.

Isay, R. (1989). *Being homosexual: Gay men and their development.* New York: Farrar, Straus, Giroux.

Isensee, R. (1991, 1997). *Reclaiming your life: The gay man's guide to love, self-acceptance and trust.* California: Alyson Books.

Janoff-Bulman, J. (1992). *Shattered assumptions: Towards a new psychology of trauma.* New York: The Free Press.

Kluft, R. P. (1993). Basic principles in conducting the therapy of multiple personality disorder. In R. P. Kluft & C. G. Fine (Eds.), *Clinical perspectives on multiple personality disorder* (pp. 19-50). Washington, DC: American Psychiatric Press.

Kluft, R. P. (1996). Treating the traumatic memories of patients with dissociative identity disorder. *American Journal of Psychiatry, 153,* 103-110.

Kluft, R. P., & Fine, C. G. (Eds.) (1993). *Clinical perspectives on multiple personality disorder.* Washington, DC: American Psychiatric Press.

Lew, M. (1988). *Victims no longer: Men recovering from incest and other sexual child abuse.* New York: Harper Collins Perennial.

Lindsay, D. S., & Read, J. D. (1994). Psychotherapy and memories of childhood sexual abuse: A cognitive perspective. *Applied Cognitive Psychology, 8,* 281-338.

Linehan, M. M. (1993). *Cognitive-behavioral treatment of borderline personality disorder.* New York: Guilford.

Loftus, E. F. (1993). The reality of repressed memories. *American Psychologist, 48,* 518-537.

Malyon, A. K. (1982). Psychotherapeutic implications of internalized homophobia in gay men. *Journal of Homosexuality, 7,* 59-70.

McCann, T., & Pearlman, L. (1990). *Psychological trauma and the adult survivor: Theory, therapy, and transformation.* New York: Brunner/Mazel.

Meichenbaum, D. (1994). *A clinical handbook/practical therapist manual for assessing and treating adults with post-traumatic stress disorder (PTSD).* Waterloo, Ontario: Institute Press.

Messer, S. B. (1986). Behavioral and psychoanalytic perspectives at therapeutic choice points. *American Psychologist, 41,* 1261-1272.

Morin, S., & Garfinkle, E. (1978). Male homophobia. *Journal of Social Issues, 34,* 29-46.

Neisen, J. H. (1993). Healing from cultural victimization: Recovery from shame due to heterosexism. *Journal of Gay & Lesbian Psychotherapy, 2,* 49-63.

Nicolosi, J. (1991). *Reparative therapy of male homosexuality.* Northvale, NJ: Jason Aronson.

Phillips, M., & Frederick, C. (1995). *Healing the divided self: Clinical and Ericksonian hypnotherapy for post-traumatic and dissociative conditions.* New York: Norton.

Pillard, R. (1996). Homosexuality from a familial and genetic perspective. In R. P. Cabaj & T. S. Stein (Eds.), *Textbook of homosexuality and mental health.* Washington, DC: American Psychiatric Press.

Pope, K. S., & Brown, L. (1996). *Recovered memories of abuse: Assessment, therapy, and forensics.* Washington, DC: American Psychological Association Press.

Pope, K., Sonne, J. L. & Holroyd, J. (1993). *Sexual feelings in psychotherapy.* Washington, DC: APA.

Putnam, F. W. (1989). *Diagnosis and treatment of multiple personality disorder.* New York: Guilford.

Ross, C. A. (1989). *Multiple personality disorder: Diagnosis, clinical features, and treatment.* New York: Wiley.

Ross, M. W. (Ed.) (1988). *The treatment of homosexuals with mental health disorders.* New York: Harrington Park Press.

Salter, A. C. (1995). *Transforming trauma: A guide to understanding and treating adult survivors of child sexual abuse.* Thousand Oaks, CA: Sage.

Schwartz, M. F. (1992) Sexual compulsivity as post-traumatic stress disorder: Treatment perspectives. *Psychiatric Annals, 6,* 333-338.

Schwartzberg, S. (1996). *A crisis of meaning: How gay men are making sense of AIDS.* New York: Oxford.

Schwartzberg, S., & Rosenberg, L. G. (1998). Being gay and being male: Psychotherapy with gay and bisexual men. In W. S. Pollack & R. F. Levant (Eds.), *New psychotherapy for men.* New York: Wiley.

Shapiro, F. (1995). *Eye movement desensitization and reprocessing.* New York: Guilford.

Shidlo, A. (1994). Internalized homophobia: Conceptual and empirical issues in measurement. In B. Greene & G. M. Herek (Eds.), *Lesbian and gay psychology: Theory, research, and clinical applications.* Thousand Oaks, CA: Sage.

Shilts, R. (1987). *And the band played on: Politics, people, and the AIDS epidemic.* New York: St. Martin's Press.

Silverstein, C. (Ed.) (1991). *Gays, lesbians, and their therapists.* New York: Norton.

Spiegel, H., & Spiegel, D. (1978). *Trance and treatment: Clinical uses of hypnosis.* Washington, DC: American Psychiatric Press.

Stein, T. S. (1996). A critique of approaches to changing sexual orientation. In R. P. Cabaj & T. S. Stein (Eds.), *Textbook of homosexuality and mental health* (pp. 525-537). Washington, DC: American Psychiatric Press.

Stein, T. S., & Cohen, C. J. (Eds.) (1986). *Contemporary perspectives on psychotherapy with lesbians and gay men.* New York: Plenum.

Steinberg, M. (1993). *Structured clinical interview of DSM-IV dissociative disorders (SCID-D).* Washington, DC: American Psychiatric Association.

Van der Kolk, B. A., McFarlane, A. C., & Weisaeth, L. (Eds.). (1996). *Traumatic stress: The effects of overwhelming experience on mind, body, and society.* New York: Guilford.

Wachtel, P. (1977). *Psychoanalysis and behavior therapy: Towards an integration.* New York: Basic Books.

Watkins, J., & Watkins, H. (1991). Hypnosis and ego-state therapy. In Keller & Heymans (Eds.), *Innovations in clinical practice: A source book.* Professional Resources Exchange.

Weitzenhoffer, A. M., & Hilgard, E. R. (1962). *Stanford hypnotic susceptibility scale, form C.* Palo Alto, CA: Consulting Psychologists Press.

Yapko, M. D. (1994). *Suggestions of abuse.* New York: Simon & Schuster.

Eye Movement Desensitization and Reprocessing in the Treatment of Traumatized Gay Men

Dennis Balcom

SUMMARY. Gay men suffering from traumatic experiences can benefit from Eye Movement Desensitization and Reprocessing treatment (EMDR). In the past decade the theory and practice of EMDR has expanded to address acute and chronic childhood and adult traumas, substance misuse or abuse, identity issues including shame and self-esteem, and health issues. Through a process of accelerated information processing, traumatic memories are desensitized and reprocessed, resulting in less distress for the client in the present and future. EMDR can also be useful for developing internal resources and for exploration of relevant themes for the client. Further attention is needed in exploring the use of EMDR for gay men traumatized by hate crimes, sexual issues resulting from traumatic experiences, and internalized homophobia. *[Article copies available for a fee from The Haworth Document Delivery Service: 1-800-342-9678. E-mail address: <getinfo@haworthpressinc.com> Website: <http://www.HaworthPress.com>]*

KEYWORDS. EMDR, gay men, trauma, addiction, shame, health

Eye movement desensitization and reprocessing (EMDR) is a promising new treatment for a variety of issues, shown to be particularly helpful to traumatized clients. In treating gay men with acute or

[Haworth co-indexing entry note]: "Eye Movement Desensitization and Reprocessing in the Treatment of Traumatized Gay Men." Balcom, Dennis. Co-published simultaneously in *Journal of Gay & Lesbian Social Services* (Harrington Park Press, an imprint of The Haworth Press, Inc.) Vol. 12, No. 1/2, 2000, pp. 75-89; and: *Gay Men and Childhood Sexual Trauma: Integrating the Shattered Self* (ed: James Cassese) Harrington Park Press, an imprint of The Haworth Press, Inc., 2000, pp. 75-89. Single or multiple copies of this article are available for a fee from The Haworth Document Delivery Service [1-800-342-9678, 9:00 a.m. - 5:00 p.m. (EST). E-mail address: getinfo@haworthpressinc.com].

chronic trauma symptoms, EMDR can sometimes offer immediate and prolonged relief from trauma related distress. EMDR treatment methods can also be effective with this population in the treatment of addictions, the enhancement of gay identity through increased self-esteem and decreased internalized shame, and health care in general with an emphasis on pain management.

EMDR is a well researched and documented treatment model with demonstrated effectiveness with Post-Traumatic Stress Disorder (PTSD) (Forbes, Creamer, & Rycroft, 1994; Lipke & Botkin, 1993; Lohr, Kleinknecht, Tolin, & Barrett, 1996; Marcus, Marquis, & Sakai, 1997; Metter & Michaelson, 1993; Montgomery & Ayllon, 1994; Oswalt, Anderson, Hagstrom, & Berkowitz, 1993; Paulson, 1995; Puk, 1991; Renfrey & Spates, 1994; Rothbaum, 1997; Shapiro, 1996; Wilson, Silver, Covi, & Foster, 1996; Wilson, Becker, & Tinker, 1995; and Wilson, Becker, & Tinker, 1997a).

This paper will describe the theory and practice of EMDR, present a survey of its applications to traumatized gay male clients, and offer an illustrative case study to highlight the utility of EMDR. Based primarily on the clinical and supervisory experience of the author, this paper is the first known report focusing on EMDR with traumatized adult gay male clients. The material discussed may also have important applications to adolescent gay males, and bisexual and transvestite men who have experienced trauma.

EMDR: THEORY AND PRACTICE

The descriptive words inform the method: eye movement, desensitization, and reprocessing. Eye movements in conjunction with the conscious awareness of a painful memory are believed to desensitize the memory, rendering it less intense. Reprocessing is posited, as new positive information is developed by the client. EMDR utilizes aspects of other psychotherapeutic theories and practices such as behavioral, cognitive, and hypnotic aspects (Lipke, 1997). The underlying theory of EMDR incorporates three essential components: neuro networks, bilateral stimulation and accelerated information processing.

Advances in neuropsychology relating to memory indicate the storage of information (memory) in the brain in networks of neurons (neuro networks) (Bergmann, 1998; Bremmer, Krystal, Southwick, & Charney, 1995; Kempermann & Gage, 1999; Lindsey, 1999; Pitman & Orr, 1995;

Shapiro, 1995; Rossi, 1999). Memory is distributed throughout the network and brain in state specific form as it was encoded, at the time of the traumatic incident (Van der Kolk, 1994). Consequently, EMDR hypothesizes that traumatic memories are not processed in the same way as normal memory (Shapiro, 1995). Thus, the traumatic memory is experienced as present reality.

The primary goal of EMDR treatment is to assist in the processing of the traumatic memory in order for it to become (1) less affective intense or intrusive; (2) experienced as in the past rather than in the present; and (3) to optimize current and future functioning. Desensitization and reprocessing is accomplished through the process of bilateral stimulation. The three forms of bilateral stimulation presently in common use are eye movements while holding the head steady; audio tones alternating in each ear; and tactile stimulation of the palm of opposite hands, alternating hands. Two forms of bilateral stimulation can be used at the same time. Bilateral stimulation is understood to activate both hemispheres of the brain, leading to the development of new neural connections while attending to the traumatic memory (Rossi, 1999).

The third component, accelerated information processing, is believed to occur through the bilateral stimulation of the brain hemispheres. Increased blood flow to both hemispheres may be seen through brain scans (MRI, PET) during eye movements. New neuronal connections are instantly made in the memory network, the result of the accelerated information processing (Rossi, 1999). Accelerated information processing also occurs because the standard EMDR trauma protocol is multi-modal. It asks the client to focus on an image of the trauma (visual), a negative belief about the self resulting from the trauma (cognitive), the emotion experienced with the current recollection of the trauma (affective), and the body location (sensation) related to the trauma experience/memory (Shapiro, 1995, 1998). The client consciously holds these components in his awareness while he receives bilateral stimulation from the therapist using one of the three forms mentioned: visual, audio, or tactile. This focus by the client of the various aspects of the traumatic experience creates a holistic awareness which stimulates more brain activity.

During desensitization, between sets of the bilateral stimulation, the client reports on his awareness during the process. His awareness could be a thought, feeling, body sensation, memory, color, or nothing.

Three areas of charge criteria are monitored throughout the EMDR treatment: (1) when the client reports a differentiation of past and present (e.g., *"It's behind me now"*); (2) the experience of active choice (e.g., *"I can live in the present"*); and (3) accurate attribution of blame (e.g., *"The perpetrator was responsible, not me as a child"*).

Additionally, two scales are used at the beginning and end of each EMDR session. The Validity of Cognition Scale (VOC) asks the client to indicate how true they believe their chosen positive cognition statement to be (e.g., "I'm safe now.") using a scale of 1 to 7 (1 completely false, 7 completely true). The VOC provides a baseline and may be used as an indicator in the change towards a positive self-statement/belief. The second scale, Subjective Units of Distress (SUDs) asks the client to relate their current experience of distress regarding the traumatic experience using a scale of 0-10 (0 is no distress or neutral, 10 is the worst possible distress imaginable). In combination, these client self-reports and observations by the therapist can give ongoing feedback to guide the treatment.

EMDR, initially seen as a short-term treatment for PTSD, has been expanded to include other protocols and variations. The standard EMDR trauma protocol is described above and continues to be the foundation for the treatment (Shapiro, 1995). An important addition to EMDR is the protocol for resource installation, which assists the client in developing internal resources, typically prior to using the standard protocol. Resource installation is a protocol developed to help clients have a firm basis from which to do the deeper desensitizing and reprocessing work. In resource installation the client develops positive allies, tools, or assets in order to feel more capable. One common resource is of a mentor or protector, either in actuality or in imagination, as is the development of a "safe place." Resource installation in some situations is the entire treatment. In other situations it is woven into the ongoing treatment (Leeds, 1998; Schmidt, 1999).

Another use of EMDR is for exploration, to follow where a particular theme, feeling, belief, or body sensation might lead. Exploration is useful for clients when they have trauma symptoms but no clear recollection of the traumatic experience(s). For some men, this is a self-stated goal (see case study following) while for others it may assist in moving the treatment forward when at an impasse. The search for unrecovered memories outside of these two examples, and without the client's cooperation, would constitute a misuse of EMDR.

Finally, there are new applications of EMDR known as "innovative use" in which practitioners adapt the model, include other theories, or experiment with new techniques in expanding the method (Balcom, 1998; Hassard, 1993; Manfield, 1998; Martinez, 1991; Schmidt, 1999).

EMDR was initially formulated as a brief treatment, beginning with an assessment, followed by a few treatment sessions, and concluded with a termination/review/reassessment meeting. Treatment sessions are preferably 90 minutes in duration to ensure the completion of a target memory. Longer-term use of EMDR is also common, particularly for clients with chronic trauma histories. EMDR can be titrated to suit the client's capacities for therapy, although, as with any treatment method, it may not work for everyone, or in every set of circumstances.

In the early days of EMDR the procedure was only of eye movements, with the clinician sitting adjacent to and facing the client. The clinician would instruct the client to focus on the trauma scene, negative cognition, emotion and body sensation, and "follow my fingers" (moving horizontally, vertically or diagonally). Any one or combination of these four content areas can give access to the neuro network and accelerated information processing. Technology has improved and replaced the hand movements (saving the clinician from overuse injuries and fatigue) and many clinicians and clients now prefer to use the Eyescan or the Tac/Audio Scan. These devices duplicate in a more regular fashion the stimulus of the hand movement (the Eyescan), with audio tones available through headphones, or the tapping on the client's palms (the Tac/Audio Scan) again with audio tones available. These devices are non-intrusive, clients can regulate the speed and duration of each set of stimuli, and clients can choose which stimuli best suits them. Audio tapes (Grant, 1997a, 1997b) can be assigned as self-help and self-soothing devices for use by clients.

Considerations in referring gay men to EMDR include the knowledge that EMDR is most effective for treating symptoms of anxiety or post-traumatic stress disorder such as intrusive images, flashbacks, and nightmares. It is the current treatment of choice immediately following a recent traumatic event. EMDR is helpful for those men who have recovered memories of past traumas, or who wish to explore missing aspects of their lives (see case study). When a client is at an impasse in a current therapy, or has a history of multiple treatments without progress, EMDR can act as a catalyst. Finally, if a client is fixated on a negative belief, such as "I am inadequate," EMDR is appropriate. EMDR is contraindicated for men with seizure or neurological disorders, and cardiac or eye problems. EMDR treatment can be emotionally and physically intense, sometimes with unpredictable results. Caution is advised for clients involved in legal actions in which memory may be an issue. Informed consent by the client is a prerequisite to treatment.

APPLICATIONS TO TRAUMATIZED GAY MEN

Gay men, beyond the usual and non-discriminatory plethora of opportunities to be traumatized in American culture, also have a specific and unique vulnerability to be traumatized by virtue of living in a heterosexist and homophobic society (Dunkle, 1994; Neison, 1993). Gay men may enter EMDR treatment with consciousness of a specific recent traumatic event, a known series of traumatic experiences, or complaining of various symptoms which might indicate a traumatic history but without clear memory of an event. Symptoms might include self-injury, high-risk behaviors, and dissociative states.

Traumatic events might be located in any developmental period of the man's life and continue to have profound disruptive effects in self-care, relationships, spirituality, career or health (any one or all of these domains). The near universality of assaults suffered by gay men would indicate a significant proportion of those entering psychotherapy would probably have some traumatic experiences. New traumatic experiences may befall the client during the course of treatment.

The major aspects of trauma EMDR can be helpful with for gay men are: (1) the actual traumatic experiences, either those in general that anyone could experience such as surviving a natural disaster, or those in specific instances that such as in bias-related assaults (physically, verbally, or psychologically) and, (2) the ancillary aspects of trauma such as addictions, shame, identity issues, and health issues especially regarding pain management.

EMDR is a dynamic and natural healing process. By changing one aspect of the neural network (i.e., a traumatic memory), clients sometimes report changes in other domains of concern as well. In general, as trauma experiences are desensitized and reprocessed, overall improvement can be noted beyond the specifically targeted issue. For some clients, resource installation or exploration of issues may suffice.

Other clients may need to return multiple times to the traumatic scene to continue desensitization, as in cases with severe childhood traumas which persisted for long periods of time (e.g., through childhood into adolescence). Traumas deliberately perpetrated as an attack on gay identity or gay sexuality which result in internalized homophobia may be more difficult to reprocess or desensitize, for some clients.

Traumatic Experiences

Gay men generally present for EMDR treatment with complex histories and complicated current situations. Traumatic histories might encompass both the general and the specific, with associated issues of identity or addiction. One important question with multiply distressed clients is where to begin. Will the client benefit most from targeting the traumatic experiences? Would he be best served by installing resources so he can tolerate the trauma work? The confluence of EMDR and trauma theories and practices offers appropriate cautions about readiness for EMDR. These cautions need to be exercised in conjunction with the therapist's comfort and style, along with the client's goals, awareness, and resources. An active mutual decision as part of the assessment process can guide the initial EM sessions, with periodic reevaluations of in- and between-session changes.

The nature of the traumas that may be addressed with EMDR include childhood neglect and abuse, both physically and sexually, within the family and by other care givers. They span the range from single incidents to repetitive experiences of being victimized or being forced to abuse other children. Witnessing the active abuse of others, either children or adults, without feeling empowered to intervene is another common trauma that has numerous applications to gay men. Childhood abuse or neglect can be physical, including for example: tissue damage, broken bones, starvation, sensory deprivation, or sexual torture. Psychological abuse may be directed at the identity of the child and may manifest in low self-esteem, self-hatred (including internalized homophobia), passivity or aggressiveness. Identity confusion may also result both in terms of gender (e.g., *"Am I a boy or a girl?"*), and sexuality (e.g., *"Am I gay, bi, or straight?"*). The traumatic experiences of adult gay men also include being raped, physically assaulted in a hate crime, emotionally or psychologically humiliated or shamed, or feared.

Ancillary Aspects of Traumatic Experiences

Substance misuse or addiction is frequently co-assembled with trauma, either as a factor in the actual trauma (e.g., driving under the influence and having an accident) or as a coping method following the traumatic experience. Substance abuse issues may include the misuse of prescription medications as well as illegal substances.

Sequential detoxification of multiple addictions, withdrawal, maintenance of a harm reduction life-style, and relapse prevention are the core elements in attending to addiction issues relative to trauma (Cain, 1991; Cook, 1991; Daley, 1989; Dusoe & Boswell, 1995; Irvin, Bowers, Dunn, & Wang, 1999; Kitchen, 1991; Marlatt, 1990; Popky, 1995; Potter-Effron, 1989; Shapiro, Vogelmann-Sine, & Sine, 1994). Two other aspects are worth noting: the concurrence of trauma while under the influence, and the role of substances as self-soothing mechanisms to cope with the traumatic experiences.

When treating traumatized gay men already in recovery from substance use or abuse, a cautionary note in the assessment phase/informed consent is to warn that EMDR treatment may stimulate old addictive patterns, wishes, cravings, or behaviors. The practical solution to this potential difficulty is to have good resources in place (e.g., AA, other concurrent therapies), a relapse prevention plan prior to beginning the eye movement (EM) treatment, and attentive checking in with the client to assess if addictive urges or thoughts have arisen during the processing.

EMDR's effectiveness in treating symptoms of PTSD, and the high correlation between trauma and shame (Catherall & Shelton, 1996; Courtois, 1992; Wong & Cook, 1992), suggest EMDR could be an effective treatment for reducing shame and enhancing self-esteem. The link between shame and trauma has been noted clinically and incorporated into several psychological and neuropsychological models (Courtois, 1992; Nathanson, 1992; Tompkins, 1987; Van der Kolk, 1996, 1994). Virtually all traumatized patients have some degree of internalized shame (Courtois, 1992). In addition, shame is often a key component of addictions, anxiety disorders, depression, major mental illness, sexual identity or dysfunction, and personality disorders (Brown, 1988; Kaufman, 1985; Krugman, 1995; Leeds, 1997; Manfield, 1998; Nathanson, 1992; Rothbaum, 1997; Schenk & Everingham, 1995; Wernick, 1993; Wong & Cook, 1992; Zangwill, 1994). For gay men in general, shame may become over time a component of self-identity and may further be included in self-loathing, internalized homophobia, and account for a closed self-referential loop which perpetuates a hostile self-identity (e.g., *"I'm ashamed of what happened to me. It must have happened to me because I'm worthless. Therefore, I am ashamed of being worthless and I deserve what happened to me."*).

Self-esteem is the opposite of internalized shame (Cook, 1991, 1989). It represents "an individual's sense of personal worth that is derived more from inner thoughts and values than from praise and recognition from others" (Barker, 1987). Shame reduction and self-esteem enhancement from EMDR treatment can potentially benefit many gay men regardless of whether shame is addressed directly or indirectly in treatment (Balcom, Call, & Perlman, 1999). The author typically uses the Internalized Shame Scale (ISS) (Cook, 1989) prior to EM treatment and again during termination to allow the client to see the changes in his scores. The ISS has two sub-scales, Internalized Shame (0-96) and Self-Esteem (0-24).

Health issues abound for traumatized gay men in two directions: first, the actual traumatic injuries to body and soul which can be accompanied by acute and chronic pain, suffering, or disability; second, the neglect of self due to the devaluating often accompanying the trauma. This may take the form of failing to follow through on appropriate medical treatments (e.g., medication, physical therapy), by tolerating high degrees of discomfort or pain, not seeking attention soon enough (e.g., disease progression), or fear (sometimes terror) at the medical or self-care procedures, especially when the treatment procedure resembles or stimulates the actual trauma (physically or emotionally).

Fortunately, EMDR can offer some relief to those men dealing with health and pain issues. EMDR has been reported as beneficial in the treatment of medical phobias, chronic pain management, and in the relief of acute symptoms (Grant, 1998; Hekmat, Groth, & Rodgers, 1994; Lohr, Tolin, & Kleinknecht, 1995; Montgomery & Ayllon, 1994; Van der Kolk, 1994 and Wilson, Becker, & Tinker, 1997b). As with the treatment choices regarding trauma and addictions, the decision to focus on health issues needs to be considered in the overall context. These four issues (trauma, addiction, identity, and health) can be interwoven in complex ways; attention to one domain can greatly shift another.

Cautions for EMDR Treatment with Gay Men

EMDR may not be appropriate for clients currently using benzodiazepines and other medications, which may inhibit processing and/or life stability/safety. One specific aspect of EMDR treatment is the physical proximity of the therapist and client. The standard protocol for EM is for the therapist to sit adjacent to the client, and move his (therapist's) hand about 18-24 inches from the client's face. In contrast to traditional distance in psychotherapy this can afford an opportunity for more intense closeness or for heightened anxiety, for either client or therapist. The issues of attraction, transference, and counter transference need to be adequately addressed in all components of EMDR treatment with traumatized gay men.

The question of where to begin focusing on the treatment can be addressed as a symptom, as a theme, or as a question to be explored. In temporal terms it can begin (and alternate or flow in either direction) from past, present and future. It can be seen as a primary/solo treatment or as concurrent with other ongoing treatments.

CASE STUDY: MR. G.

Mr. G., a gay man in his early thirties, was referred by his group therapist for EMDR. He was a college educated businessman with a history of childhood abuse complicated by adolescent and adult alcohol addiction. He had been abstinent from alcohol for the previous six years. At the beginning of treatment he was living with his domestic partner and they were mutually physically and verbally abusive. Although Mr. G. believed he had been abused as a child, he did not have any recollection of specific events. He presented with multiple symptoms of PTSD, including startle reactions, hypervigilance (especially if someone was behind him and out of his eyesight), sleep disturbance, panic attacks, and intrusive thoughts about being intruded upon.

His goals for EMDR were to reduce the "triggers" for the startle reactions and, if possible, to fill in the "missing pieces of the puzzle" regarding the mysteries of his earlier life. In addition to his group therapy he attended AA 3-5 times a week and was considering a psychopharmacological evaluation. Mr. G. and his partner were referred for couples therapy regarding this domestic violence. This additional treatment overlapped briefly with the EMDR treatment.

In the first EMDR treatment session Mr. G. focused on an adult scene in which he was triggered at a party by someone touching his buttocks without his permission. He panicked and left the event. This specific incident was chosen by Mr. G. because it continues to distress him, and because it represented a general theme of being triggered, panicking, and leaving social events.

In the standard protocol he identified the worst part of the experience as the sequence when he was undesirably touched and then "freaked out!" His negative cognition (belief) about himself in this experience was "I'm powerless and voiceless." His preferred positive belief was "I can say no." He initially rated this statement as a VOC of 1. He felt "anxious, jittery, and flighty." He rated his distress as a SUDs of 7-8, and experienced the distress in the center of his chest.

During the processing in this first 90-minute treatment session he experienced sadness, anger, anxiety, and began to verbalize "no" to himself. He recalled self-soothing as a five year old by covering himself with a blanket, and by repetitive rocking. He imagined himself saying "I can get up and walk away." In the middle of the session he focused on the pain: "Oh God, it hurts!" At the end of the session he returned to the positive beliefs of "I can say stop now. I can choose. I can say no."

Mr. G. showed many signs of desensitizing and processing in this session: he moved from the initial image of the unwanted touch to other images, and he exhibited a range of emotions and thoughts. His VOC had increased from 1 to 6-7, and his SUDs decreased from 7-8 to 1. At the beginning of his second session these scores remained the same. Two of the three change criteria were satisfied (choice–I can choose, time–I can say stop now).

In the next three treatment sessions Mr. G. followed up on the themes of anxiety and powerlessness. His VOC and SUDs scores consistently moved in the right direction, and he felt more empowered and safe in the world. He said he "felt more alive." A particular note of interest is that he felt more connected and cared about by his friends and his family of origin.

In four EMDR treatment sessions Mr. G.'s scores on the ISS indicated positive change: a 20-point reduction in internalized shame (43-23) and an increase in self-esteem (19-21). At three-month follow-up Mr. G. indicated these improvements had persisted. His group therapist concurred with Mr. G.'s self-report.

CONCLUSION

Gay men suffering from traumatic experiences are also vulnerable to addictions, self-esteem and shame issues associated with either the trauma or with gay identity, and a range of health issues. EMDR appears to be helpful in all of these areas as noted in clinical reports. Further research is needed to determine the benefits of EMDR treatment for traumatized gay men, in particular for those traumas perpetrated as a hate crime.

REFERENCES

Balcom, D., Call, E., & Pearlman, D. (1999). EMDR treatment of internalized shame. Unpublished manuscript.

Balcom, D. (1998). Coordinating inpatient EMDR treatment in ongoing outpatient treatment, *EMDRIA Newsletter, 3*, 25-27.

Barker, R. (1987). *The Social Work Dictionary.* Silver Springs, MD: National Association of Social Workers.

Bergmann, U. (1998). Speculations on the neurobiology of EMDR. *Traumatology, 4*, 1-15.

Bremmer, D., Krystal, J., Southwick, S., & Charney, D. (1995). Functional neuroanatomical correlates of the effects of stress on memory. *Journal of Traumatic Stress, 8*, 527-553.

Brown, J. (1988). Shame, intimacy, and sexuality. In E. Coleman (Ed.), *Chemical dependency and intimacy dysfunction* (pp. 61-74). New York: The Haworth Press, Inc.

Cain, R. (1991). Stigma management and gay identity development. *Social Work, 36*, 1, 67-73.

Catherall, D., & Shelton, R. (1996). Men's groups for PTSD and the role of shame. In M. Andronico (Ed.), *Men in groups: Insights, interventions, and psychoeducational work* (pp. 323-337). Hyattsville, MD: APA.

Cook, D. (1989). *Internalized shame scale.* Wisconsin: University of Wisconsin-Stout.

Cook, D. (1991). Shame, attachment, and addictions: Implications for family therapists. *Contemporary Family Therapy, 13*, 405-419.

Courtois, C. (1992). Shame as a basic dynamic of sexual abuse: Implications for treatment. *Developments: The Newsletter of the Center for Women's Development at HRI, 3*, 3, 1-4.

Daley, D. (Ed.) (1989). *RELAPSE: Conceptual research and clinical perspectives.* New York: The Haworth Press, Inc.

Dunkle, J. (1994). Counseling gay male clients: A review of treatment efficacy research: 1975-Present. *Journal of Gay & Lesbian Psychotherapy, 2,* 1-19.

Dusoe, M., & Boswell, R. (1995). The use of self-efficacy training in the treatment of relapse-prone individuals. *EAPA Exchange, 25,* 6-9.

Forbes, D., Creamer, M., & Rycroft, P. (1994). EMDR in PTSD: A pilot study using assessment measures. *Journal of Behavioral Therapy and Experimental Psychiatry, 25,* 113-120.

Grant, M. (1998). *Pain control with EMDR.* Denver, CO: Mentor Books.

Grant, M. (1997a). *Pain control with EMDR.* New Harbinger Publications (audio tape).

Grant, M. (1997b). *Calm and confident with EMDR.* New Harbinger Publications (audio tape).

Hassard, A. (1993). EMDR for body image. *Behavioral Psychotherapy, 21,* 157-160.

Hekmat, H., Groth, S., & Rodgers, D. (1994). Pain ameliorating effect of eye movement desensitization. *Journal of Behavioral Therapy and Experimental Psychiatry, 25,* 121-130.

Irvin, J., Bowers, C., Dunn, M., & Wang, M. (1999). Efficacy of relapse prevention: A meta-analytic review. *Journal of Consulting and Clinical Psychology, 67,* 563-570.

Kempermann, G., & Gage, F. (1999). New nerve cells for the adult brain. *Scientific American, 280,* 48-53.

Kitchen, R. (1991). Relapse therapy. *EMDR Network Newsletter, 1,* 4-6.

Krugman, S. (1995). Male development and the transformation of shame. In R. Levant & W. Pollack (Eds.), *A new psychology of men* (pp. 213-257). New York: Basic Books.

Leeds, A. (1997, July). In the eye of the beholder: Reflections on shame, dissociation, and transference in complex post traumatic stress and attachment related disorders. Paper presented at EMDR International Association Conference.

Leeds, A. (1998). Lifting the burden of shame: Using EMDR resource installation to resolve a therapeutic impasse. In P. Manfield (Ed.), *Extending EMDR: A casebook of innovative applications* (pp. 256-281). New York: W. W. Norton.

Lindsey, J. (1999, June). A cognitive neural network: Levels of processing approach to understanding EMDR. Paper presented at the EMDR International Association Annual Conference.

Lipke, H., & Botkin, A. (1993). Case studies of eye movement desensitization and reprocessing (EMDR) with chronic posttraumatic stress disorder. *Psychotherapy, 29,* 591-595.

Lipke, H. (1997). A four activity model of psychotherapy and its relationship to EMDR and other methods of psychotherapy. *Traumatology, 2,* 2.

Lohr, J., Tolin, D., & Kleinknecht, R. (1995). EMDR of medical phobias: Two case studies. *Journal of Behavioral Therapy and Experimental Psychiatry, 26,* 141-151.

Lohr, J., Kleinknecht, R., Tolin, D., & Barrett, R. (1996). The empirical status of the clinical application of EMDR. *Journal of Behavioral Therapy and Experimental Psychiatry, 26*, 285-302.

Manfield, P. (Ed.) (1998). *Extending EMDR: A casebook of innovative applications.* New York: W. W. Norton.

Marcus, S., Marquis, P., & Sakai, C. (1997). Controlled study of treatment of PTSD using EMDR in an HMO setting. *Psychotherapy, 34*, 307-315.

Marlatt, G. (1990). Cue exposure and relapse prevention in the treatment of addictive behaviors. *Addictive Behaviors, 15*, 395-99.

Martinez, R. (1991). Innovative uses. *EMDR Network Newsletter, 1*, 5-6.

Metter, J., & Michaelson, L. (1993). Theoretical, clinical, research, and ethical constraints of the EMDR technique. *Journal of Traumatic Stress, 6*, 413-415.

Montgomery, R. & Ayllon, T. (1994). EMDR across subjects: Subjective and physiological measures of treatment efficacy. *Journal of Behavioral Therapy and Experimental Psychiatry, 25*, 217-230.

Nathanson, D. (1992). *Shame and pride: Affect, sex, and the birth of the self.* New York: W. W. Norton & Co.

Neisen, J. (1993). Healing from cultural victimization: Recovery from shame due to heterosexism. *Journal of Gay & Lesbian Psychotherapy, 2*, 49-63.

Oswalt, R., Anderson, M., Hagstrom, K., & Berkowitz, B. (1993). Evaluation of the one-session eye movement desensitization reprocessing procedure for eliminating traumatic memories. *Psychological Reports, 73*, 99-104.

Paulson, S. (1995). EMDR: Its cautious use in the dissociative disorders. *Dissociation, 8*, 32-44.

Pitman, R., & Orr, S. (1995). Psychophysiology of emotional memory networks in posttraumatic stress disorder. In J. McGaugh, N. Weinberger, & G. Lynch (Eds.) *Brain and memory: Modulation and mediation of neuroplasticity* (pp. 75-83). New York: Oxford University Press.

Popky, A. (1995). *EMDR Integrative Addiction Treatment Model.* Unpublished manuscript.

Potter-Efron, R. (1989). *Shame, guilt and alcoholism.* New York: The Haworth Press, Inc.

Puk, G. (1991). Treating traumatic memories: A case report on the eye movement desensitization procedure. *Journal of Behavioral Therapy and Experimental Psychiatry, 22*, 149-151.

Renfrey, G., & Spates, R. (1994). EMDR: A partial dismantling study. *Journal of Behavioral Therapy and Experimental Psychiatry, 25*, 231-239.

Rossi, E. (1999, June). Does EMDR facilitate new growth in the brain? Paper presented at the EMDR International Association Annual Conference.

Rothbaum, B. (1997). A controlled study of eye movement desensitization and reprocessing in the treatment of post stress disordered sexual assault victims. *Bulletin of the Menninger Clinic, 611*, 317-334.

Schenk, R., & Everingham, J. (Eds.). (1995). *Men healing shame: An anthology.* New York: Springer Publishing Company.

Schmidt, S. (1999). Resource-focused EMDR: Integration of ego state therapy, alternating bilateral stimulation, and art therapy. *EMDRIA Newsletter, March*, 8-25.

Shapiro, F., Vogelmann-Sine, S., & Sine, L. (1994). Eye movement desensitization and reprocessing: Treating trauma and substance abuse. *Journal of Psychoactive Drugs, 26,* 379-391.

Shapiro, F. (1995). *Eye movement desensitization and reprocessing: Basic principles, protocols, and procedures.* New York: Guilford.

Shapiro, F. (1996). EMDR: Evaluation of controlled PTSD research. *Journal of Behavioral Therapy and Experimental Psychiatry, 27,* 209-218.

Shapiro, F. (1998). EMDR: Accelerated information processing and affect-driven constructions. *Crisis Intervention, 4,* 145-157.

Van der Kolk, B. (1994). The body keeps the score: Memory and the evolving psychobiology of post-traumatic stress. *Harvard Review of Psychiatry, 1,* 253-265.

Wernick, U. (1993). The role of the traumatic component in the etiology of sexual dysfunctions and its treatment with EMDR. *Journal of Sex Education and Therapy, 19,* 212-222.

Wilson, S., Silver, S., Covi, W. & Foster, S. (1996). Eye movement desensitization and reprocessing (EMDR): Effectiveness and autonomic correlates. *Journal of Behavioral Therapy & Experimental Psychiatry, 27,* 219-229.

Wilson, S., Becker, L., & Tinker, R. (1995). Eye movement desensitization and reprocessing (EMDR) treatment for psychologically traumatized individuals. *Journal of Consulting and Clinical Psychology, 65,* 1047-1056.

Wilson, S., Becker, L., & Tinker, R. (1997a). Fifteen-month follow-up of eye movement desensitization and reprocessing (EMDR) treatment for posttraumatic stress disorder and psychological trauma. *Journal of Consulting and Clinical Psychology, 63,* 928-937.

Wilson S., Becker, L., & Tinker, R. (1997b, June). EMDR treatment of phantom limb pain. Conference report regarding EMDR treatment of 6 patients with phantom limb pain. EMDR International Conference, San Francisco USA.

Wong, M., & Cook, D. (1992). Shame and its contribution to PTSD. *Journal of Traumatic Stress, 5,* 557-562.

Zangwill, W. (1994). EMDR and shame: A brief report. *EMDR Network Newsletter,* Issue 3, 13.

Variety Is the Spice:
Survivor Groups
of Mixed Sexual Orientation

Patrick A. Meyer

SUMMARY. Group treatment presents a number of healing opportunities for survivors: in the company of others who have experienced similar trauma, survivors can publicly break the silence about their experiences, compare and contrast experiences and survival strategies, and step out of isolation. A therapy group can become a safe environment for building intimacy and assisting survivors in tolerating emotional intensity and working through issues of shame. Group therapy has been found to decrease the incest victim's sense of isolation and promote his/her interpersonal experimentation with more adaptive attitudes and behaviors. Groups composed of survivors of mixed sexual orientations conserve resources and provide an invaluable tool in building support, understanding and sense of community. While potentially challenging, mixed sexual orientation groups can offer priceless opportunity to bring out subtle and terrifying issues often triggering members' fears including those associated with shame, guilt, sexual stigma and self-esteem. Carefully facilitated, these issues can lead to greater levels of intimacy within groups and a deeper understanding of the nature of one's wounds from sexual abuse. *[Article copies available for a fee from The Haworth Document Delivery Service: 1-800-342-9678. E-mail address: <getinfo@haworthpressinc. com> Website: <http://www.HaworthPress.com>]*

KEYWORDS. Group psychotherapy, isolation, sexual orientation, sexual trauma, shame, stigma

---

[Haworth co-indexing entry note]: "Variety Is the Spice: Survivor Groups of Mixed Sexual Orientation." Meyer, Patrick A. Co-published simultaneously in *Journal of Gay & Lesbian Social Services* (Harrington Park Press, is an imprint of The Haworth Press, Inc.) Vol. 12, No. 1/2, 2000, pp. 91-106; and: *Gay Men and Childhood Sexual Trauma: Integrating the Shattered Self* (ed: James Cassese) Harrington Park Press, an imprint of The Haworth Press, Inc., 2000, pp. 91-106. Single or multiple copies of this article are available for a fee from The Haworth Document Delivery Service [1-800-342-9678, 9:00 a.m. - 5:00 p.m. (EST). E-mail address: getinfo@haworthpressinc.com].

While group treatment for male survivors of childhood sexual abuse is often found by practitioners to be an important and effective intervention, little has been written on the subject. Group treatment presents a number of healing opportunities for survivors. In the company of others who have experienced similar trauma, survivors are offered an opportunity (sometimes the first of such) to publicly break the silence about their experiences. The group provides an opportunity to compare and contrast experiences and survival strategies, and to step out of the isolation that survivors often use protectively. Properly facilitated, a therapy group can become one of the safest environments for building intimacy and assisting survivors in tolerating emotional intensity.

Group therapy is seen by some as the treatment of choice for addressing interpersonal problems of the incest survivor (Herman & Schatzow, 1984), as group treatment's specific focus on incest can counteract an incestuous family's denial of the problem (Goodman & Nowak-Scibelli, 1985). Further, it can assist the survivor in relieving the sense of stigma resulting from abuse experiences (Courtois, 1988). Group therapy has been found to decrease the incest victim's sense of isolation and promote his/her interpersonal experimentation with more adaptive attitudes and behaviors (Deighton & McPeek, 1985; Tsai & Wagner, 1978). Drawing from the trauma model, group therapy offers a milieu for "debriefing" and catharsis, often freeing up energy that can be directed toward healing the wounds from sexual trauma and for moving beyond survival strategies and behaviors.

Group treatment also offers the opportunity for working with relational and transference issues, as these issues are often played out with group therapists and other members of the group. Yalom (1985) indicates that group therapy provides "the generation of corrective emotional experiences (and the) patient's discovery through reality testing, of the inappropriateness of his or her interpersonal experiences." Yalom (1985) identifies the benefits of the group format for instilling hope, building interpersonal learning and catharsis. The milieu creates a clearing ground, a mode of support and a forum for feedback from others who have had similar experiences. It can also mimic the family of origin and, with effective facilitation, promote healthier forms of interpersonal communication. Group treatment is one of the most direct methods of intervention when working with shame, a powerful and stultifying symptom of the survivor experience.

The issue of group composition and diversity is a challenging one for male survivors that becomes even more complicated when sexual orientation is considered. As resources for male survivors are often limited (particularly in small population centers), a group composed of survivors of mixed sexual orientations conserves such resources and provides an invaluable tool in building support, understanding and sense of community. Homogeneity in groups generally lends itself to cohesiveness yet often lacks the necessary tension that brings out subtler issues.

There is a wealth of information on the impact of ethnicity and race upon group process. Groups mixed in racial/ethnic background lead to greater cohesiveness born out of the process of this tension resolution. Utilizing specific models, one can extrapolate these concepts to the issues of sexual orientation. This paper will incorporate one such model as an example in assessing impacts and developing interventions in work with male survivor groups dealing with the issue of mixed sexual orientation.

The dynamics of oppression, whether based on race or sexual orientation, often follow similar patterns of expression. In this society, minorities are attributed features that highlight their differences from the Eurocentric, heterosexual norm. The dynamics of oppression often follow the themes of attributing various stereotypic characteristics, such as sexual aberration (e.g., gays and racial minorities are hypersexual), and non-traditional gender role behavior (African American women are more masculine than women of European descent, gay men are viewed as effeminate). In the extreme, these attributed traits are often animalistic and dehumanizing and are used to limit access to resources, mobility, power and control. Within group process these tools of oppression surface as group members struggle with their own issues of affiliation, safety, power and control.

This paper will explore the issue of sexual orientation in groups and the impact of mixed sexual orientation on long-term psychotherapy groups with male survivors. While potentially challenging, these issues can be fruitful areas of concern, triggering members' fears and bringing out more subtle and terrifying issues: those associated with shame, guilt, sexual stigma and self-esteem. Carefully facilitated, these issues can lead to greater levels of intimacy within groups and a deeper understanding of the nature of one's wounds from sexual abuse. The challenge for facilitators involves careful screening of potential members, awareness of the manifestations of these issues within the treatment group itself, and skillful bridging of the issue of sexual orientation and its relationship to self-concept and sexual health. The facilitator's role at each stage of development within the group establishes an egalitarian atmosphere which can promote deep psychological growth, self-understanding and acceptance.

The material presented in this paper is drawn from both personal experiences as a facilitator of survivor groups and workshops, and client surveys, individual therapy sessions, a literature research and consultation with a wide variety of colleagues working in the field. For the past thirteen years this author has conducted a number of long- and short-term psychotherapy groups, workshops and individual therapy services for male survivors of childhood sexual abuse. One of these groups has operated for nine years and with the same client population for the last five. Another group is operating in its third year. These groups have demonstrated benefits from the use of an incremental, time-limited 12-meeting model followed by a two-week break and then another session of 12-meetings establishing both a boundary for individual goals and drawing from the benefits of a long-term therapy model.

COMPOSITION OF GROUPS

Group composition can present a delicate challenge for the mental health professional. While there is little written on the impact of sexual orientation on the process or outcomes of group psychotherapy, mixing groups (especially men's groups with a population of mixed sexual orientation) can be highly beneficial to the therapeutic process. I have found that survivor groups with membership of mixed sexual orientation (when carefully facilitated) can at times lead swiftly to addressing the issues of stigma, shame and the many unspoken questions about the impact of the sexual abuse on sexual orientation.

As Yalom (1985) suggests, "time and energy spent on delicately casting and balancing a group is not justified given our current state of knowledge; the therapist does better to invest that time and energy in careful selection of patients for group therapy and in their pre-group therapy preparation." Experience shows that much of the success of the group relies on the attitudes and mores established in the pre-group interview.

The Pre-Group Interview

While it is difficult to predict group behavior, diagnostic interviews can be helpful. A pre-group interview assessing family history, coping strategies, previous group experience and stage of recovery from incest and sexual abuse is essential and can begin to measure the successful integration of new members into a group. As it may be perceived, however, as a judgment of character, it should be framed as an attempt to assess the "goodness of fit" for both the individual and the group. The interview includes a screening for characterological issues, substance overuse, past perpetrator behavior, and history of suicidal ideation and hospitalizations. In group interviews, it is also useful to ask the question "How would you feel about working in a group with both gay and non-gay men?" The responses are often a strong predictor of in-group behavior around this issue.

As with any therapeutic interaction, this interview serves both as a diagnostic tool, an intervention, and an opportunity for the survivor to assess his own progress in recovery. The mention of sexual orientation in this assessment is worded in such a way as to normalize the experience of groups containing homosexual and non-homosexual members. Among other factors, this sets the stage for greater cohesiveness and can introduce members to the issue of sexual orientation, within the group. While it could be said that it pushes the agenda of the therapist, careful attention is paid within the group to promoting a safe atmosphere where deepest concerns about a variety of issues, including sexual orientation, can be addressed.

Responses to the question range from a flat "Oh, no problem . . . " to "Gee, I never thought about it . . . " As the conversation continues one is able to incorporate previous knowledge about the client's defense structure, as indicated in responses to other questions, to the current response regarding sexual orientation. Clients may be "okay" with the issue because they are anxious and/or want to be accepted. Given that this client population tends to be compliant, it is helpful to explore the issue, particularly focusing on the potential member's ability to understand his inner motivations and to assert himself in interpersonal dynamics.

There are some who explicitly indicate that this would not be an appropriate match. Yet even with these potential clients the opportunity arises for a fruitful discussion exploring the sexual orientation question for the individual.

In groups of male survivors who are fairly new to the issue, this question brings out a variety of defensive postures for the clients ranging from denial and minimization to reaction formation. It is important to remember that silence has often been the defense of choice for a survivor. In these groups the question itself invites the opportunity to explore the issue, which, as in most men's groups, usually arises in the early sessions of group meetings as the issues of affiliation and later, intimacy arise (Garland, Kolodny, & Jones, 1965).

Close assessment of an individual's interpersonal behavior in other settings closely approximating the therapy group can help assess in-group behavior (Yalom, 1985). The behavior of an individual is understood to show consistency over time despite the variety of people with whom s/he interacts. It is with this notion in mind that we explore an individual's role and behavior in other group experiences, for example, previous treatment groups, twelve-step programs, family and work.

Diversity in Groups

Drawing from the literature, it is clear that there are mixed opinions regarding the impact of diversity in groups. As Shriver (1998) notes, it is out of the diversity of experience and perceptions of group members that "the challenge of groupness emerges." The theme of "value in diversity" rests on a hypothesis that ethnic diversity can produce tangible, positive effects on organizational outcomes (Shriver, 1998). The "variety of perspectives and experiences represented on heterogeneous teams contributes to the production of high quality ideas." Moreover, the variety in perspectives can stimulate further thought production by group members. This can be true for sexual minorities in groups as well: the issue of sexual abuse, as well as the diversity itself, offers a forum for exploring issues of both sexual orientation and sexual intimacy from a variety of perspectives. The key lies in careful facilitation by group leaders in encouraging the development of group intimacy via respect and appreciation of diverse points of view, including the potentially divergent views of sexual minorities.

As with the dynamics encountered in groups of mixed racial and ethnic composition, it is important to attempt inclusion of more than one individual of the same sexual orientation. Single individuals often are called upon to bear the impossible task of representing the entire minority and are subject to scapegoating given their role of being perceived as different from the group norm.

There are two areas in the field of sexual abuse recovery/treatment groups where diversity in the composition of membership may become problematic. These include the progress and stage of recovery and past history of perpetration. Diversity in the amount of recovery and treatment one has experienced as a survivor of sexual abuse/incest can dramatically impact the outcome of the group. Clients in earlier stages of recovery tend to cling to old survival strategies and often unconsciously. This can slow the process in a group dominated by members with a longer treatment or recovery history and distract the group from its goals. Conversely, a group population composed primarily of survivors with little recovery can frustrate a member with a longer-term treatment history.

For reasons of safety I have found it useful that non-offending survivors and survivors with histories of perpetration be separated. This tends to promote an ability to explore issues specific to the population with less threat of shame or fear of perpetration. The groups are advertised as "open to non-abusing survivors only" or "for survivors who have abused others." The question is also explored in the pre-group interview with an attempt to normalize both experiences.

SEXUAL ORIENTATION AND MALE SURVIVORS

Generally, there is a mixed reaction to the impact of sexual orientation on male survivorship. Clearly there is a high incidence of sexual abuse being perpetrated upon young gay boys (see James Cassese's introduction to this collection). Often acts of attention, particularly in the area of sexuality, may be looked upon by gay boys as a release for unresolved and unfulfilled sexual tensions. Conversely, heterosexual boys may interpret the acts of a perpetrator upon them as indications that they are homosexual.

The implications upon heterosexual and homosexual survivors in their adulthood is powerful. For some heterosexual males abused at a young age by males, an assumption follows that the survivor is homosexual. This often leads to a "pseudohomosexuality" in adulthood or to sexual acting-out that focuses primarily on same-sex partners. In recovery the question remains, *"Am I truly homosexual or simply hiding from heterosexuality?"* For others a reaction formation occurs that often leads to violent acts against gay men or those one perceives as threatening to one's sexual orientation.

For many, however, the troubling questions remain: *"Am I gay? Why am I gay? Do my experiences of being abused by men (or women) in my youth make me gay?"* These questions often lurk below the surface in male survivor groups and are exacerbated by the confusion survivors often have fusing intimacy and closeness with sex. For many, the commonalty is in the boundary violation that occurred at a vulnerable time when much needed attention by others was confused by sexual activity at an inappropriate age. The answers to these questions may be perceived as an unbearable horror and the queries remain private and unspoken. It is at certain points in group development–particularly those moments when the group moves toward greater intimacy–that these questions are raised, both directly and indirectly. This has been observed by the author as a phenomena that arises in all men's groups, but becomes particularly troubling for male survivors.

Men are socialized by the dominant culture to link feeling with action. When intimacy develops in the all-male group setting, often questions or statements about homosexuality consequently arise. One interpretation is that this is a manifestation of the developing intimate feelings being experienced by men in the groups. The metacommunication is that *"If I have these intimate feelings toward the group and other male members, they should be expressed/explored through action"* (i.e., homosexual behavior). Given the nature of the male survivor experience and the confusion with boundaries and safety that arise when feeling intimate, this can be terrifying. Some members may wish to bolt from treatment, some grow silent and withdraw, others may become judgmental or angry. Within the group process, repeated references to homosexuality or questions about homosexuality are often aired. By carefully identifying the nuances and metacommunication about the group process relating to this issue and by normalizing the experience, one can both build greater understanding of the dynamics of male intimacy and move the group toward a greater sense of safety and respect for differences in intimate expression.

Growing Up Gay

The experience of growing up gay in a world dominated by heterosexual bias and oppression is a complicated and painful one. From a very early age a child learns to hide his/her homosexual feelings. For some, the suppression becomes a complete mask (from self and others) and for others it remains a vague (or not so vague) secret. The manifestation of this disguise is highly dependent on the personality structure of the individual, ethnic and class differences and the environment.

Regardless of how this awareness is expressed (or suppressed) the gay child holds a belief that he is flawed in some fashion or another. This belief is reinforced by the environment from a variety of sources including family members, the media, educational and religious institutions and peers. Richard Isay (1989) discusses the powerful role and impact of the father-son relationship for male homosexual children. He points to the idea that on some level, the father of the homosexual son develops a conscious or unconscious awareness of the child's sexual orientation. Through thought, word and deed, a father may consequently distance himself from his son. The son in turn interprets this behavior (again, often on an unconscious level) as a sign that he himself is flawed.

This experience of "flawedness" leads the child to develop certain negative assumptions about his self-esteem and his capacity to develop normal relationships with people outside the family constellation. Shame about oneself consequently develops. Indeed, this very experience and the subsequent attempts to seek out the love and positive attention of other males often lead the homosexual child to potential victimization (Cassese, 1993).

Within group treatment this is often acted out in relation to the facilitating therapist or leaders within the group. Members may seek the support and guidance of facilitators, or may need to misunderstand or misinterpret interventions in order to blame the group therapist.

ISSUES THAT BUILD GROUP COHESION

As the group moves through stages of development toward an increasing sense of trust and intimacy, often the subtler impacts of sexual orientation of the individuals within the group begin to appear. Utilizing any stage model of group development can be helpful in examining this process. This article will draw upon the model developed by Garland, Jones and Kolodny (1965) to illuminate the issues. These authors propose that the group encounters five stages of development: Pre-Affiliation, Affiliation, Power and Control, Intimacy, and Termination.

The issue of sexual orientation will be initially broached in the Pre-Affiliation stage when questions of appropriateness of fit are aired (both in the pre-group interview and the first sessions). Spoken and unspoken questions about safety amongst other men, about the sexual orientation of group members and about the leaders' ability to facilitate potential differences will arise. Doubts may be raised about the members' sense of belonging to the group. Since survivors often use silence as a chief defense, the facilitator may have to raise the issues normalizing such fears.

As the group moves into the Affiliation stage, issues of power and control and questions about both the safety and the sexual orientation of individual members often occur. While sometimes these thoughts remain unspoken, they are at other times aired via challenging homophobic remarks or by questions about one's own orientation. Here those members with more recovery experience and those gay/bi men who are more secure in their orientation may help to set the norm.

The challenge for the facilitator lies in assessing members' withheld emotions and judgments about sexual orientation. It is in these first stages that the issues of fear and judgment are most evident. By educating the group on the role of judgment as a protective defense the discussion may be opened. In these early stages questions of gender role and stereotypes are usually addressed.

Safety

The key issue that leads to successful facilitation of any group of survivors (and in particular, a mixed group of survivors), is the issue of safety. The group facilitator often bears the focus of the effort. By processing individual members' specific needs in terms of safety, group members appreciate the benefits of boundary setting and assertiveness.

In my experience, establishing a group "Bill of Rights and Expectations" has often been a fruitful endeavor in this area. It is introduced in the pre-group interview and developed in the first and second sessions by group members. This can include such statements as "I have the right to pass if called upon by other group members"; "I have the right not to be touched unless I give permission"; "I have the right to a different opinion and will strive to understand differences I have with other members"; "I understand I am expected to attend all sessions clean and sober"; and "I will report any outside contact with other group members." Once decided upon, the "Bill of Rights and Expectations" is written up and distributed to all group members.

Perhaps the greatest challenge to safety is the fear, again unspoken, that one will be attacked or perpetrated upon. It is for this reason that the author introduces the rule of no-touch in the pre-group interview and again in the initial stages of the group. Within the group metacommunication this might be articulated by such statements as "You touched me deeply when you said that about me . . . ," "Get screwed!" or by the non-verbal protecting of one's person with pillows, or layers of clothing. This can be especially troubling for survivors in the initial stages, especially for heterosexual survivors when there are openly gay men in the group. Here again, naming the possibility of this underlying process can lead to a fruitful discussion and boundary-setting. Most often, it is the repeated test of time together that establishes a true sense of bodily safety.

Intimacy

As the group moves through issues of power and control, and the challenging of leadership and roles are resolved, the arena opens for a phase of deepening intimacy. It is in this phase of group development that some of the deepest work is sometimes achieved. Usually by this time many of the issues of homophobia have been directly or indirectly aired. Group members often disclose issues that may have been kept hidden before.

Experience shows that gay/bi members of the group tend to hesitate to discuss relational issues. It is here that the facilitator often bridges the experiences and problems brought up by heterosexual members with the experience of homosexual members. Identifying common themes and normalizing their occurrence in both gay and non-gay relationships greatly add to the exploration and self-disclosure of gay/bi clients. The facilitator must pay special attention to the discomfort some gay members may feel about the airing of heterosexual issues and bring this dynamic into the discussion.

While some members remain quiet, another presentation style often exhibited by gay/bi clients in this phase is the strident or provocative "in-your-face" attitude. Here the challenge is to help these clients identify the dynamics underlying such behavior and to assist them in being more fully open and vulnerable with other members of the group.

Seduction and Victimization

Closely related to the issues of intimacy and closeness are those of seduction by and revictimization of the survivor, whether literal or metaphoric. Survivors often learn to seduce others to distract from a perceived threat of closeness/intimacy or harm/annihilation by the perpetrator, facilitator or group member using sexual or topical diversions. The result often leads to a sense of victimization by both the seducer and those who have been seduced and can threaten the safety of the group. This behavior occurs in both heterogeneous and homogenous groups. However, given the subtleties and complexities of homophobia, such behavior, unless carefully confronted, can threaten the closeness and intimacy of the entire group experience and can be used to reinforce stereotypic assumptions by group members.

In groups of mixed sexual orientation such behavior tends to follow the symbolic or non-verbal form of seduction. Careful attention by the facilitator to the dynamics of seduction, whether it is acted out via caretaking, provocative behavior, non-verbal gesturing or other behaviors, is essential. One can reinterpret the experience and lead to a generalized group learning that benefits all members and avoids the potential for attribution, blaming and the ensuing shame and guilt.

Shame

Shame is one of the most powerful affects dominating our experience, particularly in Western culture. Shame is the common element that is shared by both survivors of childhood sexual abuse and gay men and lesbians. In a culture that strives for perfection and dictates a presentation of flawlessness, shame is the ultimate taboo.

While rarely talked about and difficult to understand, the experience of shame dominates the experience of both gay men and lesbians and survivors of childhood sexual abuse. It is that common sense of flawedness and of wounding that can build cohesion within a group of mixed sexual orientation. The key lies with the ability of the facilitator to promote both a personal and group awareness of its activation, to build upon this awareness and its impact in the process of developing intimacy and closeness.

Following the Nathanson model (1992), shame is the expression of the wounding of self, a narcissistic wound. For gay men, this experience frequently begins at an early age with the awareness of a sense of unique difference. Not all gay men as children are aware of why they feel this difference. Anecdotal reports often trace the beginnings of this awareness in early childhood when preferred play activities conflict with culturally dominated dictates of "normalcy" and the phenomenon of "gender appropriate" behavior. The homosexual child is often shamed and ridiculed for his/her preferences. This awareness of "differentness" is internalized as a sense of flawedness (and as previously mentioned may be reinforced by the father-figure) and the child learns to hide his/her preferences. This activity sets the stage for the development of a false self organized around the efforts to hide this sense of difference.

Survivors often engage in similar activities, organizing behaviors and sense of public self in such a way as to hide the shameful experience of the abuse. While the injuries may occur at different stages of one's development, because of the nature of the wounding (i.e., a sexual flaw or offense), the defense structures that develop bear a strongly similar resemblance. The key in group facilitation is to identify the common defense patterns via the process of group interaction and to build upon this sense of commonalty. In other words, the facilitator can build cohesion by using the relationships within the group to identify the patterning of affects, including shame, that dominate an individual's presentation and process. Key in this process is the ability to identify mechanisms of hiding and avoidance of intimacy. As Kaufman and Lev (1996) point out, the "principal effects of shame on the self are hiding, paralysis and a feeling of being transparent."

There are two elements that can help facilitate this process. One is to identify common triggers that activate shame responses within oneself and the other is to identify common responses to the shame. Shame triggers can come from a variety of sources: a look, a comment, or simply the discussion of a topic that brings the individual in touch with shame. Naming the process often normalizes it and establishes a sense of safety to discuss the issue. It is important to remember that a key issue for survivors is silence.

Utilizing Nathanson's (1992) "Compass of Shame" can also be an effective tool. The Compass identifies four common responses to a shaming event or trigger. One can direct one's energies outwardly toward others (attack other), inwardly toward self (attack self), one can avoid the feelings, or one can withdraw oneself from the shame affect. By identifying this process one can help facilitate the group process toward greater awareness of shame affects and towards commonalty and differences in response to triggers.

Shame responses to sexual orientation issues can be an insightful (as well as inciteful) point of focus for the group. Such responses often are characterized by the following issues: a belief one's sexual orientation has been affected by the abuse, a fear of perpetration by other members of a same sex group, homophobic rage, excessive caretaking of those members of the group perceived as "more defective," self-esteem issues, and denial and avoidance. Each of these issues offer topics rich in both personal and interpersonal material for the group process, broadening the understanding of sexual oppression and moving to a more egalitarian view of self and of life.

Self-Esteem

The entire concept of self-esteem can build a sense of commonalty among group members. These issues arise more clearly in the intimacy phase of group process as members shed defenses and articulate their concerns. Here again the concept of bridging of experience lends itself to building greater self-awareness. For example, one can utilize the experience of growing up gay as an excellent example of the impact that feeling flawed can have on one's development and relational styles. This can be translated to the experience of incest and sexual abuse and often lead to a healthy discussion of the entire concept of wounding.

Another topic often fruitful in this bridging process is that of the "internal critic" which helps identify the manner and style of personal oppression and can again be translated to the experience of larger societal oppressions as well.

Sex

The topic of sex is often a "final frontier" explored in mixed groups be they mixed gender or mixed sexual orientation (aside from the early stages where limits are often tested). The exception, of course, is when the group has members who self-identify as sexual addicts. Here, the topic may be raised with bravado or shame, but the discussion is often kept at a less threatening level, describing sexual behavior as a symptom but avoiding deeper affect.

The deeper, more self-revelatory discussion about sex often appears in the later stages of the Intimacy phase when the awareness of the group's termination becomes more evident. While often frightening for men, the open disclosure of sexual styles and issues tends to lead to greater compassion for self and others. Here the groundwork established in the earlier phases of development promoting an accepting and egalitarian atmosphere is most useful. The discussion tends to be marked by a testing phase and then full disclosure. Here, too, provocative language can test the group and the facilitator, but often appears to be male bravado and defensive positioning.

The key again lies in finding the commonalties of experience, particularly in relation to the affective experience group members have regarding sexual intimacy. One effective intervention has been to help members explore how their sexual behavior parallels the abuse, and how it shields from deeper intimacy in sexual relationships. For example, be it homosexual or heterosexual cruising, fetishism or maladaptive sexual play, pursuing the activity itself may be seeking the same results. Identifying the commonalty of the strategy in a non-judgmental fashion leads to a deeper acceptance of oneself and an identification of the common struggles survivors encounter in sexual intimacy regardless of sexual orientation. This, in turn, offers the potential for a type of disclosure, closeness and understanding that most group members have never experienced. The key here is the opening of self in a safe and supportive atmosphere without the fear of shaming or reenactment of the original wounding of the sexual abuse.

CONCLUSION

While challenging, the facilitation of survivor groups with populations of mixed sexual orientation can be a rich and rewarding experience. The experience of growing up in a homophobic society has great parallels to the experience of growing up as a survivor of childhood sexual abuse. When brought to the awareness of the group, this understanding can lead to deeper intimacy and compassion among group members.

The role of the facilitator in promoting an egalitarian and compassionate atmosphere at each step of the process is crucial. By naming the issue from the beginning in the pre-group interview the stage is set for promoting increased intimacy, understanding and self-acceptance. The facilitator's role in the bridging of experience between gay and non-gay clients continues to ease the process.

Finally, careful understanding of the nuances and unique manifestations of intimacy and shame issues with these populations allows the facilitator to identify their presentation in the group process, building greater cohesion, closeness and understanding. What is learned by group members along this road becomes invaluable to their experiences in their world.

REFERENCES

Cassese, J. (1993). The invisible bridge: Childhood sexual abuse and the risk of HIV infection in adulthood. *SIECUS Report, 21*, 4, 1-7.

Courtois, C. (1988). *Healing the Incest Wound.* New York: Norton.

Deighton, J. and McPeek, P. (1985). Group treatment: Adult victims of childhood sexual abuse. *Social Casework, 6*, 403-410.

Garland, J. A., Jones, H., & Kolodny, R. L. (1965). A model for stages of development in social work groups. In S. Bernstein (Ed.), *Explorations in group work.* Boston: Boston University School of Social Work.

Goodman, B. & Nowak-Scibelli, D. (1985). Group treatment for women incestuously abused as children. *International Journal of Group Psychotherapy, 35*, 531-544.

Herman, J., and Schatzow, E. (1984). Time-limited group therapy for women with a history of incest. *International Journal of Group Psychotherapy, 34*, 605-616.

Isay, R. (1989). *Being Homosexual.* New York: Farrar, Straus & Giroux.

Kaufman, G. and Lev, R. (1996). *Coming out of shame.* New York: Bantam.

Nathanson, D. (1992). *Shame and Pride: Affect, Sex and the Birth of the Self.* New York: W. W. Norton.

Shriver, J. (1998). *Human Behavior in the Social Environment.* Needham Heights: Allyn and Bacon.

Tsai, M. M. & Wagner, N. N. (1978). Therapy groups for women sexually molested as children. *Archives of Sexual Behavior, 7*, 417-427.

Yalom, I. (1985). *The theory and practice of group psychotherapy.* New York: Basic Books.

Beneath Contempt:
The Mistreatment
of Non-Traditional/Gender Atypical Boys

Franklin L. Brooks

SUMMARY. There is a need for increased awareness of the vulnerability of non-traditional/gender atypical (NTGA) boys to be physically, sexually and emotionally abused. Non-traditional/gender atypical male behavior refers to behavior that society usually labels as "sissy" and inappropriate for boys to display. Because NTGA behavior in boys and men is despised in our society, males who behave in feminine-identified ways are at high risk for being stigmatized, ostracized, and abused. A major factor that contributes to this unsafe environment is a patriarchal system that enforces sexist and misogynist attitudes. Because patriarchy devalues and denigrates females and things feminine-identified, boys who display NTGA are looked at as breaking male gender role boundaries. Violence is often used against these boys as a way to punish the misbehavior and also to teach other boys "the rules" for socially acceptable male behavior. The assessment of past physical, sexual, and emotional abuse with NTGA males must include sensitive questions regarding the response to their NTGA behavior. Adults, especially men, need to become allies for these boys and intervene on their behalf when the boys are being abused or mistreated. Men need to overcome the process of fear and intimidation associated with the devaluing of things feminine-identified which prevents them from identifying and empathizing with NTGA boys. Men will benefit from understanding that rigid adherence to gender behavior stereotypes limits their ability to identify with NTGA boys and prevents men from protecting NTGA boys. *[Article copies available for a fee from The Haworth Document Delivery Service: 1-800-342-9678. E-mail address: <getinfo@haworthpressinc. com> Website: <http://www.HaworthPress.com>]*

[Haworth co-indexing entry note]: "Beneath Contempt: The Mistreatment of Non-Traditional/Gender Atypical Boys." Brooks, Franklin L. Co-published simultaneously in *Journal of Gay & Lesbian Social Services* (Harrington Park Press, an imprint of The Haworth Press, Inc.) Vol. 12, No. 1/2, 2000, pp. 107-115; and: *Gay Men and Childhood Sexual Trauma: Integrating the Shattered Self* (ed: James Cassese) Harrington Park Press, an imprint of The Haworth Press, Inc., 2000, pp. 107-115. Single or multiple copies of this article are available for a fee from The Haworth Document Delivery Service [1-800-342-9678, 9:00 a.m. - 5:00 p.m. (EST). E-mail address: getinfo@haworthpressinc.com].

107

KEYWORDS. Non-traditional/gender atypical behavior, childhood physical, sexual and emotional abuse, gender identity, gender roles, sissy, feminism

Because of rigid gender roles, a binary model of gender, and inflexible rules for male and female behavior in this society, any male child (or adult) who differs from the male gender norm behavior is at increased risk for mistreatment. One of the social functions of the persecution of "the sissy" is to force other boys into gender role compliance. Most boys can recount a personal experience with either being picked on by peers because of suspicion of "being a sissy" or have witnessed other boys being mistreated. The message is clear: either conform or pay the price of social isolation, persecution, and even violent confrontations, causing injury and in extreme cases, death.

Popularly known as sissies, non-traditional/gender atypical (NTGA) boys have endured centuries of societal condemnation and ridicule, as well as physical and emotional abuse. They are one of the most stigmatized groups in society, and as a stigmatized group, they have suffered from mistreatment, social isolation and ostracism by their peers. The plight of these boys, until recently, has been ignored. Often derided as "freaks of nature" or otherwise less than human, they remain socially apart and are often persecuted by their peers and adults. Many of these boys suffer a torturous childhood and grow into adulthood suffering a series of traumatic events related to their non-traditional/gender atypical behavior.

The societal mistreatment of girls and women underlies the mistreatment of non-traditional/gender atypical boys. Within a patriarchal social system, things identified as "female" or "feminine" are devalued, while things considered to be "male" and "masculine" are overvalued and preferred. Since this promotes devaluing of things labeled feminine, including overt, observable "feminine" behaviors, boys who behave like girls are looked at with contempt, both for being different and for choosing to behave in scorned, devalued and "second class" ways.

Adults, including parents, often do not defend these boys from persecution. Instead, they leave them to fend for themselves in school and in the community. Sometimes, parents and other family members participate in the mistreatment. NTGA boys are often scapegoats in their families. Like other children who are different, they are at higher risk for physical, emotional and sexual abuse. Indeed, the contempt that these boys experience is a form of sexual abuse, as it is often accompanied by derogatory remarks centered on the boys' sexual orientation, sexual abilities and other aspects of sexual functioning.

Many of these boys experience both physical and emotional abuse during incidents of being "picked on." However, the euphemistic phrase "picked on" hides the seriousness of most attacks that NTGA boys experience.

The basic problem these boys face is rooted in the misogynist, sexist reaction to their NTGA behavior. The notion that non-traditional/gender atypical behavior might be a natural variant of gender behavior has rarely been explored.

Often, non-traditional/gender atypical boys are thought of as genetically flawed or otherwise biologically "defective." Because their allegedly "feminine" behavior is often cited as evidence of this defect, these boys are trapped in a no win situation. They can be understood to be acting and behaving naturally despite society's demands they change to "normative" male gender behaviors. On the one hand, society says "be yourself"–then persecutes these boys when they are being themselves.

Even in the gay male population, where acceptance of feminine-identified behavior in men might be expected, there can be strong negative reaction to "queens'" and their perceived "extreme" behavior. Indeed, a whole gay male sub-culture of hyper-masculinity worship is reflected in gay male pornography, advertisements, and other media which idealize and promote super muscular body structure, hyped masculine language and behavior based on the stereotypic masculine behavior in dominant society. Both the glorification of masculinity and the exclusion of things feminine are prevalent in these examples, which show the lingering influence of misogynist and sexist values in the gay male community.

Why has society allowed mistreatment of these boys and men? The major factor has been the ingrained and seemingly indestructible forces of sexism and misogyny and the patriarchal power structure that enforces and reinforces strict gender role compliance. These powerful influences have also made NTGA boys' lives a living hell, not unlike their sisters, mothers, aunts and grandmothers.

This group of boys has been targeted by society to help maintain rigid gender roles. Through verbal and physical harassment, NTGA boys are publicly humiliated, embarrassed and taunted as a means to eliminate them as a role model for other boys. There is no desire for other boys to go through this type of mistreatment. This abusive and painful process is observed by all boys and is a warning to them–do not display these behaviors or else! The overt feminine-identified behaviors are also related to denigrated feminine-identified personality characteristics such as physical weakness, emotional lability and overall personality inferiority.

Most girls and NTGA boys know from an early age that they are different and have less value in society. They are constantly exposed to negative, disparaging messages about themselves. As adults, women and NTGA men are subjected to social institutions that reinforce negative social sanctions based on social values that denigrate and devalue things feminine-identified. NTGA boys, like girls and women, bear the brunt of societal scorn and dislike for things female.

Rigid adherence to traditional gender roles and the institutionalized response to gender atypical behavior hurt all youth, boys and girls. Further complicating this situation is the belief that all NTGA boys are homosexual. This belief confuses the issues related to NTGA boys and only increases the stigma associated with both groups. Some research has shown that up to two thirds of non-traditional boys are homosexual. This leaves one third who are not. How do we account for this behavioral variance across all boys?

The American Psychiatric Association (APA) is an example of a social/medical institution that upholds and reinforces societal gender roles. The APA Diagnostic and Statistical Manual of Mental Disorders (DSM-IV) lists Gender Identity Disorder as a diagnostic category. However, the diagnostic criteria can be misused to label as pathological behavior that is not problematic to individual boys and men. Most NTGA boys are brought to counselors and other mental health professionals because of difficulties in school or at home. Although the child is typically presented as the problem, in my experience the child has been brought to counseling because of the reaction of others to the NTGA behavior. The boys themselves may be experiencing discomfort with their gender. That would be expected, especially if they are in the category of the boy who, from an early age, feels strongly that he is a girl trapped in a boy's body. I have noted in my counseling work with numerous NTGA boys that the diagnosis of gender identity disorder often has more to do with the discomfort of the adults, including mental health professionals, surrounding such children rather than with difficulties the NTGA boys identify. The problem these boys are often struggling with is a socially constructed problem, including feelings of shame produced by the negative reaction and virulent disgust directed towards them by others, including their own parents.

In 1997, I led a workshop on NTGA boys held in rural Maine. A thoughtful and caring foster parent was describing the non-traditional behaviors of her 8-year-old foster son. She described a well-adjusted young boy who happened to enjoy dressing in girl's clothing, and yet was willing to accept the limits placed on his cross-dressing by his foster parents. The foster family, including the foster father, accepted this behavior and helped the boy acquire clothing and toys that satisfied his desire to cross-dress and cross "play." As we discussed the situation, the foster mother said she was uncertain why he had been diagnosed with a Gender Identity Disorder. I told her I didn't know either, as the foster family and the boy seemed to accept the behavior, make adaptations for it, and integrate it into the family's life.

My suspicion is that because the boy experienced difficulty with how to be a boy (gender dysphoria), he was misdiagnosed with Gender Identity Disorder. However, the boy identified his own problem as how to meet his needs for cross-dressing and cross-play. This case illustrates what I have observed: many NTGA boys are not upset with their NTGA behavior. In fact, they want to be able to express themselves as females. They need, as do traditional boys, supportive, non-judgmental adults to assist them in their activities. The foster parents in this case are to be commended for their common sense and their courage to support their foster son despite pressure to label his behavior as pathologic and help change his behavior to "normal" male-identified behavior. The foster parents' compassionate approach to this situation is one to be admired.

History has shown how powerful a psychiatric diagnosis can be. A recent example is the American Psychiatric Association's removal of homosexuality from its list of mental disorders. Before 1973, thousands of homosexuals were labeled as mentally ill, and this medical label justified harsh and cruel treatments, including electroshock therapy, recommended as treatments to "cure" homosexuality. Thanks to pioneers like Evelyn Hooker and others, homosexuality was "de-pathologized" and is no longer listed as a disorder in the DSM. However, it was not until 1995 that the American Medical Association condemned their earlier policy of changing sexual orientation and now recommends that the goal of therapy be to "become more comfortable with (one's) sexual orientation and understand societal responses to it" (Hausman, 1995).

With regard to NTGA behavior, however, our society is still struggling to come to terms with the fact that there is a continuum of gender-based identity and gender-based behavior rather than a fixed polar divide between male and female behavior.

The social forces that cause the pathologizing and, therefore, the marginalization of this group include the powerful process of stigmatizing that Erving Goffman (1963) describes in his groundbreaking book *Stigma: Notes on the Management of a Spoiled Identity.* Goffman, citing the primary social need of human beings to belong to a group, investigates how people go to great lengths to prevent being marginalized or rejected from community life.

Almost no professional social work literature exists on boys who display non-traditional, gender atypical behaviors. These boys' mental health needs have been neglected because they are a stigmatized minority whose issues make many people in society uncomfortable, professionals included. Many adults, especially men, find themselves unable or unwilling to defend these boys when they are ostracized in school and community. As one of the most stigmatized of all oppressed groups, "sissies" carry society's projected fear of things feminine-identified along with projected homophobia and a more general discomfort with human sexuality.

Mick Coleman (1986) discusses the need for a more sensitive and thoughtful response to boys who do not behave according to socially prescribed gender role expectations. Feminist theory, gender studies, and the emerging field of transgender studies have succeeded in bringing gender issues to the forefront in academic and other institutions. As is often the case, elementary and secondary educational institutions are not affected as soon, or to the same degree, as post-secondary schools by institutional change. Because elementary and middle schools are traditionally more conservative and resistant to social change, it is not unusual for NTGA children to be left on the margins of school life. Anecdotal evidence points to many NTGA boys finding some semblance of acceptance from other marginalized students, usually girls. While social scientists have studied the effects of gender bias and discrimination on girls, comparable research has not been conducted with respect to NTGA boys. There has been research conducted in schools to measure the effects of homophobia on lesbian, gay and bisexual youth. In these studies, reference is often made to NTGA behavior being related to increased harassment of sexual minority youth. Further research should be conducted to clearly identify NTGA behavior as a primary underlying cause of homophobic reactive behavior.

The extent of the mistreatment of NTGA boys is widespread and nearly universal in the United States. It is rare to hear any "sissy" boy or man talk about a positive experience growing up with these behaviors. Some boys make it through relatively safely, perhaps if they attend private schools or are otherwise in a protected environment. The overwhelming majority of boys experience negative responses to their non-traditional behavior, most of which is initially related to the belief that they are homosexuals. Many of these boys express NTGA behaviors from early in their lives. Also, most were aware of the mistreatment of other boys displaying NTGA behaviors.

Studies on suicide among gay male youth identify an increased risk of suicide for gay male youth with NTGA behavior. Remafedi, Farrow, and Deisher (1994) describe the increased risk of suicide attempts for gay male youth in general and even higher risk for youth who identify themselves as androgynous or feminine in their behavior. Using the Bem androgyny scales, Remafedi found that youth who measure more feminine in their behaviors attempt suicide at a higher rate than those who describe themselves as more masculine. Remafedi also found that these same youth had more problems at school and at home and were more likely to have had contact with the mental health system. These youths were also more likely to have "come out" as gay to their parents at an earlier age and to have had more difficulty because of negative parental reaction to their coming out. These youth are at higher risk for abusing substances at an earlier age than their age peers.

Moreover, many children who have been abused and neglected are at risk for continued abuse and neglect unless adults intervene on their behalf, identify the abuse and help the child recover from the abuse.

Another area of concern for NTGA boys is the development of a shamed identity, that is, a core identity based on a devalued and despised stereotyped feminine-identified behavior pattern. Public humiliation and family rejection often shape this identity formation. These consequences include impaired and delayed development, interpersonal relationship difficulties and the inability to trust others and the social environment.

NTGA boys face increased risk for self-destructive behavior, including self-mutilation and self-inflicted injury in order to change one's gender to conform to one's internal sense of gender. Some boys try to remove their penis and testicles in an attempt to become female and also to remove the hated body parts which are a constant reminder of their "mistaken" gender. Some NTGA boys believe their male genitalia have caused them to be subjected to public humiliation and therefore look to the removal of the genitalia as a means to self-acceptance, social acceptance and personal safety.

NTGA boys often must deal with social rejection, abandonment by family and friends, isolation from peers and a future that appears perilous, dangerous and without hope of reprieve from constant harassment.

Amazingly, NTGA boys are resilient and able to function in often hostile environments. Many gender atypical and non-traditional boys have led successful lives, only to be ostracized and persecuted for their alleged gender "crimes," that is, their gender non-conformity. For example, Truman Capote and other middle- or upper-class "dandies" were often socially sought after, limited to a great degree their entertainment value. Their privileged social status often protected them from the full hostility and hatred directed toward them, but not always, as Capote found out.

In a longitudinal study of NTGA boys and men, Money and Russo (1979) found that the one factor the men identified as most important to them throughout their adolescence was the presence of at least one adult who took an interest in their well-being and accepted their NTGA behavior unconditionally. I have also found that at least one interested supportive adult taking an interest in a NTGA boy's life can be a transformative experience in the lives of NTGA boys. It is also necessary for adults to prevent abuse of NTGA boys, as NTGA boys, like other children, cannot be solely responsible for their own safety.

Several issues related to the safety of NTGA boys need to be further addressed. The safety of NTGA boys is a community responsibility. Schools and other community institutions are often hostile and unsafe for NTGA boys. The need for education regarding safety for NTGA boys needs to be on the agenda of schools and youth-serving agencies.

Who are the adults who will defend and intervene on behalf of NTGA boys? We need to assess and evaluate the characteristics of those adults who are able to understand the problems of and have compassion for NTGA boys. What are the qualities and characteristics of adults who do accept NTGA boys? How do we identify those qualities and characteristics to enable their further development in adults?

The ability of NTGA boys to grow into healthy adulthood is severely limited in our sexist, homophobic and heterosexist culture. The plight of these boys has gone unnoticed for too long. It is up to all adults to understand this plight and begin intervening on NTGA boys' behalf. A primary goal will be to reduce the contempt and hatred directed toward these boys so they can live in safety. They deserve the right to develop identities based on self-love, wholeness and acceptance of themselves as competent, vital, worthy and valuable human beings.

REFERENCES

Coleman, M. (1986). The mistreatment of non-traditional boys: A minority in need of reassessment. *Child Welfare, 65, 3*, 252-259.

Goffman, E. (1963). *Stigma: Notes on the management of a spoiled identity.* Englewood Cliffs, NJ: Prentice-Hall.

Hausman, K. (1995, Jan. 20). AMA reverses stand on homosexual issues. *Psychiatric News, 30*, pp. 1 & 18.

Money, J., & Russo, A. J. (1979). Homosexual outcome of discordant gender identity/role in childhood: Longitudinal follow-up. *Journal of Pediatric Psychology, 4*, 29-41.

Remafedi, G., Farrow, J. A., & Deisher, R. W. (1994). Risk factors for attempted suicide in gay and bisexual youth. In G. Remafedi (Ed.), *Death by denial: Studies of suicide in gay and lesbian teenagers* (pp. 123-137). Boston, MA: Alyson Publications.

Illusions of Intimacy

Don Wright

SUMMARY. Gay men share the common human need for meaningful intimate contact in which the connection is genuine, open and honest. This need can be frustrated, complicated and undermined by a sexual trauma history. The child's sense of personal boundaries, of sexual integrity and of affectional relationships is deeply impacted by a sexual trauma. The child learns that his needs become secondary to the offender's and as a result the victim learns to barter with his sexuality to get those needs met. The offender may foster a sense of isolation in the child, creating a perspective of the world that is harsh and dangerous, so that the child becomes terrified of abandonment. Homophobia is understood to be a "sexuality abuse" and as a result gay men often come in contact with other survivors. As a result, distinguishing between sex and love and recognizing genuine intimacy become difficult. This creates a spiral of difficulties whereby gay men may take enormous risks to "belong" or to avoid abandonment, often with profound consequences in terms of health and self-esteem. *[Article copies available for a fee from The Haworth Document Delivery Service: 1-800-342-9678. E-mail address: <getinfo@haworthpressinc. com> Website: <http://www.HaworthPress.com>]*

KEYWORDS. Boundaries, gay men, homophobia, intimacy, self-esteem, sexual trauma, sexuality abuse

An advertisement depicts two attractive nude men reclining in an intimate embrace. One man cradles the other's head against his chest as the second man, lying against the first embraces him around the

[Haworth co-indexing entry note]: "Illusions of Intimacy." Wright, Don. Co-published simultaneously in *Journal of Gay & Lesbian Social Services* (Harrington Park Press, an inprint of The Haworth Press, Inc.) Vol. 12, No. 1/2, 2000, pp. 117-126; and: *Gay Men and Childhood Sexual Trauma: Integrating the Shattered Self* (ed: James Cassese) Harrington Park Press, an imprint of The Haworth Press, Inc., 2000, pp. 117-126. Single or multiple copies of this article are available for a fee from The Haworth Document Delivery Service [1-800-342-9678, 9:00 a.m. - 5:00 p.m. (EST). E-mail address: getinfo@haworthpressinc.com].

waist. Both men have their eyes closed peacefully with contented expressions on their faces. The caption reads: "The place to meet. The place to cuddle. The place to . . . " The rest is left for the reader to fill in. The imagery and the verbs "meet" and "cuddle" suggest a meaningful, tender contact between two men. Yet, this is an ad for a bath house, places often notorious for anonymous, multiple sexual encounters. Thus, on the one hand, emotional intimacy is suggested, while on the other, sexual adventure. One can assume the duality is intended. The positioning of the two men and the choice of words suggest something beyond physical contact. The possibility of emotional intimacy or perhaps even love is implied; whereas the nudity and the fact that it is an ad for a bath house offer casual sex. The gay man's desire for emotional connection and often misguided search for intimacy in casual sexual encounters are portrayed in this type of advertisement. It illustrates the confusion between sex and intimacy with which gay men often struggle.

Gay men share the common human need for meaningful intimate contact in which the connection is genuine, open and honest; one in which they are seen and appreciated for who they are. Unfortunately there are several factors which undermine gay men's ability to find this kind of intimacy: (1) socialized homophobia; (2) the confines of traditional male roles; (3) the prevalence of childhood sexual and physical abuse; (4) the highly sexualized nature of contemporary gay culture; (5) the cultural obsession with youth and beauty; (6) the lack of intimate gay role models; and (7) the prevalence of HIV and other serious STDs. These are some of the major forces compromising the search for true intimacy.

It is beyond the scope of this paper to attempt to address all of these factors; however, I will examine the impact of historical childhood sexual abuse as manifest in the struggles of gay male survivors in their search for genuine intimacy. This paper discusses the tendency to avoid desired genuine emotional connection in favor of illusions of intimacy as a phenomenon resulting from the blurred boundaries from childhood sexual abuse.

Beginning with the devastation of an abusive childhood, there is an accumulative effect obscuring the path to a healthy fulfilled adulthood. The lack of early boundary development provides a poor basis for establishing personal boundaries within the broader, flexible boundaries of gay culture. Fears of abandonment springing from childhood experiences with offenders (and later reinforced as an adult with a series of sex partners) may serve to undermine the survivor's confidence to assert himself with regard to intimacy. Childhood abuse-related shame reinforced in adulthood by socialized and internalized homophobia also seriously impedes a survivor's ability to establish positive self-esteem. All of these factors and a lifetime of relationships based on sexual accommodation, in combination, result in an adult gay male with a limited concept of genuine intimacy and a basic distrust of anything that professes to be intimate.

In addition to socialized homophobia, gay survivors of childhood sexual abuse are burdened with a constellation of abuse-specific issues. To begin with, child sexual abuse by its nature fundamentally violates personal boundaries prior to any conscious development or awareness of them. This violation of the child is both physical and psychological and the child is both physically and psychologically unable to stop the abuse from occurring. In other words, the child is unable to separate himself from the sexual agenda of the perpetrator. Particularly in cases of incest, interpersonal boundaries are non-existent or limited to the needs of the offender(s). Identity is limited to a definition which is in keeping with how the offender manipulates and controls the child and the purposes that child serves for the offender. Within an incestuous home, the manipulation and intrusiveness are often pervasive and undermine any sense of boundaries that a healthy home life would model.

Often the only consistent boundary that exists in the incestuous home is the one placed by the offender between the offender/victim relationship and anyone outside the incestuous circle. It is not uncommon for abusive care-givers to convince the abused child that the outside world is cold, unfriendly and unconcerned about the needs of the child, and that only the care-giver truly loves him. In effect, the child caught in an abusive relationship is made to be fearful and distrustful of the outside world and is unlikely to reach outside that relationship to someone who might be understanding and intervene on the child's behalf. Consequently, the child is given a skewed idea of what a loving relationship is, and a negative view of the world outside the incestuous home. Within the closed-in confines of the offender-child dynamic, anything goes as per the whims of the offender, with little or no consideration of the well-being of the child. The imposed isolation and alienation of the child from the outside world serve to facilitate continuation of the abuse.

In the unconscious process of developing a gender identity a child looks to his own gender as a role model. In that process, any adult male figure (or significantly older adolescent) can have a great influence over how a boy perceives his place as a male in society and how he attributes meaning to life. When a boy is being abused by a male, his concept of what a male is and his relationship to other males are shaped accordingly. Likewise, his relationship to significant women will have an influence on how he perceives relationships between genders. When abused by a woman, his adult relationships to women often reflect something of the original abusive dynamic. When a boy is abused, the long-term impact on the development of gender identity and his concept of interpersonal relationships in terms of gender, is profound. This is particularly true in the case of offending parents or other care-givers.

Whereas any adult may serve to model social norms and gender-specific behavior for a child, a parent/caregiver also represents to the child security, protection, provision of needs (particularly for love and affection), a sense of belonging and recognition. When abuse is part of the relationship between a boy and his care-giver, the child is unlikely to question the lack of sexual boundaries, primarily due to a lack of comprehension of "healthy" parameters. He may also sense that to question the abuse could compromise the relationship upon which he depends. On some level, the abused child comes to understand that cooperating with sexual exploitation is often the cost attached to having his needs met (or which he hopes will be met). The offender's use of reward for compliance, withholding of attention or need fulfillment for non-compliance, reinforces the child's perception of the link between abuse and provision of physical and emotional survival needs. Consequently, the element of barter becomes part of the child's definition of loving relationships. Love is not given unconditionally. An abused child, particularly the victim of incest, may not have any other experience with healthy adults from which to draw upon in developing a concept of intimacy.

This is further complicated by the biological availability for a child to become aroused while being sexually abused. For a boy, the arousal response is difficult to hide. The offender may exploit any arousal response the boy may have in order to induce feelings of guilt and responsibility. A purely physiological response on the part of the boy is thereby defined by the offender as willing participation. In the midst of the confusion of the situation and the conflict between biology and will, the child is made uncertain of his culpability. The child may be unable to experience a sense of self as independent from those who use and abuse him.

Forced to comply, not only with the physical act of the abuse, but also with the psychological manipulations of the offender, the child's self-concept and cognitive schemas are, as a result, co-constructed by the offender. The child's identity may therefore be limited to a definition which is in keeping with how the offender manipulates and controls the child's emotional and physiological responses and by what the child is led to believe about the experience.

As an adolescent male survivor of sexual abuse approaches adulthood, he may experience considerable confusion about his sexual orientation. As he begins to identify as gay, influenced by socialized homophobia, he may internalize society's condemnation and hostility toward homosexuality. Enhanced by the confusion and shame attached to the abuse, this developmental period may become intensely distressful. Eventually, when he is more accepting of his orientation, he may look to the gay community in an effort to formulate a sense of his sexual self. As a gay male begins to consciously develop a sexual identity, many of the unresolved manifestations of childhood sexual abuse are often in evidence in current dilemmas and may influence conscious and unconscious choices he makes in the process of coming out to himself. By acknowledging his sexual orientation and in formulating a sexual identity, he may strive to adhere to what he believes gay culture dictates as normative behaviors, attitudes and beliefs. In the face of the less restrictive sexuality of the gay community, and without healthy development of personal boundaries, he may have difficulty defining himself, his relationships to others and to his sub-culture on his own terms. In the process of attempting to identify and articulate boundaries, within the sexual norms of the gay community, the adult survivor may avoid the risk of articulating his boundaries for fear of rejection or criticism, especially from those who are, or might become, his sexual partners. Once again, the demands of others take precedence over his own needs or values.

Sexuality abuse is a term that may include overt behavior (often involving physical contact); as well as many covert behaviors such as teasing a boy because he is not good at sports, is interested in theatre, gardening, cooking, or being ridiculed for having a high voice, or being thin or soft spoken. Perhaps the most devastating form of sexuality abuse to a developing young man is perpetrated by mainstream society in the form of homophobia. The effects of homophobic sexuality abuse may have deep lasting effects on a bi-sexual or gay male, undermining his sense of self as a male, and tainting what for him is a natural attraction to his own gender. Consequently, many gay men, to varying degrees, suffer guilt and shame very much the way survivors of childhood sexual abuse do. Discrimination in education, religion, work, social settings, sports and within many families, are all forms of sexuality abuse which any gay male may have had to endure.

As a result, gay male survivors frequently meet men who are also survivors or who have similar issues. These associations further enmesh each partner in the other's unresolved dilemmas. Survivors of sexual abuse almost without exception experience deep abiding guilt and shame. In many instances, the offender uses the child's shame to enforce silence. In some instances the shame that the offender feels is intuited and internalized by the child. Similarly, shame and self-contempt (internalized homophobia) are particularly common to gay men and may permeate their relationships to one another.

Gay male culture is somewhat prone to the whims of current fashion, currently focused on youth and virility. Gym-built bodies and model's faces prevail. Often when a gay man is dazzled by popular, idealized images of a desirable partner, he may not attend to the more substantial qualities of his sexual partners. When that is the case, he may continuously move on in search of the illusive perfect man. When a male survivor of sexual abuse is passed over by casual partners or left by a man he believed he had a meaningful relationship with, old pains connected to being rejected by an adult or incestuous parent are renewed. He is then left feeling valued for purely sexual reasons, reinforcing the belief that he needs to be a skillful, accommodating object in order to hold on to a man.

Just as it is common for the abuser to abandon the abused child once the victim outgrows his desirability to the offender, so, too, gay men are often abandoned by their partners for similarly appearance-based reasons. In adulthood, when abandonment occurs, the gay male's self-concept is diminished and his distrust of relationships is increased. Within either a short- or long-term connection between gay men, both parties may have fears about saying "no" or setting boundaries that they fear will be in contradiction to the expectations placed on them by their sexual partners. With neither partner able to set clear, healthy personal boundaries, the result is often high-risk sexual activity. As previously discussed, the survivor, responding to earlier constructions resulting from abusive boundary transgressions, may feel an obligation to please his partner and/or to ensure continuation of the relationship.

The tendency to view the self as only conditionally acceptable, or particularly valued in sexual terms began when an abused male's relationship to his offender was imbued with sexual energy. Many elements of a sexually abusive relationship directly or thematically involve sex. Affection, guidance, discipline, gifts, sports activities, entertainment, meals, and bedtime may all be involved in the sexual interaction as rewards, punishment, or conditions connected with sexual cooperation. The child's sexuality becomes a commodity which buys or guarantees provision of what would come naturally in a healthy relationship. The child's need for a care-giver relationship means that he can easily be exploited.

The adult gay male survivor's relationship to the gay community is also imbued with an analog sexual energy. On the most obvious level, it is sexuality which defines the gay community as separate from the heterosexual mainstream. Beyond merely the gender of one's sexual partners, there are significant differences in sexual values and norms between sexual orientations. Whereas marriage and parenting are very much a part of heterosexual social structure, these are considerably less significant within the gay male community (in some countries, like the United States, it is specifically not legal at this time for persons of the same gender to marry). This unfair difference at the same time allows for a broader range of acceptable dynamics within gay relationships. While monogamy is often expected in a committed gay union, open relationships are perhaps as common. Two men in a committed relationship may occasionally invite a third party for casual encounters. When not in a relationship, casual, "recreational" or "sport" sex appears to be generally accepted by a majority of the gay community. Most large cities have bath houses, sex clubs and cruising areas. Smaller cities may not have sex establishments, but often have cruising areas well known to local gays. Gay newspapers are full of ads, articles, calendars of coming events, all of which use sex as a selling point. The availability of casual, recreational sex, combined with the diversity of relationship choices and the sexually open nature of gay culture, does little to provide clear parameters for the survivor who has grown up without any. As it was in childhood, the gay individual's need for acceptance, a sense of belonging and personal meaning can be accessed and exploited through sexuality.

For a gay survivor of sexual abuse, the dual sexualization of his childhood relationships with offending adults and the sexually charged atmosphere of gay culture are confusingly similar. Through having been sexually abused, the male survivor may associate sex with many elements of life that would not be sexual had he not been abused. He may not be able to ask himself "What does sex have to do with this?" and therefore be unable to separate sex from something else. Differentiating between a sexuality that has been constructed abusively, and what is not sexual as well as the authentic sexuality of the survivor is often a monumental task. Selective response to sexual imagery, norms or mores within gay culture may likewise be difficult.

Gay survivors of sexual abuse are caught in the cross fire of three opposing sexual norms. At one point of the cross fire is the offender and abusive sexuality from which the child learns that exploitation, secretiveness, control and self-interest are the norm. At another point are oppressive forces proclaiming opposite gender partnering (including marriage, children and family) as the norm. At the third point, the gay community implicitly promotes casual, recreational, often multi-partnered sex as part of the norm. In the midst of these powerful, insistent pressures, forging an identity, making choices and setting personal boundaries can be extremely daunting. An adult who has survived childhood sexual abuse has learned powerlessness, silence and surrender to the imposition of stronger forces. The gay survivor may not even consider breaking free of external influences, nor to risk being in conflict with peer norms.

As a child in a sexually abusive relationship with a care-giver, to refuse to cooperate, to object, or to dare to break the imposed silence could mean a lack of approval, or worse: to be abandoned. The fear of abandonment reflects the perception, perhaps introduced and reinforced by the family, of being left alone, powerless in a dangerous world. Similarly, gay male survivors may have concerns about being ostracized by the gay community should their values diverge from community standards, alienated by heterosexual culture and left in an isolated no man's land.

Boundary confusion, often refracted through the lens of interpersonal relationships, will be traumatically influenced as discussed. The lack of early boundary development and the seemingly unboundaried gay culture; fears of abandonment springing from childhood experiences with offenders and later as an adult with a sequence of unfulfilling relationships; childhood abuse related shame reinforced in adulthood by socialized and internalized homophobia; and a lifetime of relationships influenced by (or indeed based upon) sexual accommodation will all contribute to frustrating difficulties with intimacy. This is often painful for the survivor, whether or not he has insight into the origins of this confusion. Having difficulty making choices that reflect his genuine desires and values, the survivor is brought to a place of shame, isolation and loneliness.

When loneliness, isolation or flaring up of historical pain and self-contempt become too oppressive or intrusive, gay survivors of child sexual abuse often turn to sexual behavior for comfort. Bath houses, public washrooms, parks and other cruising areas may offer a respite from loneliness and pain. While the cruising is under way, the issues that brought him there are forgotten. During the sexual interaction, the intensity of the moment provides the semblance of intimacy without the risk of emotional exposure, commitment or rejection. Low self-esteem, for some, can be ameliorated by being pursued. All too often, however, almost as quickly as the post-orgasmic slowing of the pulse, the illusion fades and loneliness, isolation and pain return now reinforced by what has been yet another reenactment of the original empty childhood sexual experience.

For some gay men, chance encounters at the baths or parks are intense, though short-lived, connections with other men. For them there can be real connection and intimacy within which there is a recognition and validation of each other and a celebration of their shared eroticism. Unfortunately, it is far more frequent for an adult survivor who has not resolved his historical pain and grief, to not have the means to make such a connection. Ironically, in the contrast between the images of joyous sexual sharing put forth in gay media and his abuse imposed psycho-emotional distress, the survivor may once again be made to feel inadequate.

Without the opportunity to work through the unresolved trauma, to reconstruct a personal paradigm, to break free of the cycle of reenactment, the adult gay male survivor of sexual abuse may spend a lifetime in a hopeless search for himself within illusions of intimacy. Community standards are likely to be confusing and highly reactive to the oppressive forces of majority culture. However, if the survivor's confusion is validated and he learns to develop clear, firm but flexible boundaries, he may develop the tools to make appropriate relationship choices that reflect his true desires and values. He may gain insight into how he barters/negotiates between intimacy and sex. He may recognize ways in which he participates in the reinforcement of a split between sex and intimacy. Armed with a new level of insight and self-knowledge, the survivor may be able to begin a cycle of change, trading illusions for authentic intimacy.

HIV and the Cycle of Trauma in Gay Men

James Cassese

SUMMARY. Forged within the sociocultural context of the collective trauma of AIDS, HIV prevention efforts became rigid, focusing almost exclusively on patient education as risk reduction. However, while some people have not been able to incorporate risk reduction into their behavioral patterns, others have indeed returned to high-risk behavior after a period of reduced risk as evidenced by the "Bareback" movement. HIV prevention education has overlooked the effect of oppression and sexual trauma on the lives of gay men, and the impact of these phenomena on the gay male's interest in, and ability to, negotiate safer sex. Sexual trauma has been shown to have a direct effect on HIV risk and seropositivity. Additionally, as sexual trauma (often in the form of homophobia) and HIV infection have numerous parallels, the gay man may have analogous ways of relating to, processing and dealing with the two phenomena. Case histories are offered to illustrate how the relationship between HIV and sexual trauma may be examined in an effort to enhance the self-esteem and self-concept of the gay man, and thereby offer greater possibilities for him to protect himself. *[Article copies available for a fee from The Haworth Document Delivery Service: 1-800-342-9678. E-mail address: <getinfo@haworthpressinc. com> Website: <http://www.HaworthPress.com>]*

KEYWORDS. Dissociation, gay, HIV prevention, HIV risk, homophobia, oppression, sexual trauma, unprotective sex

An integrative understanding of Acquired Immune Deficiency Syndrome (AIDS) in the early 1980s was thwarted by the overwhelming,

[Haworth co-indexing entry note]: "HIV and the Cycle of Trauma in Gay Men." Cassese, James. Co-published simultaneously in *Journal of Gay & Lesbian Social Services* (Harrington Park Press, an imprint of The Haworth Press, Inc.) Vol. 12, No. 1/2, 2000, pp. 127-152; and: *Gay Men and Childhood Sexual Trauma: Integrating the Shattered Self* (ed: James Cassese) Harrington Park Press, an imprint of The Haworth Press, Inc., 2000, pp. 127-152. Single or multiple copies of this article are available for a fee from The Haworth Document Delivery Service [1-800-342-9678, 9:00 a.m. - 5:00 p.m. (EST). E-mail address: getinfo@haworthpressinc.com].

kaleidoscopic presentation of illness. Emblematic of trauma, the abrupt appearance and swift spread of AIDS prohibited any but the most reactive responses. "At risk" individuals organized around emotions such as anger and compassion, and ultimately were galvanized into community organizations. Others coalesced around blame and hate.

The healthcare professions, within their respective realms, became caught between polarized activist forces. In the face of disheartening discrimination and maltreatment by some of the medical profession, advocacy groups formed. Patients became "People With AIDS" (PWAs), formally declaring their place at the decision-making table. The healthcare profession was forced to confront its own fears and biases, as it cared for an often disregarded, at times vilified, patient population. Empowered to a greater degree than any other patient population in history, PWAs made demands largely focused on symptom relief. At the same time, epidemiologists and scientists scrambled to stem the flow of an epidemic which, according to the warning signals, threatened to affect the entire world.

Nearly twenty years later, patient demographics have been somewhat modified, but the magnitude of the issues remains unaltered. Exhausted activists continue to demand new, more effective treatments. The medical establishment and the Food and Drug Administration (FDA) have stepped up efforts to make treatments more readily accessible. Pharmaceutical companies, with the most to gain by the transformation of AIDS into a chronic and manageable disease, present a friendlier front, funding benefits and launching magazines. HIV prevention efforts use outdated educational material and HIV testing and counseling to reduce HIV risk while "little evidence supports the notion that HIV antibody counseling and testing for seronegative persons . . . leads to favorable behavior change" (Holtgrave et al., 1995). Further, prevention efforts neglect certain difficult realities: while some "individuals have failed to initiate reduction in risk; others have returned to high-risk activities" (Roffman et al., 1997). To a great degree, without an update of these outmoded efforts, we are frozen in time.

What *has* changed is the far greater number of medical treatments available for AIDS. While none of these pharmaceutical agents is a cure, for the first time, "recent advances . . . have raised considerable hope for people living with HIV as well as for those at risk for infection" (Dilley, Woods, & McFarland, 1997). Perhaps not coincidentally, new groupings of gay men have emerged, this time coalescing around a different cluster of feelings. Coining terms like "bareback" or "skin-to-skin," these activists stake a claim in "sex positive" attitudes. Announcing a conscious return to anal sex without condoms (*New York Times*, 23/11/97), some of these groups represent an extreme within a trend toward high-risk behavior. Dilley, Woods, and McFarland (1997) found that 26% of HIV-negative men who have sex with men were "less concerned about becoming HIV positive because of the new treatments" and 13% of respondents indicated that they had become "more willing to take a chance of getting infected." Ekstrand et al. (1999) found that 50% of gay men in 1996-1997 engaged in unprotected anal sex, compared to 37% of the same subjects in 1993-94. Perhaps such a reaction is a legacy that might have been anticipated after fifteen years of rehashing the same prevention materials with little impact on infection rates.

Two phenomena–medications with high resistance profiles and a return to high-risk activities–threaten to reverse current medical advances. All available medical treatments for HIV infection demonstrate phenotypic and genotypic evidence of failure. For a variety of reasons, including patient adherence, HIV can "break through," that is, replicate in the presence of medical treatment designed to inhibit its life cycle (Eldred et al., 1997; Richman, 1997; Williams et al., 1997). Many of the drugs available share common mutations; if strains of drug-resistant HIV dominate, as can happen in Multiple-Drug Resistant Tuberculosis (MDR TB), successful treatment could become obsolete (Pablos-Mendez et al., 1997). Reports from the 12th World AIDS Conference in Geneva confirm that mutant strains of the virus already exist that are multi-drug resistant (Hecht et al., 1998; Hertogs et al., 1998; Shafer, Winters, Palmer, & Merigan, 1998; Wainber & Friedland, 1998). Thus the trauma repeats.

The coping strategies of treatment and prevention developed against AIDS/HIV are buckling under the strain of the trauma. Gay men are rendering themselves vulnerable to re-victimization at the hands of the virus. With the advent of a "Bareback Movement," there appears a return to the trauma, a metaphoric repetition compulsion.

At the same time, an atmosphere of greater hope presents an opportunity to examine the impact of AIDS/HIV in retrospect. Processing the history of the AIDS/HIV trauma may lead to deduction, understanding and interpretation toward greater psychological understanding and coping enhancement.

The phenomena surrounding HIV/AIDS stand in striking parallel to sexual child abuse. The literature indicates an enhanced HIV risk for those with histories of childhood sexual abuse (Allers, Benjack, White, & Rousey, 1993; Bartholow et al., 1994; Carballo-Dieguez & Dolezal, 1995; Cassese, 1993; Cunningham, Stiffman, & Earls, 1994; Elifson, Boles, & Sweat, 1993; Lodico & DiClemente, 1994; Zierler et al., 1991). Additionally, there may exist a metaphysical relationship for gay men between sexual trauma in their childhoods and AIDS in their adulthood. In this paper, HIV/AIDS as an existential reality in gay male life is examined through the lens of a trauma perspective. Suggestions for clinical interpretation and interventions are proposed.

Fragmentation is the psychological consequence of most traumas. In order to psychologically survive the traumatic event, the victim dissociates during and shortly after the event. The mind/body connection is severed by a sexual trauma, dissociation functioning to allow the mind to withdraw in order to preserve sanity; the body left behind to face the event. The shattering of thought, feeling and memory within the survivor is masked for a time by the dissociation. Amnesia, a component of dissociation, provides a respite from memories associated with the events. The dissociative phenomenon of depersonalization offers a cinema-like sense of "detachment from the self," including "a sense that one is observing the self from outside" (Steinberg, 1994).

Despite dissociation's self-preserving properties, the subsequent shattering often becomes problematic to the survivor. Depersonalization creates "a sense of physical fragmentation or separation from part of one's body, such as an absence of feeling, a feeling of numbness or disconnection from one's emotions, a feeling of being dead" (Steinberg, 1994). The natural inclination is toward re-integration. However, because only fragments of thoughts, feelings and memories remain, the survivor can only attend to pieces of the puzzle.

He frequently will review the memories to which he has access, poignantly re-playing the events leading up to the event. Dissociation, as would be true of any defense mechanism, cannot be precise, and often "blocks" of information are missing. The survivor searches for meaning, working with only fragmented material. In the absence of conscious memory, the survivor may focus on "missing time" or symptoms which intuitively resonate with the memory for which he is amnestic. Where memory is present, he is often preoccupied with replaying the events leading up to the event. Repetitive questions of "why" plague the survivor as he tries to integrate the event into his view of the world. Eventually, coping strategies develop to accommodate the incomplete understanding and memory of the event and its repercussions into ongoing life.

Resulting from a trauma, a psychological split serves to provide a framework within which the fragments can fit together without complete integration. Splitting ironically makes order from chaos by classifying things as "all good" or "all bad," without shades of grey. The anxiety of ambiguity is countered with a concrete all-or-none categorization. This creates the illusion of a structure and, implicitly, of safety. The questions of "why" in the historical context of AIDS were somewhat addressed with the discovery of the HIV virus and its likely transmission routes. The question "Why?", however, implies "Why me?" as well as "How could this happen to me?" These are existential questions inherent in a trauma reaction. The response in the 1980s was framed, however, within a psychological split. The world of science, working within this structure, responded to the "Why?" of AIDS by containing it within purely biological and behavioral contexts.

This accurate, however limited and incomplete, side of the split developed into societal coping strategies. With the discovery of the HIV virus, the research community located a focal point for treatment. Prevention efforts took the direction of education as risk reduction. This splitting of the larger social response, however, prevented collective thinking from moving beyond a narrow focus. As a result, the field of "psychology . . . has not contributed to HIV prevention at a level proportionate to the urgency of the crisis" (Kelly, Murphy, Sikkema, & Kalichman, 1993). The urgency as well as the intensity of fear and confusion involved in AIDS at a societal level, added to the rigidity of these strategies. Ironically (as would be the case for *any* coping strategy that becomes inflexible, static or solitary), this installed a time-limited value, a self-obsolescence. This has unfortunately been the case with the coping strategies of HIV prevention currently employed.

HIV prevention efforts reduced confusion by limiting the information to simple biology. Even today, some professionals believe that "faced with the enormity of the disaster and the inability of medical science today to control the AIDS virus, preventive education is our only weapon to fight this epidemic" (Isaksson, 1996). However, with little change in infection rates and a new movement toward unprotective sex, it seems clear that "information alone does not necessarily exert much influence on refractory health impairing habits" (Bandura, 1994). Sadly, however, reports from the 12th World AIDS Conference "lead inexorably to the conclusion that the best hope for easing the epidemic is still prevention" (*New York Times*, 5 July 1998). As the current precarious situation indicates, there is clearly more at play than transmission routes. New methods of coping, new methods of HIV prevention are urgently needed. Understanding the limits on the success of prior prevention efforts is vital. One of these limitations results from the over-reliance of HIV education on what Paulo Freire (1970) termed "the banking concept of education."

In the banking concept, the teacher deposits information in the empty vessels that are students. "The teacher talks about reality as if it were motionless, static, compartmentalized and predictable. Or . . . expounds on a topic completely alien to the existential experience of the students" (Freire, 1970). Freire acknowledges that some of the best intentioned teachers will fail to perceive the "true significance of the dehumanizing power" of the banking method, preserving the oppressive dynamics from which this type of education stems. As a result, the relation of oppressor in the guise of teacher and oppressed (student) remain largely intact. Any action or agency which seeks to obstruct the individual's movement to become "more fully human," to self-actualize, is oppressive (Freire, 1970). Freire's context of an oppressive dictatorship, applied to the dehumanization of sexual minorities in the United States, is glaring.

As with HIV education, when the information is "deposited" in the student-as-object, the student (a mere vessel) does not have the chance to problem-solve. As a result, inherent contradictions in the information become kindling to ignite subsequent resistance. The lack of participation of student-as-problem-solver is at the heart of the dehumanizing elements of the banking concept. Freire warns that it is only a matter of time before the "contradictions . . . lead formerly passive students to turn against their domestication."

Problem-solving played an historical role in HIV prevention. For example, safer sex guidelines were proposed by a group of gay men in a pamphlet entitled: *How to Have Sex in an Epidemic* (Patton, 1989).

Established long "*before* a virus was associated with AIDS," these guidelines have not changed significantly since publication of that information. Several of the contradictions within HIV "education" remain unresolved: the risk involved in oral transmission of HIV and the difference between exposure and infection. The information is *not* motionless, static, compartmentalized or predictable.

Risk behaviors and their motivations are confusing and at times counterintuitive. Hingson, Strunin, Berlin, and Heeren (1990) found in their sample of adolescents that "knowledge of someone with AIDS was negatively associated with condom use." Further, prevention theorists advocate "cultural competency" as a predictor of successful risk reduction interventions (Holtgrave et al., 1995; Kelly, Lawrence, & Brasfield, 1991; Schenkar, Sabar-Friedman, & Sly, 1996), yet only two of the eleven studies of theory-based counseling interventions "focused on interventions with gay and bisexual males, the population with the greatest prevalence of AIDS diagnoses in the United States" (Roffman et al., 1998). As research can offer cues to cultural competency, it would seem clear that more information is necessary to create cultural competency with regard to gay men.

As Freire might have predicted, students of HIV education are now frustrated and impatient. Groups like "Sex Panic" have actively opposed the oppressor implicit within the Safer Sex Imperative by organizing a conference in California, 1997, to discuss the behavioral mandates they perceive as oppressive (*New York Times*, 23/11/97). Their "reclaiming" the pleasure of anal sex without condoms is an effort to feel more fully "human" and in control of their sexual expression and identity. Because these men have been taught safer sex as an obligation, a backlash seems inevitable. It represents a metaphoric transference reaction in which the group becomes blind to the present dangers and reality of the here-and-now. "Depending on their nature, social influences can aid, retard, or undermine efforts at personal change. This is especially true in the case of sexual and drug practices" (Bandura, 1994). To the degree that there is now social support for *not* utilizing protective sexual practices, prior progress in terms of HIV prevention may be effectively reversed.

A few studies claiming qualified success rates with safer sex "relapse" indicate that "community support for safer sex norms" influenced the subjects' ability to manage safer sex (Roffman et al., 1997, 1998). Many of the studies that observe qualified success involve men who express a desire to reduce risk at the start of the study and have safer behavioral patterns at baseline. As evidenced by Sex Panic, however, there are some gay men who are not interested in reducing risk. Whether protective sex is inherently beneficial and ultimately self-preserving is a question overshadowed by reactions against the banking concept unintentionally embedded within HIV prevention.

Understanding these perspectives involves a deductive comprehension of the gay male experience. The oppression that is homophobia has far-reaching effects upon self-esteem, trust and self-concept of the gay child. Homophobic attacks are aimed ostensibly at what "defines" the difference: sexuality. This chronic sexual trauma has a profound effect on the interpersonal efficacy of the gay male. "Risk reduction calls for enhancement of interpersonal efficacy rather than simply targeting a specific infective behavior for change" (Bandura, 1994). As an adult, HIV infection results from acting on the sexuality ingrained and defined as taboo since childhood. This connection locates HIV transmission in the psychological context of a cycle of trauma; it echoes back to prior real or imagined "consequences" of a minority sexuality.

This traumatic spiral reverberates throughout the phenomena of AIDS and HIV. The point of convergence is the historical childhood sexual trauma of the gay male survivor. When the relationship between HIV and childhood sexual trauma has been discussed, however, the focus has usually been HIV risk and prevention efforts (Allers, Benjack, White, & Rousey, 1993; Bartholow et al., 1994; Carballo-Dieguez & Dolezal, 1995; Cassese, 1993; Cunningham, Stiffman, & Earls, 1994; Elifson, Boles, & Sweat, 1993; Lodico & DiClemente, 1994; Zierler et al., 1991). The research often addresses the difficulties in maintaining precautions or framed as "relapse prevention." In this way the categorical imperative of HIV risk reduction is unchallenged, reinforcing the all-or-none split. Such a split maintains the focus on the duality between negative and positive, overlooking that regardless of serostatus, there is an existential relation to the trauma of HIV for all gay men. This relationship exposes the difficulties of HIV prevention efforts that compel some individuals to adopt the other side of the split, and reject risk reduction outright. Thus, the ambiguity created by those "HIV-educated" people who do not reduce risk seems intolerable to those who make conscious efforts to reduce risks and those who teach HIV prevention education. The social manifestation of the split provokes a threatened outrage in some and is denied by others. Freire (1970) posits that the oppressed, "chafing under the restrictions of" the circumstances of their oppression, will "often manifest a type of horizontal violence, striking out at" each other.

The relationship between the self and HIV will, to a great degree, be idiosyncratic to the individual. HIV's location within a framework of historical individual/collective trauma provokes a psychological connection to the virus that may be beyond conscious awareness. Its nightmarish presentation inspires a collective relation to individual unconscious thoughts and fears: an infecting agent invades from intimate contact, to slowly devour defenses until death. In prisons this is illustrated by the slang term for HIV: "The Monster."

In the data collected from 87 men assessed for accuracy of recall of risk behaviors over time, Downey, Ryan, Roffman, and Kulich (1995) found a "significant association between the HIV-risk level of a behavior and the average extent to which the behavior was forgotten"; this was found to be especially true of anal activity without condoms. Moreover, "relapse" in HIV risk behavior is often reported in terms that might be interpreted as psychological defense mechanisms. Ekstrand, Coates, and Stall (1989), for example, found that some of the reported reasons for HIV risk behaviors among the men surveyed included: "intoxicant overuse; wishing not to interrupt the spontaneity of sex; belief that one would develop a steady relationship; or being caught up in the moment." Martin and Knox (1997) found that unstable self-esteem correlated with HIV risk behavior.

These factors fit into "classic" sexual trauma survivor aftereffects. Intoxicant overuse as well as low self-esteem are often associated with sexual trauma. In the case of gay men, such an aftereffect is further complicated by bars often serving as the initial social forum. Intimacy issues ("spontaneity of sex" and "belief that one would develop a steady relationship") are often associated with trauma symptomatology. "Being caught up in the moment" lends itself to a range of interpretations from denial to dissociation to poor impulse control, each of which is associated with sexual trauma. To focus on the behavior's impact on HIV risk yet ignore the underlying motivations is to maintain the information at the "banking concept" level of education.

Childhood sexual trauma has been shown to have direct effects on HIV risk. In a study of 1001 men in Chicago, Denver and San Francisco, Bartholow and colleagues (1994) found that "abused men were more likely to have engaged in at least one instance of unprotected anal intercourse during the four-month pre-study period." For some men, one instance is all it takes. Kelly, Lawrence, and Brasfield (1991), citing Kingsley (1987), reported that "urban gay men who have unprotected receptive anal intercourse with only one partner over twelve months are 300% more likely to develop HIV infection and engaging in this practice with five partners produces an 18-fold increase in likelihood of HIV seroconversion."

Zierler and colleagues (1991) found that "men who report a history of sexual abuse had a twofold increase in prevalence of HIV infection relative to unabused men." In a study of 2708 males and 2582 females grades 9-12, Lodico and DiClemente (1991) found that "adolescents reporting sexual abuse initiated sexual activity earlier (than non-abused) and are less likely to report condom use." Further, they observed that "sexually abused males are significantly more likely to report drug injection and needle sharing."

A fairly well-considered study by Cunningham, Stiffman, Dore, and Earls (1994) examined the "Association of Physical and Sexual Abuse with HIV Risk Behavior in Adolescence and Young Adulthood" in 602 individuals. The authors found that being beaten in adolescence contributed to engaging in greater HIV risk behavior in both adolescence and young adulthood. Interestingly, being raped in adolescence did *not* significantly contribute to HIV risk behavior in adolescence. In the same subjects, however, there was a significant correlation between being raped in adolescence and *subsequent* HIV risk in young adulthood. The researchers found no correlation between sexual abuse and HIV risk except when it was combined with other abuses. One interpretation of these data is that rape in adolescence has a delayed effect as it relates to HIV risk, or more likely it sets in motion a complex matrix of aftereffects that converge to create HIV risk vulnerabilities similar to the complex observed in this study with other abuses.

In other words, the symptoms and aftereffects that result from a sexual trauma may have a period where the individual gains control with specific coping mechanisms, just as the immune system is able to stave off HIV replication at first by producing CD4+ cells, cytokines and chemokines in ample volume, maintaining a balance between immune production and destruction, the so-called "set-point" (Mellors et al., 1995). Eventually, however, as with even the strongest coping mechanisms, post-sexual trauma symptoms and HIV overwhelm the mind and the body's ability to keep up. Bandura (1994) suggests that "coping efficacy may operate as a psychosocial cofactor that influences infectability and disease progression directly through its impact on immune functioning."

HIV risk, however, is only part of the picture. The psychological elements that predispose HIV risk and infection do not *cease* with HIV seroconversion. Their effect on the health of the HIV seropositive survivor may be even greater than upon that of the HIV seronegative survivor. Depression, a common aftereffect of sexual child abuse, may reduce patient adherence to medications for any number of reasons ranging from passive suicidality to fatigue. "A low sense of efficacy in coping with stressors activates autonomic, catecholamine and endogenous opioid systems that can impair immune function" (Bandura, 1991). The experience of powerlessness, endured over a long period of time, "is itself a broad risk factor that increases, susceptibility to higher morbidity and mortality rates" (Wallerstein, 1992). Antoni and colleagues (1990) found that "stressors which result in maladaptive functioning can elicit a series of psychological, neuroendocrinological and immunological events which may result in faster progression." Rabkin and colleagues (1991) found a significant correlation between stressful life events and social conflict with subsequent HIV symptomatology.

The huge number of threats and stressors on the life of gay men often result in maladaptive functioning as evidenced, for example, by the high rate of alcoholism/drug overuse among this population. Wallerstein (1992) notes that research supports the association between "chronic stressors and a range of mental, physical and behavioral health problems." Indeed, the vulnerability to discrimination and internalized homophobia prevent some men from revealing their sexual identity in their environment. In a chilling study of 80 men studied over nine years, Cole, Kemeny and colleagues (1996) found that "HIV infection advanced more rapidly in a dose-response relationship to the degree participants concealed their homosexual identity." The very survival strategy these men used to protect themselves from perceived threat in the environment ultimately contributed to their morbidity.

This phenomenon mirrors the aftereffects of childhood sexual trauma, which often initially developed as coping strategies, ultimately become rigid, unmanageable and contribute to significant problems in adulthood. In order to survive/cope with a traumatic event, one develops tools idiosyncratic to the personality of the survivor and the circumstances of the trauma. For a time, these coping behaviors serve their function. However, as they are forged in a reactive context, they rarely develop and grow at a pace equal to that of the survivor's circumstances. As with the concept of the set point in HIV, while the organism initially is able to handle the effects of the invading agent, over time its aftereffects overwhelm the coping structure. Instead of binding the fragments of the traumatized psyche, they often overshadow the other components of the survivor's personality. Inflexible, these coping strategies may function at cross purposes to the survivor's growth and healing. As such, they often tragically become the focus of critical judgment when viewed out of the context of the traumatic formation. As Herman (1992) elegantly indicates, "the psychological distress symptoms of traumatized people simultaneously call attention to the existence of an unspeakable secret and deflect attention from it." Thus, the individual whose trauma resulted in a reliance on drugs becomes labeled a "drug addict." His survival is overlooked by the entrenchment of the coping behavior. Further, because not all but some trauma results in a drug addiction, there is a greater tendency to blame the drug overusing survivor. This inconsistency enhances the confusion in disentangling the aftereffects of trauma from the genuine personality of the survivor. Aftereffects are never universal nor uniform in presentation.

Similarly, the opportunistic infections (OI) associated with AIDS do not emerge as universal or uniform. There may be common presentations, but AIDS is a syndrome comprised of a long list of possible, multifaceted illnesses. To the extent that sexual child abuse engenders vulnerabilities to HIV infection, the implication of a cause-effect relationality is plausible (see Figure 1).

Due to psychological splitting and subsequent cognitive extremes resulting from a childhood sexual trauma, there can be no one-to-one mapping relationship of HIV and childhood sexual abuse. A similar set of trauma circumstances may provoke excessive risk-taking in one survivor and risk phobia in another. The virus itself is mercurial and somewhat fragile; risk does not equate with exposure, nor does exposure always equate with infection. Two men may have equivalent risk behaviors and probabilities, while only one may escape infection.

At the same time, because the dynamics involved in both traumatic phenomena–HIV and childhood sexual trauma–contain striking parallels, an individual gay man may have analogous ways of relating to, understanding, coping, processing, and defending against *each* of these events in his life. The parallels are enhanced by the apparent relationship between the largely internal/hidden damage of childhood sexual trauma and the physical manifestation of disease in AIDS. It illustrates the "central dialectic of psychological trauma" which is, according to Herman (1992), "the conflict between the will to deny horrible events and the will to proclaim them." The survivor is often left feeling ugly, damaged and powerless, particularly for the male survivor whose inability to protect himself goes against cultural mandates. AIDS OIs physically manifest illnesses that disfigure, cripple and further occupy an already overwhelmed immune system. OIs in effect present as a metaphoric externalization/disclosure of the internalized trauma aftereffects.

Like the HIV virus itself, these aftereffects often present at symptomatology when coping mechanisms begin to lag in the face of extreme use. Immediately following a childhood sexual trauma, the survivor may present behavior that indicates the event that has taken place (acute phase, similar to acute HIV infection). This was the case, for example, with the initial focus on symptom relief in the early stages of AIDS activism. The survivors presented the indicators of the problem with no language to describe the event. Herman (1992) tells us that "the ordinary response to atrocities is to banish them from consciousness." The survivor may need to keep the event secret because he fears

FIGURE 1.

Child = = = yields = = = > Aftereffects
Sexual   HIV Risk Behaviors = = = result in = = = >HIV
Trauma   Maladaptive Functioning = = = yields = = = > Immune
                Impairment = = = results in = > AIDS

(e.g., *Intoxicant Overuse, Ineffective Coping, Anxiety*)

blame, and is ashamed. The survivor may not conceive the event itself as traumatic in that he may believe that he participated, enjoyed or even initiated it (see Introduction). It is only later, after the aftereffects of the trauma develop into problematic, entrenched behavior that the survivor presents fragmented, varied symptomatology which may or may not be attributed to the event. To extend the parallel, often actual infection with HIV is not experienced as traumatic in the moment. Only after a period during which the virus slowly overwhelms the immune system does evidence of infection surface in the form of opportunistic infections.

The setpoint, establishing a normalcy of balance between immune function and virus (Mellors et al., 1995), makes AIDS even more baffling. The transmission of the virus is unnoticeable, and may be followed by a period of acute infection which includes any combination of flu-like symptoms, rashes, or enlarged lymph glands, often undiagnosed or mistaken for a common flu. Confusingly, some individuals do not evidence noticeable symptomatology during acute infection. The remaining course of the disease has been variously characterized in stages and categories. From Gay Related Immune Disease (GRID) to AIDS to AIDS Related Complex (ARC) to Long Term Survivors (LTS) to Long Term Non-Progressors (LTNP), the shifting presentation of HIV disease has defied adequate, fixed categorization (Cassese, 1998). Similarly, the definition of childhood sexual trauma is one that is at times ambiguous, at others simplistic and ultimately contradictory.

For gay men in particular, the definition of a childhood sexual event as traumatic is difficult and confusing. For many gay men, sexual contact with another man is seen, despite age differences, as a rite of passage. In this interpretation, the yearning for male-male contact overrides the age discrepancies and the sequelae of aftereffects that often follow. The survivor may have the sense that he encouraged or seduced the older male; some survivors view the event with some affection. For some this might be true in the abstract. Events that occur in childhood or adolescence, however, are remembered by the survivor from the viewpoint of the developmental period during which the event occurred. The yearning by the gay adolescent for same sex contact is understandable and, in the context of homophobia and isolation, is often experienced as urgent. Longing acted upon, however, sets up two damaging aftereffects: impulse control difficulties and boundary problems. The adolescent experiences his impulses gratified inappropriately, yet with apparent benefits. The adult survivor subsequently has less control over managing the boundary between impulse and action. Further, steeped in the romantic intensity of adolescence, the gratification of the sexual impulse deprives the survivor of the opportunity to process his longing. The exploration of this longing ultimately would aid in the development of greater clarity between sex and affection. However, with these now blurred boundaries, through the adolescent's eyes, sex and love become equivalent terms. When the survivor has sex, he may mistake it for love and when he loves, he may believe that he must be sexual.

Boundaries between two people are exposed in both childhood sexual trauma and AIDS. HIV infection reveals an underlying behavior involving sexual contact or intravenous drug use. Childhood sexual trauma reveals the point of contact where sexual boundaries were crossed. The exposure of these points of contact are often marked by shame and secrecy. Despite the compassion of some, AIDS continues to be an illness that carries enormous stigma: a flashpoint for fear, hate and discrimination. Similarly, the male childhood sexual trauma survivor faces overlapping stigmas. The misogynist cultural expectation that boys possess a greater ability to fight back denies childhood realities of power differentials and sanctions victimization. This readies the child for a life of internalized blame and responsibility. In the case of incest, the stigma and secrecy are heightened.

The numerous parallels, thematic commonalities and shared characteristics between childhood sexual trauma and HIV infection are not lost on the gay male psyche. Each of these dual traumas, however, is singularly overwhelming and conscious awareness of a psychic relation between them may be difficult for the survivor. The gay man has had to avoid, deny or dissociate from the ridicule, violence or sexual behavior with adults experienced in childhood. The trauma of HIV may be maintained on the conscious level as an event distinct from prior traumas, despite a subtle resonance with the aftereffects created by childhood trauma. "People who have survived atrocities often tell their stories in a highly emotional, contradictory and fragmented manner" (Herman, 1992). As a result, the interpretation of the connections between the traumas and a consequent integrative understanding may be elusive. If this material has been split off and denied or repressed it resides in the unconscious. As a result, connections between HIV and childhood sexual trauma may be available only through preconscious thought or intuitive sense.

The individual may be aware of his cognitive, affective or visceral relation to each event. However, as outlined above, there is often significant material related to each of the traumas that is obscured by unconscious mechanisms. Motivations, authentic feelings, "shameful" thoughts residing in the unconscious will direct seemingly conscious behavior, such as intentional disregard for HIV risk reduction. The parallels between HIV infection and childhood sexual trauma offer a powerful opportunity to reveal the unconscious material attached to each event. In other words, the patient or clinician may have information regarding how the patient relates to childhood sexual trauma, however, their thoughts and behaviors regarding HIV infection may appear puzzling or contradictory. When held up against each other, the mirrored relation to childhood sexual trauma may unlock the unconscious motivations that direct the behavior as regards HIV.

In psychotherapeutic treatment, this relation may be explored to facilitate discussion or be used as a bridge to increase a cohesive sense of self over time. It is also a way to increase HIV risk reduction behavior, as it does not rely solely on education or moral/social obligation. It provides a level of insight into activities and behaviors that are at once seemingly self-generated and at odds with the survivor's values. As clinicians, examining these interrelationships in the lives of our individual clients or groups can provide a structure through which to organize our thinking.

As previously noted, the relationship between the individual to these distinct yet related phenomena will be idiosyncratic. Examination of the constellation of inter- and intra-relations between the self and each of the traumatic phenomena will reflect a deeper knowledge of each. This offers a possibility for the survivor to develop what Freire (1970) terms *"conscientizacao."* This refers to a critical consciousness where the individual perceives contradictions within his psycho-socio-political environment and "takes action against the oppressive elements" contained within (Freire, 1970). When the unconscious material is made conscious, and the survivor is able to cast off the oppressive elements that blind him to the reality *in which he participates*, positive change may occur. HIV prevention efforts can be enhanced through the incorporation of this material and individual risk reduction behavior may be more consistent and intentional.

The following paradigm is intended as a basic framework to be tailored to the specifications of the individual as well as the particular therapeutic orientation of the counselor. The Cognitive-Behaviorist approach might make use of the following information to help the individual to adjust cognitive schemas forged by childhood sexual trauma and reinforced by HIV. The Self Psychological approach might encourage the exploration of the relation between the self-object sphere most impacted by childhood sexual trauma and most affected by HIV respectively. In other words, it is up to the individual clinician to *problem-solve*, using the particulars of his or her clients.

Because the relationship between HIV and childhood sexual trauma in the gay male psyche is existential, the issue in ascendance casts a shadow in which the other is revealed. What is known about the relation of the self to one of these phenomena may yield content about the relationship to the other. Further, the processing and healing of one element may provide the means by which the other may be simultaneously or sequentially processed. This is illustrated in the following case, that of Derek, a 34-year-old, HIV-positive gay man.

Derek's incest history (with his brother of 9 years older, Ralph) had been addressed in prior therapies. He expressed frustration, however, that some remnants continued to plague him, and that the strides he had made were largely intellectual. He had previously been riddled with anxiety usually during and after contact with his family. After a family function two years ago, Derek became convinced that Ralph had also abused his daughter (Derek's niece). Derek expressed profound regret that he had not, up to that point, confronted his brother. He felt he had rendered his niece vulnerable to Ralph's molestation.

Shortly after this event, Derek had an opportunistic infection, Kaposi's Sarcoma (KS). He subsequently fell victim to repeated panic attacks, although his anxiety had been under control for some time, and returned to smoking cigarettes. While in some respects quite well-adjusted to his HIV status, Derek continued to struggle with regret and a profound lack of self-forgiveness for having been HIV-infected. He expressed that he "should have known better," despite the fact that he was infected at age 20. For some time after the initial lesions appeared, Derek became overcome with terror by any patch of dry skin or new freckle on his body. He constantly examined his skin for signs that another lesion was about to appear.

A co-worker's misinterpretation of Derek's friendliness for sexual attraction became the occasion for powerful insight. A few weeks earlier an acquaintance had revealed that he felt kept at a distance by Derek's upbeat and in-control manner. The co-worker expressed that she felt Derek was inviting her sexual interest with his body language and eye contact. These two perceptions combined to send Derek into a spiral of intense self-examination. "Maybe I don't even know who I am," he lamented, "What if I'm sending off these signals and I don't even know what I'm doing?" It was difficult for Derek to acknowledge that other people's perceptions may not be based in objective reality.

It was suggested to Derek that some people may interpret behaviors or gestures in their own way. What his co-worker experienced might not have been what Derek intended. At the same time, it was reflected that Derek's search for what he had done to invite this co-worker's feelings was similar to his obsessive body inspections for KS lesions. He spontaneously associated to his sexual abuse history. He recalled that shortly before his brother began having sex with him, Derek had a fantasy that Ralph had a friend who would "fall in love" with Derek and take him away from his violent home. He expressed that he never found his brother attractive, but imagined a friend who was taller, slimmer and rich. When the sexual contact subsequently began, Derek was left with the sense that he had made it happen by virtue of his fantasies. He had not told prior therapists about this connection because he thought he would "sound crazy."

Derek wondered aloud whether his fantasy about Ralph's friend had been aroused in response to an elaborate seduction by Ralph. Ralph had been taking Derek out to miniature golf, on fishing trips and long hikes in the woods. In each activity, they would be alone for hours at a time. Derek expressed emotional pain at what he terms his "naivete" about the seduction. However, for the first time, Derek observed that it would be unrealistic to expect an 11-year-old boy to perceive a seduction. "An 11 year old is just learning how to write in script, what does he know about seduction?" He also recognized that as an 11-year-old, he was vulnerable to subtle manipulations of a 20-year-old man.

This provoked a flood of tears, the first Derek had cried in any of his 10 years of therapy. He expressed that he felt grief, not only for what happened, but for the 11-year-old boy in his mind that he had held responsible for so much in his life, including his HIV positive serostatus.

Work in subsequent sessions involved applying and integrating this sense of compassion for his role in the incest to his HIV status. Recently, he said he felt less naive about the encounter during which he was infected. Instead, when he thinks of the circumstances of his HIV infection, he remembers it in the context of being quite young and infatuated with a handsome older man.

As Derek found his participation in prior therapies largely intellectual, he had not found space to examine his sense of responsibility for the incest. He indicated that he understood intellectually that he was not to blame, but at the same time found it difficult to forgive himself. His self-blame was attached to the magical thinking of an 11-year-old and as a result psychologically split off from the intellectual adult. Derek's anxious physical self-scrutiny was a poignant parallel search to discover the event before it revealed itself, as though he might ward off further lesions. At that time, however, there was no preventive approach. As was the case with Ralph's seduction, once the process was set in motion, there was nothing Derek could do to stop it.

In this respect, the re-stimulation of Derek's sense of responsibility and naivete for "not seeing the abuse coming" was played out with the surprising appearance of an opportunistic infection. Additionally, Derek believed that his not confronting the family about what happened with Ralph played a role in Ralph's abuse of his own daughter. Almost magically, KS lesions appeared on Derek's face as a metaphoric accusation/punishment.

When he eventually reviewed the consequences of his HIV status, Derek began to perceive indisputable strengths which outweighed regrets. He expressed pride in the fact that his adjustment to his HIV status had been remarkably graceful and that he remembered to take his medicine regularly. The protease-containing combination therapy treated his existing KS and appeared to completely eliminate further KS lesions. The strength of his coping in response to HIV has been applied in treatment to the consequences of the incest. In this way the two realms of trauma have been woven together to foster a greater sense of integration in Derek's self-concept.

The fragmentation that occurs as a result of sexual trauma oftentimes becomes the treatment focus. In the next case study, Antonio was traumatized by homophobic verbal assaults and physical threats disturbing his sexual and gender identities. Antonio's cultural conceptions of masculinity, self-sufficiency and the stigma of victimization created a complex defense system.

Antonio, a 36-year-old HIV-negative Italian immigrant, presented for treatment to address "relationship conflicts," which he felt were in part due to his "self-esteem issues." Antonio indicated that the problems stemmed from his need to "be a bad boy," having sexual encounters outside his relationship. Antonio observed that his "underground sexuality" was "dark, and mysterious," and acknowledged that the danger and the use of drugs made sex more exciting. Of particular excitement to him was the idea that by day he was a successful executive, by night he became a "sensual predator." He reported that he was not concerned about HIV despite his high-risk behavior (anal sex without condoms with numerous anonymous partners) as "now there are medicines and it is treatable." In addition, he described feeling beautiful and desirable in his sexuality. He further explained that his lifestyle and profession (public relations) were steeped in youth and beauty and therefore he did not have much concern for the future.

Antonio expressed not wanting to discuss his childhood because it "was a long time ago" and he had done much to "forget the past." He acknowledged that shame and sadness added to his feeling that his past was unimportant. "It's just me," he explained, "I keep moving on and never look back. I keep reinventing myself, and I've been quite successful doing it this way." Despite this, he often returned spontaneously to a memory of himself as an adolescent. He remembered that he would avoid eye contact at all costs in public, crossing the street if necessary to avoid anyone's notice. Often he retreated to his room where he would read for hours, trying to stave off feelings of depression and suicidal thoughts. Antonio was unable to explain why he never acted on his suicidal impulses. Although no particular incident stood out to him, he reported with profound shame frequent name-calling and threats from the other students. These verbal assaults were puzzling to him as he was initially popular with his peers, but as he entered early adolescence became an object of scorn and derision. This exacerbated a rift between his younger brothers and him, their witnessing the assaults adding to his humiliation.

Antonio's constant belittling and the verbal assaults against his gender ("girl" or "sissy") seemed to have provoked intense shame and fear in adolescence. Antonio viewed his coping mechanism (e.g., crossing the street to avoid contact) with even *greater* feelings of shame. This spiral of shame created an overcompensation with risk-taking behavior and seeking the validation he received for his "dark sexuality."

This patient's matrix of aftereffects fed upon itself, increasing as if to ward off the importance of his childhood parallel with high-risk behavior. The denial of his prior history was reinforced by his "reinventing" himself, an enormously successful professional. He can "forget" the young, ashamed and fearful Antonio and simply *act as* the powerful, charismatic public relations executive. The positive reinforcement that Antonio received for the denial of his past and prior selves in business applied to his sexual life, despite the excitement that the split between the wealthy executive and sensual predator aroused. The validation he received for his sexual behavior ostensibly allowed him to overlook his HIV-risk.

As his sexual contacts often occur within the context of a group, there exists an implied social validation for his sexual behavior. As a result, the social influences which could "aid, retard, or undermine efforts at personal change" (Bandura, 1994) thwarted interventions aimed at the high-risk behavior. In addition to the validation received from Antonio's sexual behavior, his defensive structure further protected him against profound feelings of depression, isolation and suicidality. The fear and loneliness Antonio felt as a teenager in a homophobic, isolating environment threatened his emotional as well as physical survival. As much as Antonio wished to deny these intense feelings and the circumstances which engendered them, he appeared to act on a reaction-formation response to fear and shame.

To address the current behavior, a possible approach is to work on the sexual trauma history in order to release some of the denial, in order for Antonio to identify areas of injury and discover alternate means of addressing those wounds. Should Antonio feel judged about his current sexual behavior, however, he will undoubtedly expect judgment and shaming about his adolescent victimization. Because of the prevalence of homophobia in the adolescent's life, appreciation of Antonio's painful experience might ironically provoke a perception that he is being judged as "weak" or "girlish."

The misogyny inherent in homophobia not only robs the individual male of ease with his own gender, but installs a judgment about "femininity." A gay male is discouraged from expressing pain from a verbal assault; it would be "girlish," perhaps implicitly validating the attack. In order to access the trauma history, a foundation of acceptance for the fragmented split-off and criticized elements of his self must be established. Antonio needs to find value in his "femininity" so that, upon exploration of the childhood and adolescent narcissistic injuries, he might have compassion for himself. During the process of exploring these adolescent sexual traumas and their subsequent aftereffects, the current material can be woven back into an integrated whole. It is at this point that Antonio's self-esteem might be more solidly increased and ultimately his risk behavior, with effort, reduced.

While there exists a potential for growth and understanding with both Derek and Antonio, dynamics are also engendered by trauma making an "absolute" cure difficult. A good example can be found in what van der Kolk (1987) refers to as "addiction to trauma":

> It is likely that after exposure to severe and prolonged environmental stress, reexposure to traumatic situations in humans can evoke an endogenous opioid response, producing the same effect as temporary application of exogenous opioids. Opioids have psychoactive properties such as anxiolytic and tranquilizing action, a reduction in rage and aggression, antidepressant action and a decrease in paranoia and feelings of inadequacy.

The gay child develops in a maelstrom of severe and prolonged environmental stress. The existence of a biochemical addiction to the soothing opioid response would offer some explanation for the entrenchment of numerous behavior management issues in gay men, including excessive risk-taking. Perhaps, as is the case with HIV illness, a solid approach in these situations is harm reduction. In a harm reduction approach, the costs and consequences of a behavior are reduced by the active participation of the subject. If the survivor recognizes that there are biochemical changes that occur following engaging in unprotected sex, for example, that are in keeping with an opioid response, the task would be to find a substitute experience that is equally exhilarating. Clinician and patient work together to explore what exactly might unlock the cycle of traumatic reenactment.

Active participation of the patient must not be lost in reducing the harm of trauma in the lives of gay men. The changes that occur, the education around the issues, cannot simply be deposited in the individual. The patient must *participate* in the resolution. In the case when a particular patient has most likely suffered sexual trauma, one effective clinical approach is to state this opinion as being based on the information the patient has presented. It is up to the client to determine his relation and ultimately his *response* to the traumatic events.

With such an approach in individual and group therapy, the response to the trauma of HIV/AIDS may be more fully in the survivor's control. Instead of acting against the oppressor and ultimately damaging the self, the survivor may be able to control his sexual behavior. He may be able to reduce internal psychological stress and stave off ill health. It is important to note that this perspective would not be possible without the full spectrum of behaviors that existed at the emergence of the trauma and returned at this point in time. It is only in retrospect, as is true with many traumas, that we can appreciate the full impact of the event and more fully understand the responses to it. This argument is not meant to victim-blame prior responses to AIDS, such as HIV education. In the moment, they were necessary and helpful. However, at this time, like many coping strategies initiated to deal with trauma, they have outlived their usefulness and need to be replaced by more effective measures. It is in this way that the cycle of trauma can be broken.

REFERENCES

Allers, C., Benjack, K., White, J., & Rousey, J. (1993). HIV vulnerability and the adult survivor of childhood sexual abuse. *Child Abuse and Neglect, 17*, 291-8.

Altman, L. (1998, July 5). AIDS meeting ends with little hope of breakthrough. *New York Times*, p. 1.

Antoni et al. (1990). Psychoneuroimmunology and HIV-1. *Journal of Consulting & Clinical Psychology, 58*, 38-49.

Bandura, A. (1991). Self-efficacy mechanism in physiological activation and health promoting behavior. In J. Madden (Ed.), *Neurobiology of learning, emotion and affect*. New York: Raven.

Bandura, A. (1994). Social cognitive theory and exercise of control over HIV infection. In R. DiClemente & J. Peterson (Eds.), *Preventing AIDS: Theories and methods of behavioral interventions*. New York: Plenum.

Bartholow, B., Doll, L., Joy, D., Douglas, Jr., J., Bolan, G., Harrison, J., Moss, P., & McKirnan, D. (1994). Emotional, behavioral, and HIV risk associated with sexual abuse among adult homosexual and bisexual men. *Child Abuse and Neglect, 18*, 9, 747-61.

Carballo-Dieguez, A. & Dolezal, C. (1995). Association between history of childhood sexual abuse and adult HIV-risk sexual behavior in Puerto Rican men who have sex with men. *Child Abuse and Neglect, 19* (5), 595-605.

Cassese, J. (1993). The invisible bridge: Childhood sexual abuse and the risk of HIV infection in adulthood. *SIECUS Report, 21*, 4, 1-7.

Cassese, J. (1999). In the eye of the hurricane: A discussion of issues for HIV+ long-term nonprogressors. In M. Shernoff (Ed.), *AIDS & social work practice: Clinical and policy issues.* California: The Haworth Press, Inc.

Cole, S., Kemeny, M., Taylor, S., Vischer, B., & Fahey, J. (1996). Accelerated course of human immunodeficiency virus infection in gay men who conceal their homosexual identity. *Psychosomatic Medicine, 58*, 219-231.

Cunningham, R., Stiffman, A., & Earls, F. (1994). The association of physical and sexual abuse with HIV risk behaviors in adolescence and young adulthood: Implications for public health. *Child Abuse and Neglect, 18*, 3, 233-45.

DiClemente, R. & Peterson, J. (1994). Changing HIV/AIDS risk behaviors: The role of behavioral interventions. In R. DiClemente & J. Peterson (Eds.), *Preventing AIDS: Theories and methods of behavioral interventions.* New York: Plenum.

DiClemente, R. & Peterson, J. (Eds.). (1994) *Preventing AIDS: Theories and methods of behavioral interventions.* New York: Plenum.

Dilley, J., Woods, W., & McFarland, W. (1997). Treatment advances may be changing perceptions of risk. *New England Journal of Medicine, 337*, 7, 511-2.

Downey, L., Ryan, R., Roffman, R., & Kulich, M. (1995). How could I forget? Inaccurate memories of sexually intimate moments. *The Journal of Sex Research, 32*, 177-191.

Ekstrand, M., & Stall, R. et al. (1999). Gay men report high rates of unprotected anal sex with partners of unknown or discordant HIV status. *AIDS (13)*, 525-533.

Eldred, L. et al. (1997, January). *Adherence to antiretroviral therapy in HIV disease.* Paper presented at the 4th Conference on Retro & Opportunistic Infections, Chicago.

Elifson, K., Boles, J. & Sweat, M. (1993). Risk factors associated with HIV infection among male prostitutes. *American Journal of Public Health, 83*, 1, 79-83.

Erdelyi, M. (1994). Dissociation, defense and the unconscious. In D. Speigel (Ed.), *Dissociation: Culture, mind & body* (pp. 3-20). Washington, DC: APA Press.

Hays, R.B. et al. (1997). Unprotected sex and HIV risk taking among young gay men within boyfriend relationships. *AIDS Education and Prevention, 9*, 4, 314-29.

Hecht, F., Kahn, J., Dillon, B., Chesney, M., & Grant, R. M. (1998, June). *Transmission of protease inhibitor resistant HIV to a recently infected anti-retroviral naive man: The UCSF options primary HIV project.* Paper presented at 12th World AIDS Conference, Geneva.

Herman, J. L. (1992). *Trauma and recovery.* New York: Basic Books.

Hertogs, K., Larder, B., Mellors, J., Miller, V., Kem, S., Peeters, F., & Parwels, R. (1998, June). *Patterns of phenotypic and genotypic cross-resistance among protease inhibitors in over 1000 clinical HIV-1 isolates.* Paper presented at 12th World AIDS Conference, Geneva.

Hingson, R., Strunin, L., Verlin, B., & Heeren, T. (1990). Beliefs about AIDS, use of alcohol and drugs, and unprotected sex among Massachusetts adolescents. *American Journal of Public Health, 80*, 295-99.

Holtgrave, D., Qualls, N., Curran, J., Valdiserri, R., Guinan, M., & Parra, W. (1995). An overview of the effectiveness and efficiency of HIV prevention programs. *Public Health Reports, 110*, 2, 134-146.

Isaksson, A. (1996). Education as a key factor in fighting AIDS. In I. Schenkar, G. Sabar-Friedman & F. Sly (Eds.), *AIDS education: Interventions in multi-cultured societies*. New York: Plenum Press.

Kaliski, E., Rubinson, L., & Levy, S. (1990). AIDS, runaways, and self-efficacy. *Family Community Health, 13*, 1, 65-72.

Kelly, J., Murphy, D., Sikkema, K., & Kalichman, S. (1993). Psychological interventions to prevent HIV infection are urgently needed. *American Psychologist, 48*, 10, 1023-34.

Kelly, J., Lawrence, J. S. & Brasfield, T. (1991). Predictors of vulnerability to AIDS risk behavior relapse. *Journal of Consulting & Clinical Psychology, 59*, 1, 163-6.

Kingsley et al. (1987). Risk factors for seroconversion to HIV among male homosexuals. *Lancet, 1* (8529), 345-9.

Leiner, M. (1994). *Sexual politics in Cuba: Machismo, homosexuality and AIDS*. Colorado: Westview Press.

Lodico, M., & DiClemente, R. (1994). The association between CSA and prevalence of HIV-related risk behaviors. *Clinical Pediatrics, 33*, 8, 498-502.

Martin, J. & Knox, J. (1997). Self-esteem instability and its implications for HIV prevention among gay men. *Health and Social Work, 22*, 4, 264-273.

McGonagle, K., & Kessler, R. (1990). Chronic stress, acute stress, and depressive symptoms. *American Journal of Community Psychology, 18*, 5, 681-706.

Mellors, J.W., Kingsley, L.A., & Rinaldo, C.R. et al. (1995). Quantitation of HIV-1 RNA in plasma predicts outcome after seroconversion. *Annals of Internal Medicine, 122*, 573-579.

Nardone, A. et al. (1997). Surveillance of sexual behavior among homosexual men in central London health authority. *Genitourinary Medicine*, June, 762-766.

New York Times, 23/11/97.

New York Times, 5/7/98.

Pablos-Menez, A. et al. (1997, February) Nonadherence in tuberculosis treatment: Predictors and consequences in New York City. *American Journal of Medicine*.

Patton, C. (1989). The AIDS industry: Construction of 'victims,' 'volunteers,' and 'experts.' In E. Carter & S. Watney (Eds.), *Taking liberties: AIDS and cultural politics*. UK: Serpents Tail Press.

Richman, D.D. (1997, January). *Resisting resistance: Strategic approaches to preventing and coping with resistance to antiretroviral drugs*. Paper presented at the 4th Conference on Retro & Opportunistic Infections, Chicago.

Roffman, R., Stephens, R., Curtin, L., Gordon, J., Craver, J., Stern, M., Beadnell, B., & Downey, L. (1998). Relapse prevention as an interventive model for HIV risk reduction in gay and bisexual men. *AIDS Education and Prevention, 10*, 1, 1-18.

Roffman, R., Downey, L., Beadnell, B., Gordon, J., Craver, J., & Stephens, R. (1997). Cognitive-behavioral group counseling to prevent HIV transmission in gay and bisexual men: Factors contributing to successful risk reduction. *Research on Social Work Practice, 7* (2), 165-86.

Schenkar, I., Sabar-Friedman, G., & Sly, F. (Eds.). (1996). *AIDS education: Interventions in multi-cultured societies.* New York: Plenum Press.

Shafer, R., Winters, M., Palmer, S., & Merigan, T. (1998, June). Multiple concurrent reverse transcriptase and protease mutations and multidrug resistance of HIV-1 isolates from heavily treated patients. *Annals of Internal Medicine, 128,* 906-911.

Smith, M. et al. (1997, April). Ziduvine adherence in persons with AIDS, the relation of patient beliefs about medication to self-termination of therapy. *Journal of General Internal Medicine.*

Speigel, D. (1994). *Dissociation: Culture, mind & body.* Washington, DC: APA Press.

Steinberg, M. (1994). Systematizing dissociation: Symptomatology and diagnostic assessment. In D. Speigel (Ed.), *Dissociation: Culture, mind & body* (pp. 59-90). Washington, DC: APA Press.

Stolberg, G. (1997, November 23). Gay culture weighs sense and sexuality. *New York Times.* Week in Review, p. 1.

Van de Ven, P. et al. (1997, December). Sex practices in a broad cross-sectional sample of Sydney gay men. *Australia & New Zealand Journal of Public Health.*

Van der Kolk, B. (Ed.). (1987). *Psychological trauma.* Washington, DC: APA.

Wainber, M. & Friedland, G. (1998). Public health implication of antiretroviral therapy and HIV drug resistance. *Journal of the American Medical Association, 279,* 24 June. 1977-83.

Wallerstein, N. (1992). Powerlessness, empowerment, and health: Implications for health promotion programs. *American Journal of Health Promotion, 6* (3), 197-205.

Williams, A. et al. (1997, July). Adherence, compliance and HAART. *AIDS Clinical Care.*

Zierler, S., Feingold, L., Laufer, D., Velentgas, P., Kantrowitz-Gordon, I., & Mayer, K. (1991, May 5). Adult survivors of childhood sexual abuse and subsequent risk of HIV infection. *American Journal of Public Health, 81,* 572-5.

Cross Cultural Perspectives in Treating the Gay Male Trauma Survivor

James Cassese
Ernesto Mujica

SUMMARY. In recent years, there has been an increased emphasis on cultural considerations in psychotherapeutic treatment. Sound psychotherapy is ideally culturally sensitive and concerned with the context within which the client developed and exists. At the same time it is often difficult for many clinicians to navigate the cultural within the psychological framework. When both patient and clinician share more than one language in common, there are a variety of subtle issues that surface. In psychotherapy, "coordinate bilinguals," those who learn their languages separately, during different developmental stages and contexts, tend to have greater access to their emotional experiences within their first language. When the client presents with a sexual trauma history, the language spoken during the abuse will also have an effect on the language used in the psychotherapy. The case history of Lucio, a Latino gay male, is discussed in terms of the cultural and psychological elements of his treatment by a bilingual North American therapist. This therapist's psychotherapeutic conceptualizations and treatment approaches are examined and reviewed in a written dialogue/ discussion with a Latino psychologist. *[Article copies available for a fee from The Haworth Document Delivery Service: 1-800-342-9678. E-mail address: <getinfo@haworthpressinc.com> Website: <http://www.HaworthPress.com>]*

Ernesto Mujica would like to thank James Cassese for his generous offer to allow us to explore his experiences as a therapist. All too often therapists are wary of having others review their case material. This is particularly true when it comes to discussions of cultural issues in the treatment, as this area remains largely unexplored, leading therapists and patients alike to feel highly vulnerable when these topics are addressed.

[Haworth co-indexing entry note]: "Cross Cultural Perspectives in Treating the Gay Male Trauma Survivor." Cassese, James, and Ernesto Mujica. Co-published simultaneously in *Journal of Gay & Lesbian Social Services* (Harrington Park Press, an imprint of The Haworth Press, Inc.) Vol. 12, No. 1/2, 2000, pp. 153-182; and: *Gay Men and Childhood Sexual Trauma: Integrating the Shattered Self* (ed: James Cassese) Harrington Park Press, an imprint of The Haworth Press, Inc., 2000, pp. 153-182. Single or multiple copies of this article are available for a fee from The Haworth Document Delivery Service [1-800-342-9678, 9:00 a.m. - 5:00 p.m. (EST). E-mail address: getinfo@haworthpressinc.com].

KEYWORDS. Bilingual, coordinate bilingual, cultural issues, homophobia, gay male, sexual trauma

INTRODUCTION

The practice of psychotherapy and psychoanalysis as we know it is relatively young, dating back to Freud's early writings in the late nineteenth century. During the past hundred years, cultural norms, traditions, and even artistic expression, have largely been understood in psychological terms from analytic perspectives as a function of underlying instinctual drives which are transformed, or sublimated, into more socially acceptable forms of expression. Psychopathology has been understood to arise from the inhibition and undue frustration of instinctual gratification, a product of repression of unconscious desires which were unacceptable to the individual and/or their social context.

The question of culture, with its attendant implications of relationality and subjectivity, renders categorical clinical formulation in terms of psychopathology difficult. The Interpersonal school of psychoanalysis, which developed in the United States during the 1930s, emphasized that, in addition to psychopathology, cultural and economic influences are integral to the shaping of character development. Harry Stack Sullivan, Clara Thompson, Freida Fromm-Reichmann, and Ericc Fromm, are generally considered the founders of the Interpersonal School. Sullivan suggests that despite how well one may be acquainted with a particular culture or individual, the most effective stance of the clinician is to place him or herself in regard to the patient with the curiosity of a stranger. In so stating, Sullivan underscores the importance of inquiry and exploration, commonly known as the "detailed inquiry," while maintaining a watchful and cautious eye for the therapist's tendency to categorize, classify and interpret (Sullivan, 1972). Not only is therapists' understanding of the patient biased by their own cultural and personal history, but the act of intervening in the therapeutic interaction also has a specific impact on what takes place, how the patient feels, and what and how the patient attends to within the treatment experience.

Context and perspective are among the most vital components to be assessed in any examination of the factors involved in sexual trauma in gay men (see Introduction). The clinician seeks to understand the patient within the constellation of early childhood events, personality development as well as sociopolitical, cultural and religious variables. A variable that is difficult to "control for" has been the cultural influences on the patient. Combined with complications in assessment of sexual trauma in gay men, the factor of cultural influence exponentially increases the complexity of issues at hand. Minority sexuality status, a history of sexual trauma and cultural issues, create a complex matrix of shifting contexts and relativity of meaning.

This paper examines the interplay of these dynamics as demonstrated by a case history of a Brazilian patient treated by an Italian-American clinician, James Cassese. The therapist will present the case and some of the cultural questions that he experienced. This is followed by clinical commentary on the material by a Cuban-American psychotherapist, Ernesto Mujica. As the authors cannot, and indeed, *do* not wish to "speak for" their ethnic subgroup, this paper attempts an open discussion. As mentioned above, the interaction of these relative variables increases the vulnerability of interpretation to subjectivity. In response, this paper was written as a discussion. It is for the reader to explore and interpret the extent and nature of the impact of culture on the therapeutic work.

In this case, the therapist and patient are both gay, Caucasian and of approximately the same age. Such similarities often serve to enhance the sense of positive therapeutic engagement. However, the extent to which this is true will also depend on the degree to which each member of the dyad identifies positively with the characteristics which they share in common. In the following case, the dynamic tension within the treatment relationship is also influenced by important sociocultural differences. For example, the therapist is a native of the United States, who is thereby able to work in his profession of choice. The patient, an immigrant, is unable to obtain legal employment due to the fact that he was admitted into the United States under a tourist visa, which having expired, makes him an "illegal," undocumented resident.

Cassese

In practice with non-American clients, I have at times questioned the limits of clinical understanding in terms of negotiating the boundaries between an individual and his culture. I noticed (particularly with Brazilian patients) intense, indeed what might be seen as entrenched, relationships between mothers and sons. Initially I viewed these relationships in the context of a possibly incomplete separation-individuation process. However, there also appeared to be a specific pattern/profile that these patients shared which seemed to transcend class, education or birth order. From my perspective, the gay Brazilian men I treated uniformly idealized their mothers, sacrificing their own identities to present a perfect "image" to her. Each of these men had fled Brazil in order to live an ostensibly "open" homosexual life in the United States, retaining their heterosexual facade in Brazil. Although aware of a certain dissatisfaction with the limits on their ability to freely discuss their lives in these relationships, these men seemed to accept it as part of a compulsory arrangement. Mother is seen as all-sacrificing, nearly deified in this, the largest Catholic country in the world. Respect for one's mother takes on an almost religious imperative.

The question of how to conceptualize common psychological events (e.g, separation-individuation) in terms of a culture seemed analogous to locating context in the sexual trauma histories of gay men. Would separation from the mother result in a disconnection from the culture? If that were to occur, what positive purpose would it serve? To what extent was the reasoning used to explain the heterosexual facade in these Brazilian men a defensive rationalization? This parallels understanding the patient's subjective experience as defining criteria for trauma. If a gay man remembers the sexual interest of an adult as "affection," how does it help/interfere with the patient's process to label it as abuse? From a clinical standpoint, obvious aftereffects may be present, but the patient may have some investment in perceiving the events according to his contemporary cognitive schemas.

In trying to maintain my perspective to approximate the experience of the client, I struggled with another seeming cultural institution that seemed to have potential traumatic effects. There exists an unwritten cultural convention in Brazil that married heterosexual males may have sexual contact with gay males. The sex that occurs, however, is limited in scope and roles and is not necessarily considered homosexual. It seems that the identity labels are unequivocal: behaviors which would seem contradictory (e.g., in the United States) have little impact upon the identity of the individual in Brazil. This phenomenon is not limited to Brazilian culture. In describing this phenomenon in Cuban culture, Leiner (1994) explains that "to have sex with another man is not what identifies one as homosexual . . . for many Cubans, a man is homosexual only if he takes the passive receiving role."

This arrangement, with its obvious advantage to the heterosexual identified, and potential risk to the homosexual partner, was emotionally and intellectually challenging to understand as an American clinician. These dynamics come into play in the case discussion to follow. As there are implicit as well as explicit sanctions against homosexuality, this configuration seemed to reward the individual who could "pass," while subjecting the "passive/receptive" partner to danger. It further seemed to be reflected in the language of Brazilian Portuguese: the married male partner retains the descriptive noun "*o homem*" (masc.) while the passive/receptive male takes on the label of "*a bicha*" (fem.).

Because I am fluent in Portuguese, I am aware that its nouns and adjectives are gendered. I wondered whether the concept of a binary-gendered language, including self-referent nouns and phrases, had an impact on the child's identity or sense of self as inherently masculine or feminine. I also wondered about the influence *machismo* had upon the child's development–specifically its effect upon the gay child's vulnerability to abuse. The impact of these considerations has at times informed and confused my understanding of client issues. What, if any, are the limits on analytic scrutiny and interpretation of client material? When does the cultural supercede the analytic?

A number of Latino clinicians with whom I discussed this seemed reluctant to assign too great a meaning to the influence of *machismo* on trauma risk. Alex Carballo-Dieguez and Curtis Dolezal (1995) established connections between sexual childhood trauma and HIV risk in Puerto Rican gay men. However, Carballo-Dieguez was, in subsequent research efforts, unable to establish any more specific connections between childhood sexual trauma risk in gay men and Latin culture. The practicing clinicians with whom I spoke countered that Latin culture was no more "*macho*" than American. I wondered about the accuracy or defensive nature of *their* responses as well as *my* questions.

In order to be empathic with patients, the clinician must understand the highly personal meaning that the *patient* assigns to the elements in his life. This involves being attuned to the meaning derived from the patient's past cultural milieu as well as the current one. At the same time, the work of psychotherapy includes a certain amount of interpretation in terms of health and pathology. It became clear to me that in practice, culture can never be free from subjective interpretation. I wondered whether I was reluctant to interpret in order to be culturally sensitive and, as a result, less clinically effective.

Were there times, in deference to culture, I was overly reluctant to examine issues in order to be "culturally sensitive?" Might I have overlooked potentially rich clinical material by assigning it the category of culture? For example, I had learned to appreciate South and Central American *Spiritismo* and *Santeria* as religious constructions. The relationships and transactions within these religions also appear to lend themselves to unique expressions of personal dynamics. However, because these religions were not my own, I have hesitated to analyze the material from any other than a "hands-off," ergo "culturally sensitive" perspective. To what degree would I be likely to consider an issue in a cultural context for a non-American client, and in clinical terms in an American? Could that lead to different goals, if not expectations for these clients? Hypothetically, therefore, expectation for self-actualization might be different for a patient based more on culture than personality development. Ironically, a quest for cultural sensitivity might therefore result in a disservice to the non-American client.

The following case, that of Lucio, will first present the points of tension in the clinical work, with an eye toward some of the cultural dynamics. This will be followed by Dr. Mujica's clinical commentary.

Lucio

Lucio, a 33-year-old male homosexual, was referred to me within a community clinic by a physician from whom he was receiving treatment for asymptomatic HIV infection. Our work began at that clinic, and after I discontinued working there, Lucio moved to my private practice. The referring physician at the clinic had reported that Lucio had only recently discovered his HIV status, and was bi-sexual. A tall, slender man, Lucio's presentation was somewhat flat, and he was preoccupied with fears about the confidentiality of his interactions with the medical staff. He eagerly accepted psychotherapy as provided in the clinic setting, but indicated a certain amount of suspicion that he would not be required to pay for the treatment.

After I disclosed that I am gay, Lucio revealed that not only was he gay, but he had known his HIV seropositivity for six years prior. This event had in fact prompted his move to the US from abroad in order to escape what he considered an inevitable revelation of his sexuality via his health issues. He indicated a long-term depression and unstable self-esteem which had been the cause of much suffering for most of his life. He reported that when he looks in the mirror he sees an "old" "ugly," "skinny thing." His depressive symptoms included difficulty maintaining hygiene (despite that his presentation was always neat and well-groomed); constant hunger (which he would rarely satisfy, instead having a "glass of milk" for a meal) and sporadic impotence. He attributes this symptomatology, in part, to the fact that he has to work for a living in the United States. In South America, Lucio was part of an affluent family whose life included servants, and having all his expenses covered by his parents. He contrasts the luxury of having a car that was completely maintained by the family, for example, with having to clean toilets in this country. He interprets this contrast as the cost of being gay and having to leave home in order to find community. His status in this country was, at the time, undocumented, and he feared deportation. He has made it clear that he would suicide before returning to Brazil. He reported that he dislikes other Brazilians and observes that he has no interest in Brazilian culture (including food, music, media, etc).

Born the youngest of a family with eight children, Lucio observes that he was very close to his mother growing up, and resented his father for making his mother "miserable." The parents have only divorced since Lucio left South America. The mother is extremely financially successful; the father is barely able to keep his head above water. Lucio describes his sibling relationships as "not close," while at the same time he maintains weekly telephone contact with them. His mother is described as a sensitive woman at the mercy of an insensitive and oafishly chauvinistic husband. At the same time, Lucio does not appear to note the apparent contrast between this view of her, and her actual behavior. The mother owns a multi-million dollar business which she created from the ground-up. Harshly critical of her children, she "keeps them in line" with the threat of her disapproval. He remembers that when he was seven, he kissed his father good night before going to bed, and his mother became furious. She fumed that "men do not kiss men" and he was forbidden from that moment on from expressing any physical affection toward his father. At this point, he has not discussed his sexuality nor his HIV-infection with anyone in the family. He suspects that his parents are aware of his sexual orientation.

Lucio remembers as a child having sexual interest in boys, and in the tiny town in which he grew up, had oral and anal sex with a group of older boys who were friends of his brother. He was surprised when this sexual activity was reported by the boys (and some adults in the town) who ridiculed him for being the "passive." He was from that moment on vilified, although the other boys with whom he was sexual suffered no repercussions. He also reports that he finds no reason to assign relevance from these events to his current life. He has remarked "Maybe I was just a bad horny little faggot."

He reported an incident from a depressed period during his adolescence. Despondent, Lucio told his mother that he had a monster inside him that he wanted to destroy. He is certain that they both knew he was referring to his homosexuality. She responded: "Just kill it, Lucio, and be done with it already."

This patient has difficulty finding appropriate romantic involvements, although he indicates that his goal in life is to "get married" with a man. He rejects partners if they have any mannerisms which he would consider feminine. In his home country, he was brutally beaten publically by military police after he was caught having sexual contact with another male in a movie theater when he was 17. He also reported that his sexual partners of choice were often from the military police, but would be unable to have sex if they expressed the wish to be passive sexually with him.

Currently, Lucio's sexual life is limited to anonymous sex. If he is the "active"/penetrating partner, he feels disgust and rage at his partner when they are through. After, Lucio prefers that they not speak to him. If they do, he observes that he sometimes has the fantasy of murdering them. He has not been able to maintain "safer sex" precautions and observes that if his partner uses condoms, Lucio is unable to maintain an erection. He indicates that this is emblematic of his corruption, and insists I see him in those terms. Indeed, any attempt to indicate positive regard on my part has been met with silence or outrage. He also becomes upset if men "look at him" on the street, observing that he thinks they must think he is "gay" or "ugly."

During the course of the twice weekly treatment, Lucio was often silent during the session, quietly making faces, sticking out his tongue, puckering his lips or raising his eyebrows. These gestures, while puzzling, were also quite endearing. At times, after a lengthy silence, he would suddenly ask: "Do you think I'll ever get better?" He was often abruptly defensive, and almost any intervention was translated into a judgment. If I repeated exactly what he had said to me, he heard an inflection that implied that I thought it should be otherwise. This made it difficult to remain empathically attuned to him, because any attempt to reflect or clarify was experienced as criticism by Lucio.

He describes that it is often difficult for him to remember to brush his teeth, much less take his medicines. As a result of incorrect dosages, this patient has become resistant to a number of the current HIV medications. He is on the last available combination, which he has acknowledged taking inconsistently.

GENERAL CLINICAL DISCUSSION

The points of tension between the analytic and cultural have arisen both within my own thoughts and have been voiced by Lucio as well. I have wondered to what extent can this patient, within his cultural context, be prepared to separate from his mother and accept himself? What is the meaning of his rejection of all things Brazilian, from friends to food? Lucio does not wish to speak Portuguese with me, and rejects any implication that any of his behaviors or motivation are culturally influenced. In the context of this aversion to any exploration of the cultural, to what extent can the trauma be extracted from the setting within which it is steeped?

One of my hopes of an empathically accurate treatment of this patient was that he internalize the clinician as a positive self-object to sustain him as he repaired childhood injuries. This took on an added sense of urgency, because the patient was undocumented and HIV positive. His options for staying in the United States were severely limited. If some of these psychological conflicts and interpersonal issues were addressed (e.g., closeness with his family, intimacy with a partner, or abreactive trauma work), in the event that he was forced to return to Brazil perhaps he would understand that he possessed options other than suicide.

I hoped that once a level of trust had been established in the therapeutic relationship, he would then be able to examine the relationship with his parents with greater clarity. It appeared that Lucio's sense of himself was based upon a reflection of his mother's view of him as weak, needy and bothersome, and reinforced by the sexual events with the older boys. His relationship choices were often with men who were harshly critical or friends who appeared to find Lucio's needs excessive or inappropriate. I therefore prioritized the recognition/resolution of the internalized damage to Lucio's self-esteem and self-concept as an area that potentially would ameliorate his support network, his romantic choices, and his relationship with his family. As his mother was among those who ridiculed and shamed Lucio after his sexual contact with the older boys, his relationship with her seemed an efficient focus for treatment. However, I anticipated that an exploration of his relationship with his mother might be painful for him: it might create the occasion for her to be seen as imperfect. Ironically, should Lucio more fully separate from his mother, indeed not see her as all-good all-sacrificing, he would be at odds with a culture that requires this perspective of, at least, its male children. It has not been clear what prompts this perception of his mother as so vulnerable, when she is clearly a powerful woman.

How much of his view of her is culturally informed and how much related to her depression? How much of his mother is he seeing, and how much of the icon of the long-suffering *Mae* (mother)? If he begins to see her differently would he be, culturally speaking, a "bad son"? The danger here would be that this shift would give his ongoing sense of badness the chance to attach to another emblem of his wrong-doing. I considered that a negotiation of the cultural within the clinical needed to be established. Lucio would need to feel as though his separation from her were not culturally aberrant. I recognized that my hesitancy in approaching this with Lucio is different than it would have been if Lucio were North American.

I did not hazard a question, for example, on the discrepancy between his presentation to the physician as bisexual and to me as homosexual. I understood it as the natural pseudo-paranoia of an immigrant. Although the information had not been revealed at that point, I had a sense that he might also be undocumented. I imagined that, as such, he would not be likely to reveal something that might render him vulnerable to discrimination.

At one point, however, I tried to explore with him the meaning of his silences. The wordless quiet was troubling. I was concerned that my reluctance to address it indicated a collusion with his defenses. I suggested that we "try to understand what the silence means." He appeared to be furious, abruptly left that session, and missed the following. At the start of the subsequent session he announced that it would be his last, lamenting that he was "beyond help." Again he abruptly stood up, only shortly into the session, and left.

I was puzzled and concerned. However, I also sensed that we were in the arc of some transformation in our clinical relationship. Two weeks later he called to make another appointment, reporting that he felt "more depressed than ever." When he returned to treatment, he insisted that he pay more and see me less. He doubled the fee and made it a point to pay in advance. From that point on, he began to speak more in the treatment and examine himself with greater depth. He observed that "paying so little I felt bad telling you things, now I feel like I'm paying you more so you have to hear what I want to say."

I understood this to some degree in the cultural context of an immigrant who wanted to be treated like everyone else, which was expressed by his wanting to pay the same fee as others. However, it also seemed to illustrate Lucio's fragile psychic structure which was enormously reactive to narcissistic injury. A small slight sent him reeling, and he had clearly felt injured by having the silences addressed. In observing them, as well as when I mirrored his statements, he experienced criticism. To be seen, it appeared, was to be judged.

From a Self Psychological perspective, the child's nascent grandiosity requires notice in order to develop into healthy self-esteem. When Lucio was noticed, it was always in terms of his badness or difference. Lucio's idealizing needs were similarly frustrated. In the idealizing sphere the child wishes to merge with the parent in order to absorb the adult's capacity to tolerate and soothe strong emotion. It is through the Idealizing Sphere that the individual learns to be aware of, experience, and express his feelings. While Lucio seems to have tried to idealize his father, he was often deprived of this chance.

There existed a family myth that the father was just a "nice guy" (understood to mean a "nobody"), something Lucio is terrified will be true of himself. He often returns to a fear that he is boring. My attempt to examine the silence held up a critical mirror to him, producing a powerful reflection of worthlessness and feelings of inadequacy. As he was unable to reflect upon his silence in a non-judgmental manner, he interpreted it as meaning that he had nothing of interest to offer–that he was indeed boring. In addition to the immigrant context mentioned above, his increasing his fee while reducing his frequency of sessions reduced his "burdening" me and gave him something to offer (money).

Money has been a recurrent issue in the treatment. Having money is associated with his mother and not having it aligns him with his father's shortcomings. The eldest brother (and, in Lucio's view, the mother's favorite) had often joked that the father is a "nice guy." The implication was that the father is weak and foolish and everyone takes advantage of him. (Interestingly, I wonder if the father's "niceness" in the cultural context of being against the normative *"machismo"* or aggressiveness, may ironically make him "bad.")

In idealizing the mother, Lucio internalized a depressed and critical self-object. The original idealizing self-object informs the individual's ability to tolerate strong emotion and to soothe himself. Lucio's mother's attention was one of criticism, and his merging with her included this view. Lucio, however, has not spontaneously noted his mother's depression, but has indeed concurred with my suggestion that she may have been depressed. This internalized mirror views himself as bad and wrong. When people look at him on the street, he thinks they are "disgusted" by him. He is noticed, but *when* he is noticed, he is seen as bad or disgusting. This is reinforced not only by a mother who blithely suggested that he murder a part of himself, but by a culture that rewards his invisibility and discourages his visibility. As a result, Lucio's normal need to express himself and assert his views/wishes has been transformed into a fear of self-expression and a need to hide. The rewards of hiding are further reinforced by mother, family and culture.

Lucio has wondered why "I feel like I'm punishing myself." His ability to provide basic self-nurturing is impaired: he deprives himself of food or medicine, or takes his medicine incorrectly knowing that resistance can occur. With regard to unprotected sex, he regrets only the risk to his partner, seemingly unconcerned by his own risk. His romantic choices often fit her profile: dynamic, successful, hyper gender-identified people who seem indifferent to Lucio, belittle him and ultimately leave him. The maternal parallels are not lost on Lucio who seems to undermine the power of this insight with a powerless lament:

"What do I do about it? I can't help myself!" (from choosing these men).

I have understood these attractions and disregard for his own safety as a partial reenactment of the dynamic with the boys from his childhood. He is already infected: the toxic one; the "horny little faggot"; the boy who wants to kiss his father; the adolescent with the monster inside that he should "just kill already." He worries that he will never be able to be in control of his sexuality (and ability to take precautions against infection). This may have its roots in his natural desire for closeness with his father, the normalcy of which was implied by his mother to be unnatural. That the rest of the family belittled the father underscores the message that Lucio's wishes were abnormal. Further, the episode with the older boys traumatically sealed within him this sense of self as inherently bad.

It is unclear how the cultural might be included in this psychological understanding of Lucio's choices with regard to men and sex. The actual circumstances of Lucio's environment make it difficult to draw an accurate analogy to an American client. The sexual trauma that Lucio suffered as a child with the other boys would not have been possible in the same way in United States. The other boys *could* not have revealed Lucio's being the sexually receptive partner without suffering some stigma themselves as well. In the hierarchy of sexuality in the *Brazilian* culture, there is room for same-sex sexual activity where both partners are not subject to the same level of scrutiny and judgment. Interestingly, a few of the other Brazilian men that I have treated have endured strikingly similar circumstances in different parts of that country. In the United States, by contrast, same-sex relations are universally judged.

A fundamental difficulty involved approaching the trauma with Lucio, while appreciating the cultural context within which it occurred. Lucio learned from this event that there are different standards by which people are perceived. The older boys got away unscathed, but he endured ridicule and shaming from those around him (including his family and especially his mother). With the police, the older man with whom he was being sexual was able to escape the police, while Lucio was beaten in the face with a club. This repetitive pattern of victimization contains the dynamics that are reenacted with such uncanny precision that coincidence seems unlikely. Lucio appears actively involved in the pattern, being sexual, for example, with Military

Police while rejecting situations which do not play out the elements in the correct format.

In order to address some of the cognitive results of this recurrent pattern, the patient would re-formulate the thinking that was established by the trauma and maintained by its memories. In Lucio's case, there are cultural arrangements which acknowledge/accept that this unequal pattern of sexual relation is an existential possibility between *homem* and *bicha*. With an American, conversely, the universality of the bias against homosexuality allows for the possibility of an adult rejection of that inequality based on its obvious inequity. The mixed message in the cultural *homem/bicha* relation conveys that same-sex relations are under some circumstances allowable. They become wrong only if one happens to be the *bicha* (whose desires within the pair are considered to be "wrong"). How, as a clinician, can this be addressed, while not implying judgment about the culture that allows it? To what extent should it be examined? At what point does the culture become "off-limits"?

In the case of Lucio, he avoids all things Brazilian. He prefers to speak to me in English rather than Portuguese. He has few Brazilian friends, and obsessively clings to all things American. It is unclear whether this reflects solely his distaste for Brazilian things or a longing for that culture which is so intense that it makes the examination of the cultural issues intolerable.

Mujica

In this discussion I will highlight some of the transference and countertransference aspects which may be related to cultural influences on the patient's and therapist's experiences within the treatment relationship.

In examining the multiplicity of cultural influences within any treatment relationship, it is important to consider the cultural background of the therapist, the patient, and the cultural context within which they find themselves at present in the treatment relationship. The first two sources of cultural influence are more readily considered, and relate to the predominant sociocultural background of each member of the dyad. However, the sociocultural context of the treatment relationship is often overlooked despite its importance. During the initial phases of treatment, when the therapeutic relationship and the meaning of the patient's experience of being in therapy is often loaded with anxiety, the sociocultural context of the treatment is particularly significant.

For Lucio, the initial context of his treatment, a community clinic, has implications for the ways in which he experienced his therapist's interventions. Lucio initially discloses that he is bisexual when he is interviewed within the context of the community clinic. He exhibits mistrust of the fact that he would not be required to pay for therapy at the community based health center. Once he is within the context of his therapist's private practice, he reveals that he is gay. The issue of his initial suspiciousness and reluctance to state his sexual orientation may reflect some of his ambivalence about being gay. It is also, however, likely to be indicative of his distrust of authority and of the mental health profession. Though the therapist in this case is openly gay, the patient may nonetheless be prone to reasonable suspicions concerning the therapist's understanding and treatment approach. He may wonder how it is possible that someone in this profession could have escaped the inherent homophobia which has been associated with the mental health field in general.

Furthermore, as a foreigner, as a gay man, and as an undocumented immigrant, he may fear maltreatment and deportation as well. These are not irrational fears, but express a convergence of his own sense of discomfort with himself, with his accurate assessment of the potential hostility and rejection which may befall him for the mere reasons of his social status and sexual orientation. Fortunately, his therapist is sensitive to these issues and does not treat Lucio's suspiciousness and guardedness as a symptom of his illness, or resistance to treatment. Misunderstanding of a patient's behavior as pathological, when it consists of largely appropriate responses from the perspective of his own cultural background, or appropriate responses to unusual circumstances, can often lead to errors in diagnosis, as well as trigger the patient's wish to terminate treatment prematurely.

We learn that Lucio tends to choose men who use him sexually but are not emotionally available to him. He is prone to seeing himself as "gay and ugly," words which may be synonymous to him. We learn that his father was kind but distant, and that his mother contributed to the distancing between his father and him by drawing on a readily available sociocultural taboo against homosexuality. This is a good example of how his mother was able to use a social taboo against homosexuality in order to distort and hinder his expression of affection for his father. As a seven-year-old boy, he sought a goodnight kiss from his father, for which both he and his father were chastised and humiliated by his mother. This incident is not only an example of his mother's prohibition of his affection for his father, but also an example of how his natural longing for affection toward his father was sexualized and pathologized by using social taboos and biases.

Lucio's early childhood experience of being sexually penetrated by older boys, and then publicly humiliated, further pathologized his desire for closeness, acceptance and childhood exploration of his body and sexuality. He becomes the pawn of the older boys, who enact the social denigration of homosexuality, and perhaps deny their own homosexual feelings by abusing Lucio. His desire for closeness and sexual exploration with other boys is turned upon him for the purpose of scapegoating, through humiliation and further isolation. He is ridiculed for having been the passive *"bicha,"* a feminizing term which aims to strip him of his masculinity, self-assertiveness and pride. The path is further paved for him to associate his desire for intimacy and sexual pleasure with self-denigration and worthlessness.

One of the most recurrent issues in working with survivors of sexual abuse concerns their persistent range of difficulties with developing and sustaining self-esteem. Though this topic is discussed elsewhere, I would like to highlight some of the aspects which have to do with social and cultural factors. First of all, abuse of a child always takes place within the context of society. In addition, it takes place within the context of a specific relationship to the perpetrator(s), family, and others who may be conscious onlookers, knowing but not seeing, not telling, and not protecting. The fact that all forms of abuse take place within the context of the larger society plays an important role in influencing the young child to feel that he is worthless in relation to others who were not abused. The recurrent questions of "why me" become self-attacks: "because I am bad," "because I deserved it." As a result, the child seeks to maintain a sense of hope and control over future abuse by believing that he may be able to influence the perpetrator through his actions. Furthermore, the child learns to experience himself as soiled and damaged, not fit for belonging to society. When the abused child also happens to be gay, his sense of being damaged and unworthy are intensified by the rejections which he encounters regarding his sexual orientation.

For Lucio, a positive identification with his father as a source of affection and self-esteem is also undermined by the family myth that his father is "a nice guy," which is understood within their family to signify he is "a nobody." James Cassese notes that interestingly, the father's "niceness" in the cultural context of being against the normative "machismo" or aggressiveness may ironically make him "bad." I would argue that this is not so ironic, and that in fact this is also quite common in the United States, where being known as a "nice guy" can also be used to signify that one is "not so smart" or a "dope," a "wimp." Once again, his father's capacity for caring and goodness is portrayed within the family, primarily by his mother, in a negative light. This portrayal underscores that his father's kindness is a sign of weakness, not unlike his capacity for affection which is labeled as a sign of femininity and shameful homosexuality.

Indeed the term *macho*, which means "male" in Spanish, is deceptively useful in the United States for making that which is familiar, yet unacceptable, foreign. At times I have considered this term as the North American way of emotionally distancing from what is perceived as "bad masculinity" by making it foreign. *"Macho"* qualities can thereby be experienced as having been introduced from the outside, belonging to another culture. This is not unlike the way we have also experienced HIV as coming from the outside. As a nation, we delude ourselves into thinking that the HIV virus could not have developed in our own people, that it is the product of evil forces, of the sin of others–foreigners.

Sadly, it makes sense that Lucio's experience of feeling disgusted when other men look at him is rooted in the multiple rejections he has experienced for his being gay. It is interesting to note that the particular word which he uses, which in its Latin root refers to "bad taste," indicates a rejection of Lucio's natural desire (*dis* refers to negation, reversal or absence of an action, *gustus* means *taste*). The desire to taste expresses a wish to take in, to incorporate and savor. Lucio has learned to respond to his own desire by anticipating rejection at a visceral level. However, disgust is also a precursor to vomiting, a rejection of that which is experienced as bad-tasting or poisonous. I believe that Lucio's use of this word is over-determined by the multiple experiences of rejection he has had, as well as by the phobic rejection of his own desire for intimacy and sexual contact with other men.

In keeping with this theme, Lucio has also learned to experience disgust and express denial concerning his own body. Tragically, this negative self-regard and disdain may play a major role in his not being able to consistently protect himself and others from contracting STDs and HIV infection. With regard to the latter, it might be fruitful to explore the specific meanings which becoming HIV positive have for him, as well as the meaning of his infecting others. I speculate that this is a means by which he further expresses hostility towards himself and others, and additionally, that it is a means by which he expresses his longing to become a "member" of those who belong to the identifiable HIV positive group. This would make explicit his sense of being damaged, while simultaneously providing a sense of belonging. How does he perceive those who are positive? Had he secretly longed to become one of them, to get special status and special attention? Could this be a way of manifesting the anger and resentment he has harbored all his life for having been estranged from his father and sexually abused by others? Is he enacting society's hatred against homosexuals–that indeed he should not exist? Does he ever get the message, or feel like the world would be a better place without him? These are likely to be painful issues to explore, and I would do so only with careful attention to the patient's ability to cope with the anxiety and emotional turmoil that may emerge during such inquiry. However, such inquiry may help him recognize the reasons for which he continues to place himself and others in danger. He may then more consciously proceed to explore less self-destructive ways of expressing the feelings he has denied himself from asserting more openly, while also working more consciously to engage in safer sex practices.

It is also noteworthy that another aspect which may contribute to Lucio's not protecting himself concerns his tendency to dissociate. One's tendency toward dissociation is often exacerbated as a function of immigration, living in a different culture and using a second language. Furthermore, dissociation is a major defense associated with a history of sexual abuse, and can strongly contribute to individuals' inability to take action to protect themselves when faced with future threatening situations. With regard to Lucio, he may experience dissociation during sexual situations as a way of participating while also maintaining a sense of himself as separate and protected from the actual interaction with his sexual partner.

Finally, I will directly address some of James Cassese's questions garnered from this text as well as during conversations regarding this paper.

Cassese

At what point does the cultural become "off-limits" in psychotherapy?

Mujica

This is a frequently asked question by many clinicians who are interested in taking the influence of culture into account in their work. I believe that nothing is off limits in terms of our expressing curiosity and exploration. Asking questions in an open-ended manner is helpful. For example, "how do you feel that the closeness which you have with your mother has affected you in your relationships with others?" In reality, however, patients will often pick up on the fact that you think there is something wrong, that you are critical of something they consider harmless. At this juncture it is best to be candid about the issue in order to not add to the patient's sense of confusion and mystification. I may ask the patient: "How do you feel about my having asked you that question?" Furthermore, it is sometimes helpful to express one's concern more directly, e.g., "I come from a different culture, where men tend to emphasize their emotional independence from their mothers. I find that I am concerned with your closeness to your mother. I wonder whether you may be limiting yourself from being better able to develop intimate relationships with others, but I hesitate to explore this with you because I fear my concern is a result of my bias." This allows the patient to hold a larger portion of the deck of cards in play, and may help him to take a more explorative, less defensive stance.

Cassese

It occurs to me that if I slip into the patient's first language, which in this case is also the language of the perpetrator, this will be experienced by the patient as a boundary violation. I would be speaking in the language of the perpetrator before the patient is ready to do so himself, before he invites me into that part of his experience. I have also considered that the patient's first language is more likely to encode the traumatic material. In effect, one might say that the first language contains the traumatic material in a manner that is dissociatively encoded. In contrast, Lucio's second language is the language of psychotherapy and offers an opportunity to reflect upon these issues.

Mujica

Lucio is aware that Portuguese is his therapist's second language. The power imbalance that currently exists within the treatment (in that James is more fluent in English than Lucio), would shift if the language switches to Portuguese. Were they to conduct more of the treatment in Portuguese, Lucio could experience himself as being in a position of dominance over his therapist, which may feel uncomfortable for him for numerous reasons. By conducting the sessions in English, it may be that Lucio is able to maintain a greater sense of reliance on and support from his therapist. Though he may be better able to express himself in Portuguese, Lucio may feel he is better understood by his therapist in English. He may feel better taken care of in English, as his therapist is also more likely to feel he has greater access to a broader range of emotional sensitivity and professional ability in English rather than Portuguese. These are some of the many themes that may emerge as the experience of language use and switching is explored.

Using another language is not unlike casting another light to obtain a second profile of the same subject. If Lucio were to switch to speaking Portuguese with James, he may learn things about James that he would rather not have to contend with at this time in their treatment. For example, he may begin to wonder how it is that James learned Portuguese. Certainly, one does not become fluent in a second language without significant effort, requiring considerable motivation. Lucio may wonder what motivated James to learn Portuguese. He may suspect that James may have family in Brazil, or perhaps that he lived there previously, or that he has a Portuguese-speaking partner.

It is generally good advice to stick to the *patient's* language choice when both patient and therapist are fluent in more than one language. Language switching should generally follow the patient's lead. Multilingual clinicians tend to agree unanimously with this technical position (Perez-Foster et al., 1996).

When we speak of first and second language we are making a distinction which indicates that both languages were learned at different times during the person's development and within different social, cultural, and even emotional contexts. The later in life that the second language is learned the greater will be the emotional resonance or connectedness of the first language over that of the second. The first language is privileged over the second insofar as it more consistently elicits a stronger affective response, as well as more deeply felt bodily sensations and perceptual experiences associated with early memories. Those who learn their main languages during the same early developmental stages, prior to age five or six, are considered "compound bilinguals." They are more likely to have equal access to similar emotionally relevant associations in both languages. This is especially true if the languages were spoken equally within their significant relationships. In psychotherapy, "coordinate bilinguals," those who learn their languages separately, during different developmental stages and contexts, tend to have greater access to their emotional experiences within their first language. However, coordinate bilinguals may use the greater emotional distance available to them in their second language to bolster their ability to maintain secondary process thought, thereby maintaining an enhanced sense of safety from being flooded by their emotional experience.

I have worked with several coordinate bilingual patients who, like Lucio, have chosen to conduct psychotherapy in their second language at various times during the treatment, despite the fact that they were more fluent in their first language. In all cases where this has occurred patients have reported a history of trauma, namely, physical and/or sexual abuse in their early history and country of origin. These patients have indicated that speaking in their second language, English, permits them to discuss emotionally painful issues with a greater sense of control and greater emotional distance from the impact of the original trauma.

For example, a woman who had been repeatedly sexually abused by her father during childhood clearly stated that she wanted to get as far as possible from the abuse she had suffered. She stated that she had left her country of origin in order to have a new life, that she felt much safer, and less of a potential victim, when she speaks in English. Two gay patients also come to mind, for whom Spanish was also their first language. One man told me that he preferred to use English during our sessions because of the severity of abusiveness he had experienced in his country of origin due to the severe homophobia that was prevalent in his family and culture. He poignantly expressed in English that he could talk to me without too much difficulty about being called a "faggot," but that it would take a long time in treatment before he could use the same word in Spanish (*maricón*, which he did not verbalize in Spanish at the time). He explained: "I don't want to open the door to those feelings. Maybe I'd start crying and couldn't stop. It's too painful and makes me very angry." A second gay man with a childhood history of sexual abuse, who has done much of his healing by reading self-help books in English and by participating in 12-step programs such as Sexual Compulsives Anonymous and Al-Anon, stated: "I don't have the words of my recovery from my sexual abuse in my first language. English has been the language of my recovery." Both of these men cautiously expressed an interest in expanding their exploration to increase their use of their first language in psychotherapy, and have gradually been able to do so.

With regard to the transference-countertransference engagement, language switching may become the means by which an aspect of the patient's trauma becomes reenacted within the treatment. I concur that the therapist's switching into the patient's first language, without the patient having done so first, can constitute an experience of boundary violation. The meaning of this experience is, of course, specific to the particular patient and therapist given the context of their personal histories as well as the history of their therapeutic engagement up until that moment. Language switching may also represent a seductive ploy to intensify the visceral and emotional experience in the moment, which may have negative and/or positive consequences to the treatment depending upon the therapist's ability for introspection and capacity to take responsibility for whatever impact his actions have upon the patient's experience.

Another point worth keeping in mind is that the first language is not only more likely to be closer to the experience of trauma, but also to negative self-experiences. Negative self-esteem and self-blame are often a consequence of post-traumatic reactions. Self-blame and self-denigration are often associated with feelings which arise from victimization, such as intense fear, helplessness and hopelessness. Lucio's first language is more likely to tap into feelings of negative self-esteem and unworthiness which are associated with the original abusive experiences as well as with the repeated experiences of internalized shame and self-blame. Futhermore, this is augmented by the intense homophobia which Lucio associates with his first language and culture of origin.

Lucio might experience James as yet another perpetrator should James switch into using Portuguese before Lucio speaks Portuguese himself. Though James may consciously decide to follow Lucio's lead in this respect, he may nonetheless "slip" into speaking Portuguese. If so, it is important to open the dialogue for Lucio to express how he feels about this in the moment. One may ask: "What is it like for you when I speak in Portuguese? How do you feel in relation to me when I switch into Portuguese without your having done so first?" Lucio may state that it makes no difference to him, in which case he may not be ready to discuss the details of this experience. However, having asked these questions communicates to Lucio that one understands and is accepting of the fact that he may feel differently about speaking English or Portuguese, and that the action of switching from one language to another can elicit a change in one's emotional experience, and in the emotional state of the relationship. By addressing these experiences in the moment in which they occur, one can begin to slowly work through in the *here and now* of the therapeutic relationship past traumatic experiences of seduction, boundary violation, and shifts in control and power.

Cassese

In the context of an aversion to any exploration of the cultural, to what extent can the trauma be expected to be extracted from the setting within which it is steeped?

Mujica

I recognize that, for Lucio, the very act of pursuing an analysis of his experience in relation to categorical terms (e.g., Brazilian/American, Gay/Bisexual/Straight, Victim/Perpetrator), may set into motion his defensive operations. I suspect that he correctly anticipates that once he is categorically labeled he is more vulnerable to being re-victimized and shamed. Another factor that may be playing an important role in his guardedness when discussing issues of culture may concern his fear of experiencing himself as different from his therapist. Numerous reasons may motivate this possibility, including a fear of experiencing heightened negative transference feelings if he experiences his therapist as "other" and different from himself. He may feel more vulnerable, in this respect, toward engaging in more hostile projections, becoming more likely to experience his therapist, for example, as a potential perpetrator or as a rejecting parental figure. Accordingly, Lucio may be protecting his sense of closeness to his therapist; he may protect his positive experience of his therapist in order to enhance his sense of safety, as well as his potential for developing greater feelings of trust, idealization, and identification, in a way that he was not able to achieve with his father.

Another aspect to this issue may concern his desire to take distance from identification with his culture of origin. Identifying himself as a New Yorker, or better yet, a gay New Yorker, may hold more positive forms of self-affirmation. I suspect that as a gay New Yorker he is able to uphold a more hopeful and uplifting self-image, and a more integrated, less threatened sense of self than when he thinks of himself as a Gay Brazilian. As such, I imagine that the more humiliating and undermining self-experiences associated with epithets such as "*bicha*" are more likely to surface. He may become less defensive about addressing cultural issues as he progresses toward more stable, positive self-esteem, hand in hand with his identification as a gay man, and as a worthwhile human being who is worthy of respect and love. However, much of the therapy may take place in English before Lucio feels secure enough to discuss his experiences in Portuguese.

Cassese

Would separation from the mother result in a disconnection from the culture? If that were to occur, what positive purpose would it serve? To what extent was the reasoning used to explain the heterosexual facade in these Brazilian men a defensive rationalization?

Mujica

Generally, if the patient is unwilling to discuss issues of culture, the therapist does best to be respectful of the patient's wishes and follow the patient's lead. It may well be that Brazilian men who maintain their sense of "heterosexuality" by emphasizing that they play a "dominant," or "active"/"insertive" role during sexual contact with other men are largely rationalizing and negating their own homosexual desires. However, sexual contact is also used as a form of aggression, most obviously during acts of sexual abuse. Within Lucio's recurrent abusive relationships with men, it is understood that the positive esteem and status of one partner is to be maintained at the expense of denigration of the partner who is identified as homosexual–he who is receptive in oral or anal sex must suffer the consequence of humiliation.

It is curious to consider that a more reciprocal form of sexual contact, such as mutual masturbation or mutual fellatio, would most likely be understood as homosexual behavior on the part of both men. The implication here is that caring, and perhaps affection for the other, through concern for mutual pleasure, would undermine the higher status of the heterosexually-identified male. Thus, not caring for the other's pleasure is a prerequisite, as is denigration of the other in order to preserve one's higher status. From this perspective, it is imperative that a non-mutual form of sexual contact take place in order for one of the partners to "survive" the sexual encounter with self-esteem intact. To some extent this is true in the United States, where someone may be referred to as a "cocksucker" and thereby gay, for example, without implying that the person who is receiving fellatio is homosexual. Only the one who performs fellatio is the "fag." The experiential differences between cultures regarding these categorizations and sexual behaviors are importantly, however, a matter of difference of degree and severity.

Cassese

How can we understand the mother-child relationship in this case considering basic psychological issues as well as the cultural context which may impact the idiosyncratic formation of these dynamics?

Mujica

Psychotherapeutic treatment, when it includes the exploration of unconscious dynamics and sociocultural effects, is by its very nature subversive of cultural assumptions and norms. This is true despite the fact that social biases are also imbedded within any theoretical approach and clinical treatment. From this vantage point, cultural norms and taboos become the target of psychotherapeutic inquiry, whether one is exploring the impact of a familiar or foreign culture. Either way, one is seeking to enhance one's awareness of that which has been repressed, dissociated, or more consciously disowned.

With regard to Lucio, part of his disowned experience concerns his rage toward his mother. I would speculate that he turns this rage on himself, as he tries to protect her and their relationship, as well as protect himself from her anger. He seems to guard his closeness to her wherein he identifies with her powerful rejecting and denigrating aspects. Indeed, through support of the sanctity of respect and adoration of the mother in his culture of origin, he is dissuaded from confronting these issues. In a similar manner, Lucio has accepted, to a large extent, the homophobic attitudes of his culture of origin. He is particularly rejecting of any "feminine" characteristics he possesses or perceives in others. He denigrates himself and other men for desiring penetration during sexual intercourse. However, given the fact that he has immigrated to the United States, he is also seeking to maintain his gay identity and expand his capacity to live in keeping with his sexual orientation. Much of his suffering stems from this central conflict between his homosexual longing and his homophobia. It is perhaps inevitable that he will own more of his anger toward his mother's rejection of his homosexuality as he becomes more aware and accepting of these conflictual aspects of himself. To this extent, he will also lose aspects of his identification with his mother, and with his culture of origin, as he finds greater inner freedom from their punishing and restraining effects.

Lucio's mother, and his internalized sense of her authoritarian and shaming aspects, seem to play a major role in the way he feels about himself and others. From an early age, it appears that Lucio's mother interrupted his attempts to establish emotional closeness with his father. Lucio's mother used the readily available homophobia in their cultural milieu as a way of poisoning their mutual affection and attachment. Lucio states that, as a young boy, she shamed him when he requested a good night kiss from his father. She referred to this behavior as effeminate and essentially homosexual, thereby sexualizing otherwise normative, positive attachment between them. To the extent that Lucio has incorporated his mother's negative attitudes about his emotional and sexual desires for closeness and attachment to other men, he maintains a shaming and denigrating attitude which undermines his ability to maintain stable and positive self-esteem. This also interferes with his ability to develop intimate and loving relationships with men. Though he consciously wants to get away from the severity of condemning homophobia of his family and culture of origin, he nonetheless may be unconsciously protecting his bond to his mother by maintaining a substantial amount of homophobic attitudes himself. Ultimately, it seems that Lucio's homophobic prohibitions and shaming lead to a sense of emotional starvation, one which he acts out through periods of actual anorectic behaviors.

It also occurs to me that part of the "monster" which his mother has identified in him, and which he continues to feel is present in himself, is the "monster" which is voraciously hungry for a sense of mastery, efficacy and love, as well as open affirmation of his sexual orientation. I speculate that this "monster" is a consequence of his keeping himself from having the fullness of emotional and sexual intimacy which he craves. This same "monster" may be the aspect of Lucio which knows, but is unable to speak, of the intense feelings of anger about the emotional and sexual castration which he has experienced in his relationship with his mother. He keeps the rage and knowledge which this "monster" possesses at bay, thereby protecting his relationship to his mother, and protecting himself from his fears of further annihilation and humiliation by her. He seems to maintain an attachment to an internalized maternal self-object that possesses these characteristics. It may be most efficient and beneficial for him to attend to the ways in which he finds himself limiting his own ability to be more outspoken and honest about his feelings and desires, especially within the treatment relationship. Under what circumstances does he seem to inhibit or deaden himself? When does he engage in self-humiliation and shaming? What is he keeping himself from pursuing by engaging in these experiences? How do these issues affect the way he experiences his relationship with his therapist?

It may be that important countertransference feelings are interfering with a more explorative and less inhibited stance within the therapeutic relationship. One may explore what is impinging upon the therapeutic inquiry that may stem from the therapist's own life experience. The therapist might consider the nature of one's relationship with one's own mother. What role does one feel one's mother played vis-à-vis one's relationship with one's father, and vis-à-vis one's ability to embrace and pursue intimate emotional and sexual relations with others? At what moments during the therapeutic engagement does the therapist feel that much more is going on than is being addressed? One can attend to these experiences in the moment, despite one's usual sense of foreboding dread or sense of unknowing, by verbalizing some sense of awareness concerning the immediate experience. With regard to Lucio, this may concern, for example, a moment in which James feels that Lucio has stated something which reflects a strengthening of his attachment to his mother at the expense of self-humiliation or some other form of denial of important aspects of himself. James may feel hesitant to note this because he feels Lucio will be quickly dismissive. James may also have a sense that Lucio is aware of a good amount of what is transpiring in the moment. One might then ask: "I have a sense that a lot is going on right now that we are not putting into words. What is it that you are aware of? What is your sense of what is happening between us right now?"

Another alternative is to state more directly one's own conflictual experience in the moment: "I wanted to ask you about how your feelings of humiliation may be related to your wish to protect your closeness with your mother, but I feel hesitant to do so. I felt you would be quick to tell me that what I'm thinking and feeling is irrelevant." Exploring one's countertransference within the treatment experience is never an easy task. It often involves feeling afraid and vulnerable, as well as clumsy and inarticulate. The work needs to take place within one's own self-exploration, treatment, and supervision outside of the consulting room, as well as during the immediate experiences of heightened anxiety, avoidance, or dissociation in the presence of our patient. I believe that what is most helpful about one's ability to speak and question at these junctures in the treatment dialogue, when words seem to quickly disperse and disappear, is that we express an experience of interest and curiosity. By so doing, we encourage patients to take notice of the unspeakable, and to venture in an accepting and open-ended manner an exploration and appreciation of themselves.

CONCLUDING COMMENTS

It seems clear that the complexity of the dynamics within a cross-cultural psychotherapeutic relationship, their subjectivity and availability to interpretation make it difficult to adhere to any absolute rules regarding the clinical observations of cultural material. Concrete strategies such as following the patient's lead when both client and therapist are bilingual are helpful. However, a discussion such as contained in this paper often raises more questions than it can answer.

For example, Ernesto's comments about the use of the term "*macho*" are important considerations. In interpreting a "bad" or "other" masculinity in the term, the American use of it could also be seen as an appropriation, a metaphoric semantic exploitation. This type of colonialism/imperialism is woven into North American cultural history. From this context, could the North American political interest in cultural sensitivity be seen in another context as an intellectual attempt to colonize a foreign element? At the same time, if the first language of a bi-lingual patient could be the "language of the perpetrator," and the second language serve as the language of healing, what are the ramifications for the first language? How does the healing translate into that first language?

The complexity of issues that converge on a gay male survivor of sexual trauma who is being treated by a therapist from another culture is enormous. Differences within the psychotherapeutic dyad, as well as the issues of sexuality, culture and trauma interplay to create a delicate matrix. While Ernesto ascribes to the Interpersonal School, and James uses a Self Psychology orientation, the fundamental interest in empathy, in expressing interest in and curiosity about the patient is shared by these approaches. It appears that one conclusion we can draw from this discussion is that these questions are to be discussed and examined, as appropriate, between individual therapist and patient. It is up to the reader to decide, whether patient or therapist, how and when to approach these issues in the therapeutic relationship.

REFERENCES

Blechner, M. J. (1995). The shaping of psychoanalytic theory and practice by cultural and personal biases about sexuality. In T. Domenici & R. C. Lesser (Eds.), *Disorienting sexuality, psychoanalytic reappraisals of sexual identities*. New York: Routledge.

Carballo-Dieguez, A. & Dolezal, C. (1995). Association between history of childhood sexual abuse and adult HIV-risk sexual behavior in Puerto Rican men who have sex with men. *Child Abuse and Neglect, 19* (5), 595-605.

Drescher, J. (1995). Anti-homosexual bias in training. In T. Domenici & R. C. Lesser (Eds.), *Disorienting sexuality, psychoanalytic reappraisals of sexual identities*. New York: Routledge.

Freud, S. (1905/1962). Three essays on sexuality. In *The standard edition of the complete psychological works of Sigmund Freud, 7* (pp. 123-46). London: Hogarth Press.

Leiner, M. (1994). *Sexual politics in Cuba: Machismo, homosexuality and AIDS.* Colorado: Westview Press.

Lionells, M., Fiscalini, J., Mann, C., & Stern, D. B. (1995). (Eds.). *Handbook of interpersonal psychoanalysis.* New Jersey: The Analytic Press.

Perez-Foster, R. M. (1996). Assessing the psychodynamic function of language in the bilingual patient. In R. M. Perez-Foster, M. Moskowitz, & R. A. Javier (Eds.), *Reaching across boundaries of culture and class* (pp. 243-263). New Jersey: Jason Aronson.

Sullivan, H. S. (1972) *Personal psychopathology: Early formulations.* New York: Norton.

Van der Kolk, B. (Ed.). (1987). *Psychological trauma.* Washington, DC: APA.

New Directions for Research Examining Sexual Trauma Histories of Gay Men

James Cassese

SUMMARY. Research efforts have been unable to accurately examine the effect of childhood sexual trauma in the adult lives of gay men. Complications stemming from precise definitions of abuse, as well as the subjectivity inherent in the terms, make comprehensive research difficult. As abuse and traumatic events may sometimes be subtle and not involve overt violence, these more delicate events are often over-looked or unaccounted for. Further, because it is a complex endeavor to obtain accurate reporting from children, research efforts rely on the self-reports of adults remembering traumatic events. The symptomatol-ogy that results from trauma, including amnesia and dissociation, also affects the reliability of self-report. Additionally, gay men have been notably absent from sexual trauma research efforts for a variety of reasons. A research study which investigates childhood sexual trauma in the histories of adult gay men is discussed. Directions for future research efforts are suggested. *[Article copies available for a fee from The Haworth Document Delivery Service: 1-800-342-9678. E-mail address: <getinfo@haworthpressinc.com> Website: <http://www.HaworthPress.com>]*

KEYWORDS. Gay men, homophobia, research, sexual trauma, sexual abuse

Accurate, comprehensive research examining sexual trauma in gay men has been elusive due to a variety of factors. A sexually traumatic

---

[Haworth co-indexing entry note]: "New Directions for Research Examining Sexual Trauma Histories of Gay Men." Cassese, James. Co-published simultaneously in *Journal of Gay & Lesbian Social Services* (Harrington Park Press, an imprint of The Haworth Press, Inc.) Vol. 12, No. 1/2, 2000, pp. 183-193; and: *Gay Men and Childhood Sexual Trauma: Integrating the Shattered Self* (ed: James Cassese) Harrington Park Press, an imprint of The Haworth Press, Inc., 2000, pp. 183-193. Single or multiple copies of this article are available for a fee from The Haworth Document Delivery Service [1-800-342-9678, 9:00 a.m. - 5:00 p.m. (EST). E-mail address: getinfo@haworthpressinc.com].

183

event is, in itself, difficult to measure and codify. "By its very nature, sexual abuse is a problem that is concealed" (Finkelhor, 1986). It often occurs within a complex setting which, by design, obscures the identification of single event as "traumatic." Abusive events occur within larger contexts, and discussions of a single episode frequently include associations to other situations. A sexually traumatic event also often exists within a matrix of co-factors which themselves range from subtle to explicit, from seductive to emotionally coercive or violent. The use of the adjectives "traumatic" or "abusive" is also highly subjective and implies relativity.

The childhood sexual abuse of gay men as the focus of this type of research further complicates matters. The sexual abuse of gay boys occurs within a context, a norm of homophobic discrimination, ridicule, and violence. To single out one event as traumatic may be impossible. Additionally, the relativity of trauma can at times be confusing or counterintuitive. For example, the gay boy who is coerced into sex by an older boy or adult may remember that event with less horror than the constant ridicule and torture he suffered daily in school or at home. Even within these events, however, there exists a range. How can researchers measure ridicule and humiliation (and the frequency of those events) objectively? Does the threat of violence need to be included in order for it to "count" as traumatic?

The terminology involved in discussing sexual trauma can also become confusing or imprecise. How does abuse differ from trauma? How can either or both be measured for research purposes? Abuse itself, due to the subjective nature of the adjective, makes it difficult to define. While trauma seems to offer an implication of objectivity, it is also prone to subjective limits. The word trauma is often confined to situations that are extreme in nature. Indeed, to qualify for a PTSD diagnosis according to the APA Diagnostic and Statistical Manual of Mental Disorders (DSM-IV), for example, the individual must have "experienced, witnessed, or was confronted with an event or events that involved actual or threatened death or serious injury, or a threat to the physical integrity of self or others." The term trauma rarely captures those more subtle events which also produce traumatic aftereffects. Further complicating the terminology, the terms are often defined by researchers looking to codify and examine specific phenomena. Doll et al. (1992) imply that, in the light of those who "have criticized researchers who assume that all intergenerational sexual relationships are emotionally traumatic," it might be efficacious for research to focus on only those events that involve violence or coercive force. Herman (1992) observed that "the severity of traumatic events cannot be measured on any single dimension; simplistic efforts to quantify trauma ultimately lead to meaningless comparisons of trauma." As a result, events that clients, psychotherapists, and educators may recognize as traumatic are often unrepresented in the research literature.

This paper examines some of the complexities involved in research regarding gay men and sexual trauma. Some of the pitfalls and obstacles to accurate evaluation are discussed, and suggestions for new directions in research are offered.

One of these complexities is the absence of a clear-cut definition of sexual trauma in the non-research literature. Often the definitions are offered in the context of how those used by the author contrast with other definitions, almost invariably offering some relationality. Courtois (1988) reviews some of the research definitions of incest before providing her own:

> I use the word "incest" to describe intrafamilial sexual violation because it is the most commonly used term; however, rather than stressing the differences between rape and incest, I emphasize their similarities. Incest is a form of rape (as defined from the feminist perspective)–rape within the family, with additional potential for damage to the victim due to the relationship between perpetrator and victim.
>
> –Courtois (1988)

Courtois places "her" definition of incest within a context of those definitions already established by others. Similarly, Mike Lew (1988) in his groundbreaking *Victims No Longer* does not offer a concrete definition of abuse, but offers what he identifies as the following "feelings": "I believe that children have a right to care and protection. This right is absolute. When anyone who is in a position of greater power–strength, authority, or experience–violates that right in any way, that behavior is abusive." He then goes on to define incest in the context of that which has already been defined, and emphasizes the setting in which that type of abuse occurs.

A number of fairly comprehensive texts on the subject ironically offer *no* definition of incest or sexual trauma (McCann & Pearlman,

1990; Messler-Davies & Frawley, 1994). The variety of research studies, even those few concerning men, rarely agree on a definition of trauma. They are often contingent upon some age discrepancy between victim and perpetrator. Some studies demarcate abuse as "sexual relations" occurring when the child is less than 13 years old with someone four or more years or older (Carballo-Dieguez & Dolezal, 1995), while others increase the age of the subject to less than 16 years of age, with the perpetrator of "sexual contact" needing to be at least five years older than the subject. One research study examining the phenomenon of "why males report having liked it" defined sexual abuse as a sexual relationship before puberty with someone at least four years older (Fischer, 1991).

Even if a single definition of abuse, such as the one offered in the introduction to this collection of papers, was codified, it would still be subject to the complications of any study which relies on self-report. "There are problems to asking . . . questions of children who are currently victims. Parents would be unlikely to give permission to interview them, and children might be put in danger of retaliation if they did tell" (Finkelhor, 1986). This has placed the focus on adults being asked to remember and discuss childhood events; researchers therefore rely on a certain amount of deductive reasoning in finding applications for this information.

Herman (1992) reminds us that survivors often tell their stories in a disjointed, sometimes contradictory manner. Further, the way in which the question is posed may or may not elicit the relevant information. A questionnaire would need to be fairly exhaustive to cover the variety of manifestations of a sexual trauma. Conversely, if it is too general, the survivor may not volunteer information, or may be confused as to what the researcher is asking. The setting in which the research is conducted will also have an impact on survivors' ability to reveal and explain their traumatic circumstances. As sexual trauma almost always occurs within the context of secrecy, and much effort has been exerted over time in disguising the event, it is often difficult for the survivor to reveal the information–especially to a stranger.

Further, as dissociation is routinely activated by traumatic circumstance, the survivor's memory of such events will be limited. The survivor may be amnestic for the actual events. He may conversely remember the events, but dissociate as a result of the questions, setting, or posture of the researcher. Survivors are also particularly sensitive and vulnerable to issues of shame. For male survivors these issues are often enhanced. Stigma and shame will be exponentially increased for the survivor who is also a sexual minority (and even more so for a minority within the minority). As mentioned previously, thinking about a sexually traumatic event may also provoke associations to other events. For example, a number of men I have treated, associate to moments when they themselves were sexually inappropriate with another child, the moment that their own sexual trauma history is discussed. As these events are often sexually charged as well as shameful, the survivor often has difficulty speaking about the initial event at all. The subsequent "acting out" in his history, continues to serve to reassign blame and keep his initial victimization unclear or silenced.

In addition to shame, a variety of feelings, emotions and physical sensations may be provoked when the survivor is asked about, or is asked to think about, the sexual trauma he may have suffered. These feelings, such as fear, anger, guilt or sadness, may be so powerful that it becomes difficult for the survivor to report his history accurately. He may also feel physical sensations such as nausea, headaches, or sexual arousal, which further compromise his ability to provide candid information. Of course, any of these feelings, from shame to fear to anger, can also provoke a dissociative response.

The person who has been abused or traumatized by an adult may also have lingering issues with figures of authority. He may be overly suspicious or paranoid, or conversely may be eager to please, needing to do it "right" or be a "good boy." Issues of trust will be provoked by a formal research endeavor associated with or administered by an institution. The survivor may question the purposes of the research. For the survivor, whose boundaries have been violated, and whose sexuality and feelings have been used for the satisfaction of others, participating in a research study is a complicated prospect. It is at best unclear, at worst doubtful, whether the distrustful survivor would be likely to participate in a research effort. The survivor who tends toward people pleasing may be a more likely subject. This itself would skew the data, as the participants of such a study would not be representative of the greater whole.

However, the constraints of research are not limited to the subject/ survivor. Clinicians and researchers themselves often have difficulty with this material. Even when we want to examine this material, when we *try* to focus our attention, we are subject to induced dissociation. We can become forgetful or even suspicious. The ethical researcher who is not a clinician may also feel fearful about the subject's response to the material. What happens if something is re-triggered? What if the subject begins to relive/reexperience the trauma? The ethical researcher may be reluctant to be very specific regarding sexual trauma for fear of the subject's (or the researcher's own) safety.

Herman (1992) reminds us that "the ordinary response to atrocities is to banish them from consciousness." It would be naive to ignore that some researchers indeed have this (un)intentional banishment agenda. Some may seek to disprove sexual trauma (which, for many of the reasons outlined above, is a lot easier than it is to prove). At a conference in South America in 1998, a well-known researcher approached me reporting that he had read something I had written about sexual abuse and HIV risk behavior from 1993. He candidly admitted that he included questions in his (quite large) study of gay men regarding sexual trauma to "prove (the 'trauma community') wrong once and for all." He courageously acknowledged that the data were undeniable–that the effect of a childhood sexual trauma on HIV risk behavior was clear. This particular researcher was bravely able to acknowledge his biases and grow from them. Others, however, may not be willing to do so, and in fact, their research consequently may be severely myopic.

This type of bias may not even be conscious for the researcher. Gay men are tragically absent from the research literature regarding sexual abuse and trauma. As outlined in the introduction to this collection of papers, when gay men are discussed in relation to sexual abuse, it is almost invariably an inquiry into the etiology of the subject's homosexuality. When sexual trauma and gay men have been examined in research efforts it is often with regard to HIV risk behavior. While, as discussed in the "HIV and the Cycle of Trauma in Gay Men" paper in this volume, trauma will have an enormous and profound effect on HIV risk, that is only part of the picture. There are, however, numerous other angles from which the phenomena of childhood sexual trauma and gay men may be studied.

One notable exception to this paucity of research is that conducted by Doll et al. (1992) who developed an interesting classification system to codify the abusive nature of certain sexual events. The 1001 men in their study were over 18 years old and had reported engaging in oral or anal sex within the prior five years. Participants completed a questionnaire and were interviewed by STD clinic staff using a standard survey instrument. "To assess potentially abusive sexual contact, interviewers asked participants whether they were encouraged or forced to have sexual contact before the age of 19 with a person whom they perceived as older or more powerful than themselves. Participants were asked to self-define sexual contact for this question" (Doll et al., 1992). Participants who offered such information were then asked more specific questions including the ages of those involved at the time, gender, type of contact, and presence or absence of verbal or physical threat. It is important to note that the researchers included the *perception* on the part of the subject of the other as being "older or more powerful."

Sexual contacts with more powerful males were then categorized into six mutually exclusive areas, which ranged from invitation or request to do something sexual to anal-genital contact. "Developmental differences in defining peer and non-peer contact were accounted for by varying the age differences classified as abusive according to the age of the participant at the time of the contact: for participants 0-5 years of age, 3 or more years age difference was defined as abusive; for participants 6-11 years of age, 4 or more years of difference; 12-15 years of age, 6 or more years of difference; and 15-18 years of age 10 or more years of difference" (Doll et al., 1992). The researchers acknowledged their own limitations including that "methodological contracts . . . suggest that (their) data may underestimate the amount, or inadequately describe the full range, of abusive contact that occurred" (Doll et al., 1992). Other constraints, they observed, prevented them from gathering information about situations when "overt physical or verbal force" was present, or about sexual relations between peers.

Even with these understandable limitations, 37% of the participants reported sexual contact before the age of 19 with a partner "whom they perceived as being older or more powerful than themselves" (Doll et al., 1992). This figure is significantly higher than what has been previously demonstrated (Finkelhor, 1984, 1987). Some estimates suggest that only 2.5%-8.7% of men are sexually victimized as children (Finkelhor, 1985). At the same time, some studies have supported a higher rate for the sexual victimization of gay men as children compared with their heterosexual counterparts (Finkelhor, 1985).

In the Doll et al. (1992) study, the "median age difference between partners" for boys who were under 6 at the time of the sexual contact was 17 years, while for boys who were between 6 and 11 years old, that age differential dropped to 9 years, increasing again to 12 years for adolescents between 12 and 15 years old, jumping to 16.5 years for those adolescents abused between 16 and 18 years of age. It is interesting to note that the researchers configured an age differential that increased along with the child's age, while the perpetrator's median age difference was found *not* to follow the same pattern.

This speaks to the difficulty in assigning an appropriate age number to classify abuse. While one of the strengths of this study is its elaborate classification of abuse, it may be more useful to employ a power scale, whereby the study subjects might identify the level of power they perceived their sexual aggressor to have, as compared to their own power level at that time. For example, the school bully, football player, or hero, may be the same age as the study subject. By virtue of his status or level of confidence, however, that class hero may wield a power in the school that might align him, in the victim's eyes, with an older child.

Future research efforts might also focus on the development of terminology and scales which provide more comprehensive definitions of sexual trauma. For example, the power differential could be combined with an age differential to create a differential *profile* that could then be compared with the subject's power/age profile at the time of the event. The power differential would be defined subjectively by each subject. The information yielded might be discussed in terms of the symptomatology evidenced by the subject as an adult. For example, dissociation, anxiety and panic issues, sexual compulsivity and drug/alcohol misuse could be investigated in relation to the subjective power differential.

It might also be helpful for researchers to examine the dissociative phenomena in the lives of the study subjects, and have those participants rate their level of dissociation at the *time* of the actual interview or questionnaire completion. To address trust issues, research efforts might create linkages with mental health clinics that have a sexual abuse focus or trauma units, or mental health centers for gay men and lesbians. In this way, perhaps the clinician involved in the subject's treatment might administer the interview, or at least assist in the engagement of those clients. While this might still activate the subject's need to be a "people pleaser," the benefit of having a stronger level of trust between researcher and subject might outweigh those costs. It might also provide a safety net should the interview re-trigger any overwhelming feelings for the subject.

Involving mental health centers is an important consideration. Providers of mental health care need to be aware of the prevalence and gravity of sexual trauma in gay men. It seems likely that mental health centers which provide services to gays and lesbians would have already noted the sexual trauma history of their clients. However, services delivery might be enhanced once more accurate figures were demonstrated regarding the childhood histories of sexual trauma in gay men. Further, AIDS Service Organizations (ASOs) as well as drug treatment centers, for example, might provide skills building for their staff around these issues, once properly identified. Graduate and professional schools might also alter curricula to provide a more thorough education to their students.

Research can play a helpful role in examining some of the complexities of the clinical material. For example, as discussed, gay men (as well as non-gay men) may remember sexual encounters with an older person fondly. It would be interesting to examine the differences in symptomatology understood to develop as a result of sexual trauma in men who remember these types of sexual events fondly compared with those who remember these events neutrally or negatively. I have often noticed, for instance, that clients who fondly remember sexual encounters with adults when they were children, have similar symptomatology to those who remember them negatively. The clinical difference, however, is in the configuration of the defensive structure. Often, the person who remembers it fondly relies on greater extremes of defense combining, for example, a primitive denial with a sophisticated level of intellectualization.

A thorough examination of the effect of homophobia on the lives of gay children is long overdue. An obstacle to this type of investigation, however, is indeed its prevalence. It might be hard to codify or quantify the number of slurs, threats, or physical violence the gay child suffers on a daily, weekly, or monthly basis. A scale, however, might be developed which classifies name calling and slurs, bullying or menacing behavior, humiliation at the hands of parents, siblings and teachers, physical and sexual assaults, as well as frequency (daily, weekly, monthly). This scale might be used to discuss these types of events in the context of adult symptomatology.

While the gender of the perpetrator has been examined in terms of men in general (Condy, Templar, Brown, & Veaco, 1987), it would be interesting to note the effect of the gender of the perpetrator on gay men. Would there be an increase in shame associated with the subject's homosexuality if the perpetrator was female? Might the subject have been made to feel that he should have enjoyed it? Might the subject believe that, for example, this event caused him to "flee" into homosexuality? Indeed, it might be material for a study to examine the effect of the gender of the perpetrator on the survivor's comfort level with his own sexuality.

These may be questions that are unanswerable by researchers, or indeed by clinicians or clients. At the same time, research informs educators. It helps direct funding for social services. The limitations on research in terms of sexual trauma histories in gay men are complex; however, the need for quality efforts is at the same time urgent. With issues of drug misuse and overuse rampant in our community, with safer sex efforts being abandoned by many gay men, as well as a variety of other mental and physical health issues, the need for an accurate understanding of the effect of sexual trauma in the lives of gay men is urgently needed. Clinicians, educators, doctors, and clients *need* research to help create a foundation upon which our understanding can grow.

REFERENCES

American Psychiatric Association (1994). APA diagnostic and statistical manual of mental disorders (DSM-IV) Washington, DC: APA.

Bagley, C., & Thurston, W. (Eds.). (1996). *Understanding and preventing child sexual abuse, Vol. 2.* Vermont: Ashgate Publishing Company.

Bartholow, B., Doll, L., Joy, D., Douglas, J., Jr., Bolan, G., Harrison, J., Moss, P., & McKirnan, D. (1994). Emotional, behavioral, and HIV risk associated with sexual abuse among adult homosexual and bisexual men. *Child Abuse and Neglect, 18, 9 (7),* 17-61.

Carballo-Dieguez, A., & Dolezal, C. (1995). Association between history of childhood sexual abuse and adult HIV-risk sexual behavior in Puerto Rican men who have sex with men. *Child Abuse and Neglect, 19, (5)* 595-605.

Condy, S., Templar, D., Brown, R., & Veaco, L. (1987). Parameters of sexual contact of boys with women. *Archives of Sexual Behavior, 16,* 379-374.

Courtois, C. (1988). *Healing the incest wound: Adult survivors in therapy*. New York: Norton.

Doll, L., Joy, D., Bartholow, B., Harrison, J., Bolan, G. et al. (1992). Self-reported childhood and adolescent sexual abuse among adult homosexual and bisexual men. *Child Abuse and Neglect, 16*, 855-864.

Finkelhor, D. (1984). *Childhood sexual abuse*. New York: Free Press.

Finkelhor, D. (1985). Sexual abuse of boys. In A.W. Burgess (Ed.), *Rape and sexual assault: A research handbook* (pp. 97-109). New York: Garland.

Finkelhor, D. (1986). How widespread is child sexual abuse? In D. Haden (Ed.), *Out of harm's way: Readings on child sexual abuse, its prevention and treatment* (pp. 4-8). Arizona: Oryx Press.

Finkelhor, D. (1987). The sexual abuse of children: Current research reviewed. *Psychiatric Annals, 17*, 233-241.

Fischer, G. (1991). Is lesser severity of child sexual abuse a reason more males report having liked it? *Annals of Sex Research, 4*, 131-139.

Haden, D. (Ed.). (1986). *Out of harm's way: Readings on child sexual abuse, its prevention and treatment*. Arizona: Oryx Press.

Herman, J. L. (1992). *Trauma and recovery*. New York: Basic Books.

Lew, M. (1988). *Victims no longer: Men recovering from incest and other sexual child abuse*. New York: Harper Collins Perennial.

McCann, T., & Pearlman, L. (1990). *Psychological trauma and the adult survivor: Theory, therapy, and transformation*. New York: Brunner/Mazel.

Messler-Davies, J., & Frawley, G. (1994). *Treating the adult survivor of childhood sexual abuse: A psychoanalytic perspective*. New York: Basic Books.

Index

Abuse, defined, 185-186. *See also*
   Trauma
AIDS (Acquired Immune Deficiency
   Syndrome)
   coping strategies, 129-130
   epidemic of, 127-128
   health professions and, 128
   medical treatments for, 128-129
   opportunistic infections and,
      138-139
American Psychiatric Association,
   110-111
Amnesia, 130
Another child relationships, 176-180
Anti-gay zealots, xviii
Assessments, 51

Balcom, Dennis, 13, 75-89
Banking concept of education, 132
Bareback Movement, 129
Black, Claudia, xxi
Brazilian gay men, 156-157
Breathing techniques, 54-55
Brooks, Franklin L., 107-115

Carballo-Dieguez, Alex, 157
Cassese, James, xxii, xxiv, 1-17,
      127-152,153-182,183-193
Childhood sexual trauma
   HIV infection and, 141-143
   HIV risk and, 130,136
Clinicians
   gay affirmative, 39-41
   legal considerations for, 50-51
   providing appropriate care, 23
   role of, in treatment, 46-52

understanding survivor's authentic
      sexual identity by, 26
   vicarious traumatization and,
      13-15,52
Coleman, Mick, 112
Containment imagery, 56-57
Coordinate bilingual patients, case
      study of, 158-175
Coping strategies
   for AIDS, 129-130
   for HIV infection, 129-130
Cultural dynamics
   case study of, 158-171
   extracting sexual trauma from
      within, 175-176
Cultural influences
   case study of, 158-171
   sexual abuse survivors and,
      154-158

Depersonalization, 130-131
Disassociation, 11,42-43,130,186-187
   sexual trauma and, 11
   substance overuse and, 11
Documentation, 51
Dolezal, Curtis, 157

Ego-states
   defined, 64
   identifying functions of specific,
      64-65
   identifying specific, 64-65
   therapy, 65-66
Existentialism, 51
Eye movement desensitization and
      reprocessing (EMDR), 13,
      57-58
   case study, 84-86